IN THE DITCH
Stories of the Pacific Great Eastern Railway 1929-65

ERIC PRINCE STATHERS

Stathers & Associates LLC Publishing

© Copyright, Jacob Eric Stathers

All rights reserved. No part of this publication may be reproduced or transmitted in any form or by any means, electronic or mechanical, including photocopy, recording, or any information storage and retrieval system, without permission in writing from the publisher.

First Printing 2016

LIBRARY OF CONGRESS CATALOGING-IN-PUBLICATION DATA

Stathers, Eric Prince, 1907-1986.
In the Ditch, Stories of the Pacific Great Eastern Railway 1929-65 / Eric Prince Stathers.
pages cm.
Includes index of names.
ISBN-13: 978-0-692-56282-6
ISBN-10: 0692562826

1. Railroads – British Columbia, Canada – History I. Title
2. Railroads – Cars – Maintenance and Repair
3. British Columbia – History

Text set in Garamond
Designed by Jacob Eric Stathers, Kim Stathers, and Nicola Stathers

LIBRARY OF CONGRESS CONTROL NUMBER: 2015920057

Stathers & Associates LLC Publishing, Bellevue, Washington, 98005

Printed in the United States of America

DEDICATION

This book is dedicated to Mary Stathers, known to her grandchildren as Nana Mae.

The front cover picture of an engine on its side in the ditch was taken to the best of my knowledge north of Lillooet alongside of the Fraser River. This happened before my time with the railway but aptly illustrates the term "in the ditch" and the difficulties that the men had to overcome before they were able to get that locomotive back on the rails without the modern wrecking equipment that is available today.

It didn't help much to hear people talk about the P.G.E. as "Please Go Easy" or "Prince George Eventually", and other clever jibes, when our men were working their guts out to keep the road open without the proper equipment.

Eric Prince Stathers

CONTENTS

	FOREWORD	1
1	COME WEST, YOUNG MAN	3
2	FATE TAKES A HAND	11
3	THE BIG SNOW	23
4	UNDERWATER SALVAGE	36
5	SAVED BY THE SWITCH	47
6	MUTINY AT MILE 65	56
7	TRAGEDY AT SETON LAKE	68
8	CHEAKAMUS TO THE LAKE DISTRICT	79
9	LAKE DISTRICT DERAILMENTS	90
10	FRASER CANYON FROLICS	103
11	STORIES OF THE CARIBOO	113
12	PUSHING NORTH	123
13	DAWN OF A NEW ERA	139
14	THE BIG HOOK	151
15	RUNAWAY AT MILE 110	162
	ABOUT THE AUTHOR	172
	ACKNOWLEDGMENTS	173
	GLOSSARY	174
	INDEX OF NAMES	176

FOREWORD

It was 1956 before the trains ran from Squamish to North Vancouver, and 1958 before the highway opened. You went by boat from Vancouver to Squamish back then. I belonged to the Varsity Outdoor Club (VOC) in Vancouver, where I got to know Harold and Jack, sons of Eric Stathers. In 1954 a small party of us coming back from a trip to Mount Garibaldi missed the boat, and wound up sleeping in the Stathers' front room that night. I kept in close touch with the boys after that.

It was the banjo playing that made the book possible. Eric played a tenor banjo, and I played the standard banjo. We knew many of the same songs. The banjo was always with me on visits at Squamish to see Jack, and at Lillooet to see Harold. When I came back from England for a Christmas visit in 1970, Eric picked me up in North Vancouver and took me to Squamish for a visit. When Eric secured his summer camp at Big Gun Lake, I went along, and cut down the first tree. I took the banjo with me. We sat on the porch, and he told me stories about the railway.

Eric Stathers and Dick Lazenby, Brackendale Art Gallery, Squamish, B.C., 1979.

There were many family occasions. When Jack's daughter Lynn was married Eric and I played and sang. At Eric and Mary's 50th wedding anniversary party, my band played for the dance, and he sat and played in my chair for a couple of numbers. When Conductor Bud Butterworth retired, Eric and I played banjo in one of the Budd Cars riding from Squamish to Lillooet and back.

Eric had started with the P.G.E. Railway in September 1929 as Car Shop Foreman. He, and his team, because of their detailed knowledge of the locomotives and rolling stock, became the wrecking crew which attended accidents. In my history project about North Vancouver I was doing extensive research, part of which involved scanning all of the newspapers. The P.G.E. operated service on the North Shore between 1914 and 1928, and became connected to Squamish in 1956 – part of history. I found some train wreck stories in the Vancouver papers, and asked Eric about them. He could remember all sorts of incidents and details. I asked him to write these down, but he said no, writing was too slow and typing worse.

So I got hold of a small tape recorder and microphone. He recorded a tape, and I took it back to North Vancouver and transcribed it, adding material to link things up, and handed him the typed version. He said, "This is not right!" But he rounded up all of his old detailed notebooks, and re-told the stories in a more accurate version, which I took home and transcribed, with more linking material. He made further improvements, and had it typed in Squamish. I took a manuscript to a Vancouver publisher, who said they had no market for railroad stories. But I arranged for a copy to be put into the British Columbia Archives in Victoria. I loaned my copy to one of the P.G.E. Company Officers, Barry Hunt, who had been one of Eric's apprentices. Barry told me that he had stayed up all night reading it, and said that the accounts were as he remembered them.

Dr. A.L. (Dick) Lazenby
North Vancouver, B.C., Canada
December 2015

1 COME WEST, YOUNG MAN

1929-1930

I woke up to the sound of the huge steam whistle that dominates the town and surrounding countryside, saying in its booming voice, "Get up, lads, it's time to get up and go to work". It was another day in July 1929, in the town of Transcona, Manitoba, where the large railway shops of the Canadian National Railways are located. As I groped for my pants and shirt I had a feeling that somehow or other, this day was going to be different than those of the past five months, since my marriage to my young wife Mary. Just recently our union committee had recommended me for the new position of carman apprentice instructor for the shops. The job was to be the first step up in promotion to foreman, and possibly further up the railway ladder. Maybe this would be the day the promotion was to be confirmed.

It was only eight months since I finished the five-and-a-half year apprenticeship course, but since I had been nearly always in the top ten amongst some forty to fifty apprentices in the Railway Carman's trade, I suppose they thought me worth considering for the position. After having a good breakfast with my young and lovely wife, I toddled off to work. Early that afternoon my foreman told me that Mr. Bristol, our classroom instructor, wanted to see me. "I wonder what he wants now?" I thought. Mr. Bristol had been like a second father to me, though a rather stern one, and sometimes he would get me to do a little job that he required for the classroom. So with the foreman's permission I wended my way between the various shops until I came to the classroom, which was in the main offices of the Car Department. As I stepped through the door, after knocking and being told to enter, I saw a dark handsome man with curly hair and eyeglasses. He was gesturing with his arm, upon which was an odd hand, which had been injured somehow, and had only one remaining finger. Mr. Bristol introduced this man as "Mr. Bailey from British Columbia".

After a few pleasantries, Mr. Bristol threw a bombshell question: "Eric, how would you like to go to British Columbia and take a Car Foreman's job with the Pacific Great Eastern at their railway shops in Squamish?" After swallowing for breath, I said, "What is the Pacific Great Eastern, and where is Squamish?" I must have looked bewildered, because I had no thought of leaving the C.N.R., especially now that I had been recommended for a promotion. So he described the lovely little village that Squamish was in those days, and Harold Bailey told me about the railway, the shops, and so on, and added that the line was expected to be taken over by the C.N.R. in a short while. It was on account of that information that he had left his C.N.R. job in Port Mann a year ago, and gone to Squamish as Locomotive Foreman.

After getting over the shock, I said, "Well, I have two weeks holiday coming for this year. If you can fix it, Mr. Bristol, and get me a pass, I'll talk it over with my wife, and if she is agreeable we will go to Squamish and look the place and the job over". Mr. Bristol assured me that he could arrange things, so I left, saying that I would let him know our decision the next day.

Mary was not too fussy about leaving her mother and family and friends to go to a place so far away where we knew no one. She said, "My place is with my husband, and if you want to go, let us both go and see what is there, as this may be an opportunity that comes only once". The next day I told Mr. Bristol of our decision. He arranged for me to take my holidays immediately, and got us a pass on the C.N.R. to Vancouver.

We were both young then—22 years old—and as we had never been west of Manitoba, the journey became an exciting adventure. We had very little money. I had to wait until payday before we could go. However, instead of going coach, we blew ourselves on a berth in the tourist class accommodation that was available in those days. Tourist class was a sleeper with pullout seats covered with leatherette that made a bed and an upper berth that pulled down and made a second berth above. There was a small kitchen at one end of the car with a small cook stove and sink, and an ice box where you could keep foods cold and make light meals, and tea or coffee, etc. So after packing some clothes and making up a box of food and dishes, we started out on our great adventure.

Going across Saskatchewan and the first part of Alberta was not much of a thrill, but when we got our first glimpse of the Rocky Mountains we were awed at the size of them, and by the scenery on both sides of the train as we started to get near the coast. We were delighted and surprised to see those turbulent rushing rivers, and the clear sparkling waters of the coast rivers as they ran to the sea, so different from the placid brown streams that we had been used to in Manitoba. The huge trees and the dense foliage of the rain forest were also very different from the aspens and tree clumps on the prairies. We stayed overnight in Vancouver with people who were related to friends of ours at home, and in the morning we went to the Union Steamships docks to catch the boat to Squamish, which that day was the *Lady Alexandria*.

We bought our tickets, boarded the boat, and went up onto the upper deck to watch the different kinds of people that were coming aboard. We did not know it at the time, but it was train day up the line, and an odd mixture of humanity poured onto the boat: businessmen in suits, loggers in rough clothes carrying caulked boots and battered suitcases (some of them being helped aboard by their mates after a spree), Indians in colorful clothes, ranchers with big hats, and various other specimens of humanity. We were not too impressed by the dock area, what with broken crates, orange peel and various types of garbage floating along side of the ship, and the wheeling seagulls which every so often dumped onto the deck or onto some unlucky passenger. As one of them said to me when I met him in the men's washroom, cleaning the fertilizer off him, "Thank God that cows don't fly". However, after we left the harbour and headed out to Point Atkinson, there were a few waves, a light chop, and the smell of the sea. It was a beautiful day, and when we rounded the point to head up Howe Sound, we saw small sailboats, speedboats, and other pleasure craft dotted over the water, so that we seemed to be sailing in a green paradise where everyone was on holidays. After the ship had stopped at Bowen Island and discharged passengers and freight, the call came for lunch.

For seventy-five cents, each of us was admitted to the main dining room, with linen on the tables, good silver, and finger bowls. We had a most delicious meal of soup, a starter of fish, and the main course—a choice of two meats, desserts, and beverage. The ship moved on to Britannia, again discharging passengers, and then across the Sound to Woodfiber, where we got our first sight of Mount Garibaldi. From Woodfiber we went on to Squamish but there was no town! Nothing in sight except two long docks, with a train sitting on one and a couple of cars and a truck on the other. We were told to stay on board the ship until the train passengers and express cargo had been taken off for the train. Then we went over to the other dock and got into a taxi, and started up the dock, inland, through an avenue of trees.

As we rounded a corner and went over a bridge, there before us was the village of Squamish—a most pretty place, with a row of cottages on each side of the street, covered with climbing roses, and trellises with honeysuckle. Across another bridge was the business section of the town. It was a picture postcard scene, with all those little cottages so neatly kept set in acres of green lawns. The cattle and horses were allowed to graze at large. Each cottage was fenced and the remainder of the town had automatic mowing machines because the grass was cropped short by the foraging animals.

We met Harold Bailey at the station. Mary went on further into the town to stay with his sister, Annie Moon, and I went on to the shops with Harold Bailey on a speeder. There I met Andrew Kyle, the Master Mechanic, who was in charge of the Mechanical Department; a large, florid man who had been a machinist with the C.P.R. before coming to the Pacific Great Eastern Railway. He asked me various questions about the work I had done, which I was able to answer to his satisfaction. Then he asked me if I had any wrecking experience, and I had to say no, as only senior men went out on wrecks on the Canadian National Railway. He said, well, he thought that I could handle the job all right, and as for the wrecking duties, if I would ask him what to do and watch and ask a carman named Alex McDonald, I could pick up experience on the wrecks as they happened. However, he would have to wait for confirmation of the appointment until the General Manager came in from Vancouver in a couple of days, before I could go to work.

About then the shop whistle blew, and Harold Bailey took me around the shops. There was a six-stall roundhouse, one stall of which was planked in and used as the machine shop, a steam boiler house, a two-fire blacksmith shop, a stores building, and an extra storage shed. My domain was to be the Car shop, the coach yard and the repair tracks. The shop was a three-track shop, with part of it blocked off for the Paint shop and Sheet Metal shop, and machinery. It held six cars in the shop and about twelve cars on the repair tracks. The coach yard was very primitive, just a wooden platform on one side of the centre track, with a water line and electricity available—all in all, a very poor setup for handling passenger equipment. There was a staff of 16 people all told in the car department, about the same in the roundhouse machine shop and blacksmith, and two in the stores, making a total of about 35 or 36 employees in the shops.

The P.G.E Shops at Squamish north yard about 1936

Robert Wilson, the General Manager of the P.G.E., arrived from Vancouver on Friday, and talked to me for a while with Andrew Kyle. Turning to Andrew Kyle, he said, "Don't you think he is too young for the job?" Andrew Kyle replied, "Well, he comes to us well recommended, and I think he will do the job we want". Robert Wilson shrugged his shoulders and said, "Well, if you think so, Andy, it's all right with me". So with that I was told to report to work on Monday morning, July 21, 1929.

That Monday morning was a dramatic day in my life. I was only 22 years old and had to supervise men who were twice as old as me. Some of them were hostile because they resented an outsider coming in to take a job that they thought should have gone to them. Also, the foreman I had replaced went back to the tools and worked for me, which was not a very pleasant situation. However, after a few months of settling differences and accepting invitations for fisticuffs at the back of the shop after the whistle blew for quitting time (to which, by the way, the other parties always failed to show up), I managed to establish myself and there was no longer any doubt about who was running the Car Department.

At that time, in 1929, the P.G.E. started at Squamish and ran north to Quesnel. The North Vancouver to Horseshoe Bay section had been closed down in 1928. Freight was brought up from Vancouver on our own barge that held fourteen freight cars, and was towed by our own tug, the *Point Ellice*. Passengers arrived the way we had done, via the Union Steamships boats. There were two scheduled trains each week from Squamish to Quesnel. These were mixed trains, with both freight and passenger cars. One left Monday afternoon and came back on Wednesday evenings. The other left Squamish Thursday afternoon and came back Saturday evening.

In the summer, there was also the Fisherman's Special, which left Squamish for Lillooet on Saturday, and returned on Sunday. This train stopped to let people off anywhere they asked, and picked them up anywhere they wanted to flag the train down on Sunday. This service allowed people to fish the streams and lakes anywhere between Squamish and Lillooet, camp out overnight, and be back in Vancouver by Sunday night. For two months the P.G.E. also operated the Sunday Excursion to Alta Lake, with coaches and open-topped observation cars. Passenger came up on the Sunday morning boat, boarded the train to Alta Lake where refreshments were served, and then returned on the same day. All these mixed and passenger trains had to coincide their schedules with the Union Steamships boat times, since this was the only way to get between Vancouver and Squamish for passengers traveling up and down the line.

There was also a crew that took the way-freight up as far as Lillooet twice a week, serving every whistle stop, house or form along side of the track. The men on this train were very friendly with the people in the bush, since they relied on the railway for news and mail, as well as the food and materials they needed to live. Many a homemade pie, dozen eggs, cured hams, and other goodies were presented to the crew for the personal favours they did for the people living alongside the old Pacific Great Eastern Railway.

The railway at that time had twelve steam locomotives, numbered as follows: 3, 4, 5, 51, 52, 53, 54, 55, 56, 57, 58, and 59. Number 3 was a small 0-6-0 switcher, often used at the "North Yards" at Squamish. Numbers 4 and 5 were 2-6-2 types (that is with two pilot wheels, six driving wheels, and two trailing wheels) used primarily for switching and work trains, and were often assigned to Squamish. The 51 and 52 were lighter 2-8-0 types called consolidations, while engines 53 to 56 were heavier 2-8-0s, and the 57-59 engines were larger 2-8-2 Mikado types, powerful but slippery and used for faster trains mostly between Williams Lake and Quesnel. Engines 53, 54, 55, and 56 were standard steam locomotives, with pony trucks. These were the workhorses of the line, used mostly in mixed and passenger trains. Engines 57, 58, and 59 were the most powerful locomotives of the fleet, but they were small wheel freight locomotives that tended to slip on the heavy grades and wet rail. In fact, No. 59 was known as "Slippery Dick" to engine crews.

The passenger equipment was a mixed lot: wooden coaches 3, 4, 5, 6, and 7, tourist-class sleepers

Squamish and *Cariboo,* a better class but narrow width sleepers *Lillooet* and *Quesnel,* four wooden open-top observation cars 10, 11, 12, and 14, and a business car, *Chilcotin*. All of this equipment, with the exception of the two small sleepers, was very old and in grim shape. It was a continual battle to stop them leaking when it rained. These cars were heated by coal-burning heaters, that supplied hot water to the pipes running around the outside walls, which made it very difficult to keep them warm in the freezing weather of the north country.

Freight equipment included some wooden flat cars and boxcars, ballast cars, and outfit cars for the work trains. The only cars that were anywhere near modern were 100 steel flatcars, 40 steel frame wooden boxcars, and three refrigerator cars. Service equipment consisted of: one wooden snow plow, one battered Jordan spreader, two steam Lidgerwoods (one at Squamish and one at Lillooet), and a top-heavy steam crane of 7-ton capacity. To the best of my recollection, this is the complete list of rolling stock on the P.G.E. in 1929.

As time went by I gradually learned something about the beginnings of the P.G.E., and why the equipment was so old and tired. Much of it was left behind when the construction company folded up and left the government to take things over. The construction work never did get finished, for years and years. That railway was running on temporary track over temporary culverts with temporary curves and temporary ballast. They started off in debt and never could catch up. It's easy to draw straight lines on a flat map on top of an office desk. Railways on the prairies run pretty straight, but they still had something to learn when they got to British Columbia. On top of that, the P.G.E. was owned and operated by the provincial government—and that meant politics.

The village of Squamish was divided right down the middle between the Conservatives and the Liberals. Whichever party was in office and in power ran the town and gave out the goodies. When I went to buy fire insurance from a coal dealer who was the Conservative big boy, he said that since the Conservative government was paying my salary, and he was their representative in town, I should buy my coal from him. Later on in 1930, we were advised from Vancouver that the shop men should buy their groceries from the Conservative grocery store as well. Liberal henchmen ran the other grocery store in town. There were also a few Co-operative Commonwealth Federation (CCF) people. One of them ran the gasoline station, and also sold coal. As the man I replaced was a staunch Conservative and a great pal of the Conservative coal dealer, and three of the men in the shop were in the same group as the ex-foremen, they were doing their best to get me fired. I had to tread very carefully. Reports of my doings were going from this group to Robert Wilson at the Vancouver office, who was also a good friend of the coal dealer. I was up on the carpet in front of Andrew Kyle a number of times to answer gossip about me that this group had sent in, which in all cases was false. If I had known what a back-biting political turmoil I was going to get into, I would never have gotten off the boat, and this story would never have been written.

There was also a distinct social line drawn in town. The Merrill and Ring Lumber Company were operating in the Stawamus Valley just over the hill. The Company would not let their men use company transportation to come in to town. Only their superintendent lived in town. Soon after we came, all of their men except the repair crew moved up to a camp seven miles north of Squamish. To get in for a Saturday night binge at the beer parlour, they had to walk three miles through the bush and then walk all the way in to town or get a taxi. The store owners, officials of the railway, and senior conductors and engineers looked upon themselves as an upper class. Some of the men wore white shirts and collars, to distinguish themselves from the ordinary working stiff. I thought the town looked like a little Shangri-La when I first saw it, but after we had lived there a few months, we began to experience the turmoil underneath that beautiful exterior—and more so after the economic collapse in 1929. Still, while we would all bicker over day to day things, when anybody had serious personal trouble the whole town would rally round to help them.

The roadbed of the railway was unbelievable. It was just a glorified cowpath with rails on it, which wound over wooden trestles that shook and groaned when trains went over them. Routes went through rock cuts with sopping wet track in them, because proper ballast and drainage had not yet been put in. Parts of the track up in the Fraser Canyon were so close to the edge of the bank that you couldn't walk on the downhill side of the ties, as there was nothing there but the sloping bank. I saw places where the land had slipped away, and the ends of the ties were actually sticking out over the bank two or three inches, hanging above the steep slope into the Fraser River. The line was still in its construction stage, but as we were told that the C.N.R. would most likely be taking over in the near future, we hoped for the best.

As time went on the Depression came, the government changed, and the rumors flew thick and fast. The Great Northern was going to buy it. Then it was going to be shut down, the rails torn up, and the road bed turned into a highway. An American financier was going to take it over. He was even taken up the line by our officials and given royal treatment on our business car *Chilcotin*. One after another, the rumors came and went, which did not make us very secure about our future. In the meantime, although I had come to Squamish and was rising quickly up the ladder, I had given up a secure position with the Canadian National Railway. Sometimes I wondered why I had made such a foolish move, especially after our children started to arrive. Well, that's enough about the background of how I came to the Pacific Great Eastern Railway. It's time to tell the story of my wrecking experiences.

The very first experience I ever had came from a simple derailment. I went out with Andrew Kyle and the wrecking crew. A couple of ballast cars had gone off the track in a gravel pit. It wasn't a difficult situation, but I didn't have the foggiest notion of what to do, so I kept right alongside of Andrew Kyle as he gave the orders, and watched Scott McDonald do most of the work with the replacers. I should explain that replacers are specially-shaped pieces of metal with grooves and ridges in them, designed to guide the wheels of a derailed car up beside and above the track, so that the car wheel flanges lift back into their normal running position. In effect, the wheels are made to slip off the replacers, back onto the rails. Replacers come in pairs and weigh about 75 pounds each. One goes on the inside and the other on the outside of the rail. In those days, they were spiked on to the ties to hold them in place. More modern ones today are held in place with rail clamps and wedges, and are much easier to put in place and work with. There is also another type nowadays called butterfly replacers, which fit over the top of a rail to serve on either side of the rail.

It was generally a difficult job, spiking these replacers into position, because you had to crawl under the derailed car and try to swing your spiking hammer in a very limited space. However, the men just kept on working, using these replacers and getting the cars re-railed, with the help of the little seven-ton steam crane. I did make one contribution that day, when the crane swung around and the heavy hook at the end of the cable was going to strike Andrew Kyle in the head. Being close to Andrew Kyle, I was able to catch the hook and prevent him from being hurt.

That little steam crane was involved in the next call the wrecking crew got during my first year with the Pacific Great Eastern Railway. The crane was lifting some cement counterbalances from the side of Birken Lake to be used at the barge slips down at the tidewater in Squamish, when the crane tipped over and fell partially into the north end of the lake. Only the cab portion of the crane was in the water and the body was clear of the track. There was a good sandy beach there and lots of room around the track, so it was just a matter of the section crew moving the track over to get the line by and maintain line traffic. All we had for machinery was our old wooden Lidgerwood, run by steam. On that day I got my first experience of how to go about picking up derailed equipment with a Lidgerwood. Andrew Kyle, the Master Mechanic, pointed out a group of trees up on the side hill, over the gravel and loose rock, and told me to take a cable up around those five trees and sling a block on it so we could run a Lidgerwood cable through. We did that, and put a long sling on the block so it sat right level with the centre of the track. Then we ran the Lidgerwood cable out through that block and over to the cable on the crane. When we pulled, the crane would tip back up onto its feet again. But when we started, the anchor sling pulled over one of the five trees and its roots gave way. The sling pulled some more and the second tree pulled out, and finally we pulled out the whole of five trees by the roots. Down they came, crashing down the bank, blocking the little gravel road that went by there, and the crane had not budged.

I could see what was happening. We weren't getting enough purchase on the roots of those trees; with the sling set that way, we were just squeezing them into a bundle. So I suggested to Andrew Kyle that instead of grouping the cable around a clump of trees, we should tie two or three trees in a line. There were some good big trees up there, so he agreed that we should try it. Up the hill we went with a great long inch-and-a-quarter galvanized cable, and we wrapped the cable around those trees in a line. When the first tree started to go over, the strain would come onto the second tree, and when it moved the strain would come onto the third tree. Alex McDonald, an old-time logger on the wrecking crew, agreed that this was the best way of doing it. So we finally got those trees all tied together, and re-hung the block and reset the rigging, and on the next pull the crane came out and we finally got it back onto the track. That taught me a lesson that would hold me in good stead in later years, and I never forgot it. Our crew did not grab at a clump of trees when we needed a tail hold; instead, we used trees that could be tied together in a line, because it was the best method of obtaining a strong anchor.

It seemed like no time at all before it was Christmas—our first Christmas in Squamish. My wife and I went out for a walk in the early afternoon, and around 3:30 pm the Master Mechanic came around to say that the passenger train was in the ditch. Just north of Cheakamus station is a small creek that ran under the track, with a wooden bridge over it. The passenger train coming down the line on Christmas Day had broken through this little wooden bridge. The engineer had gotten out of it safely, but the tender (fuel car) went through the bridge and was in the water. Here it was, Christmas Day with a turkey in the oven, and I was called away to a wreck, leaving my wife Mary all by herself on our first Christmas away from home.

When the wrecking train got to the bridge, we found that it was not too serious. The tender was lying on top of the bridge, which was collapsed into the water, and the passenger train was on the far side. All the passengers had been transferred by speeder down to the docks, where they were being put onto the Union Steamships boat for Vancouver. Since it was Christmas Day, there were only a few passengers anyhow. It was a straightforward job, but we weren't equipped for working in hip-deep water. The creek was not very big, perhaps three feet at the deepest spit, but that was higher than the average rubber boots, so it meant working wet in ice-cold water. We had to set our jacks down in the creek, and jack up the tender and the timber part of the bridge. Then we slid some rails in under the tender so it could be pulled clear. The engine from our work train hooked onto the tender and dragged it on the ground along the main line, where we could re-rail it. Then the bridging department stepped in and rebuilt the bridge, and the next day the train arrived back in Squamish. We left them rebuilding the bridge and brought the work train back to the shops.

When I arrived back home at about four o'clock in the morning, there was my wife, of not much more than a year, furiously ironing clothes. Four o'clock in the morning, she had the ironing board out, tears running down her cheeks, turkey and the whole Christmas dinner spoilt in the oven, and she turned to me and said, "What a way to spend Christmas! I hope we never have to go through this again!" Life is funny. It seems that it didn't matter what we thought, we were fated to go through another Christmas wreck, as you will find in another story later on.

Still, by the time the year 1930 had gone by I was becoming more familiar with the methods we were using to re-rail cars. By working along with the men, under the supervision of Andrew Kyle, I began to feel more confident about taking command of the small wrecks that we had encountered up to that time, and I think the men were getting used to taking orders from me as to what we wanted to do. However, I was to encounter many more incidents that would tax my ingenuity, and there were no textbooks at all to help me in this part of my work. There were training manuals and procedures and a long tradition in all the crafts and trades, but never did I see any manual for wrecking gangs to help sort out those cars and engines that wound up "in the ditch".

2   FATE TAKES A HAND

March 25, 1932 and August 12, 1944

It was March 25th, 1932, in the middle of the Great Depression. Things were pretty nearly shut down in the town of Squamish. Merrill and Ring, the logging company, would shut down for long spells. The Pacific Great Eastern Railway was operating on short time, with the shops open three or three and a half days a week. There was no other industry in the town. Men were cutting alder wood in the bush to sell for $4.50 or $5.00 a cord. Welfare was very small. Only five regular train crews were working on the whole line: three crews for the mixed train twice a week, two crews for the way freights, and the rest of the operating men at the bottom of the seniority lists were down on the spare board in case somebody booked off sick.

But there were lots of fish in the rivers and plenty of game in the woods. People had time to plant and tend large vegetable gardens, which made them a lot better off than many people in the big cities. You could cut wood anywhere you liked, so fuel for cooking and heating was no problem. So even though the railroad was operating on short time, things were not too bad in the attractive rows of cottages on the main street of town, known as P.G.E. Row. In this row of cottages lived two locomotive engineers and their wives: Mr. and Mrs. Mike Powell and Mr. and Mrs. Minor Bazley.

Twice a week, crews took the day run, the mixed passenger and freight train, up the line from Squamish to Lillooet, which was the first divisional point 120 miles up the line. The train would leave Squamish about 3:30 in the afternoon and get to Lillooet about 10:30 at night. The crews would change at Lillooet, and after the trains had received due inspection, fuel and water, they ran on to the next divisional point—another 140 miles to Williams Lake. This was called the night run. Mike Powell was the engineer on the night run, and his regular fireman was Mr. Giles. Minor Bazley was at that time on the spare board in Squamish. Sometimes he would work the way freight, and because he was well up on the seniority list, he was working quite steadily.

Mrs. Powell was a very able woman when it came to handling money. The Powell's had no children, so Mrs. Powell invested their money in the stock market and kept a close eye on the newspaper reports to see how the stocks were moving. In 1932 the stock market was in very sorry shape. She called Mike up on the company telephone one day and said, "Mike, I'd like you to take a few days off to come down here to talk over our stocks situation. Maybe we'll have to go to Vancouver to straighten things out". Mike said that he would arrange to book off for one or two trips, and his fireman said that he would take off a few days as well and do a little gardening at his home in Lillooet. So Mike called the dispatcher and arranged to book off, and caught the Wednesday train down to Squamish. As top man on the spare board, Minor Bazley was assigned to take the night run for March 25th, with John Duncan as his fireman.

The regular mixed train ran with a baggage car, two day coaches, and a sleeping car behind the freight cars. It loaded passengers from the Union Steamships boat and left Squamish about the usual time. In order to work that night run, Minor Bazely and John Duncan were "deadheading"; that is to say, riding off duty on the train up to Lillooet, where they would book on to operate the same engine, which on that day was Engine 54 (of the 2-8-0 class of steam locomotives, with four drive wheels on each side). It took all that those locomotives could do to work through the grades on that end of the line. The grades on the P.G.E. were some of the toughest in Canada, averaging 2.2 percent, but in some short sections the grades were as steep as 2.6 percent in those days. A few miles out of Squamish you hit the lower part of the Cheakamus Canyon, which was 2.2 percent for forty miles, then down another section, 2.2 percent again, and up and down, up and down. There was a long section along Anderson and Seton Lakes that was 28 miles on the flat, but very curvy, and then a brief run into Lillooet. Lillooet was Mile Zero on the old highway to the Cariboo goldfields in the 1858 gold rush and has plenty of history of its own.

When the train reached Lillooet, about ten o'clock at night, Minor Bazley and John Duncan went up to take over Engine 54. This class of engine was an oil-fired steamer, which meant that the water and the fuel oil were topped up at divisional points. The engineer and fireman also went round and checked all engine bearings and running gear to see that everything passed inspection. There was a terrific storm going on with rain pelting down and it was pitch black. However, the weather is not supposed to make any difference to the railway timetable. So, with all tanks full and inspections completed, they were ready for the night run to Williams Lake. The rest of the crew included Conductor Frank Conway and Brakemen C.M. Conley and H.P. Cumming.

At Lillooet the railway is just a couple hundred feet above the Fraser River, and the line has to climb rather sharply to get onto the plateau. Inside of 30 miles, the line is about two thousand feet above the river. The steeper grades begin near Fountain, a small station that is the first stop north out of Lillooet. Just above this station lives the Fountain Indian Band. Up the hill further is Fountain Lake, and a stream draining Fountain Lake comes down a gulley to the Fraser River. To cross the gulley, the railroad constructed Fountain Bridge, and the highway ran right under one end of the bridge. The retainer wall at the foot of the bridge was on an almost sheer rock face that slipped down eight or nine hundred feet into the Fraser River.

Between Lillooet and Fountain there is a long cut bank that was known as the Shooting Gallery. It was a clay bank, which was very hard when it was dry, but got sticky and gooey when it was wet, and the rocks would work out and roll down the bank onto the track and bounce over down into the Fraser. This was one of those terrible wet nights, and the crew was on the lookout. However, they got through that part safely and didn't expect to have any more trouble. But just before they got to Fountain Bridge over the gulley that drains Fountain Lake, there was a huge rock on the track, so Minor Bazley brought the train to a full stop.

Usually on the trains in those days, the conductor and one brakeman rode at the back of the train, and the fireman and another brakeman rode with the engineer in the engine at the front. The engineer blew his whistle to signal for the brakeman to come up from the back end of the train to help clear this rock off the track. Between the four of them there were able to dislodge the boulder, roll it over the edge of the roadbed, and let it crash down the hillside to the river below. Then the four men climbed back into the cab of Engine 54, just on the lip of the south end of Fountain Bridge.

The same storm that poured rain onto the hillsides and loosened the rocks had swollen the water levels of Fountain Lake, with the result that the little stream was now a raging torrent, pounding and driving at the footings of the railway trestle. Local materials had been used as much as possible during construction days because they were cheaper and quicker to put in place. Concrete took too long. Big first-growth cedar was plentiful, so the contractors simply set big cedar blocks into the gravel and built up the base footings of the bridges from a cribwork of cedar logs and gravel. That was the way to get the line pushed through and this type of construction lasted for a long time. But eventually, the pounding and the erosion by wind and water had their effect. Under flood conditions, this little stream had washed out the gravel and the soil from under one set of bridge legs, leaving a gap with no support.

When you start up a locomotive engine on a hill, all of the weight of the engine and the whole train behind is exerting a pull on the track. This weight on the track is exerted on the bridge, and the whole pull of the locomotive wheels was acting on the bridge timbers. Engine 54 got very nearly across, up to the last bend in the bridge, right in the steepest part, when there was a tremendous cracking and shuddering. "God Almighty," said Minor Bazley, and he could say nothing further, because the engine dropped right through the bridge, onto the ground about fifty feet below and rolled partly on its side, while the tender made a half turn and landed on top of the cab, crushing the men inside. At the same time, the hot oil in the tender, which had broken away from the engine, flowed all over the cab and all over the men in the cab: Minor Bazley, John Duncan, H.P. Cummings and C.M. Conley.

There were three regular places for the men in the cab of those engines. The engineer rode on one side of the boiler, and the fireman and brakeman rode on the other side of the boiler. There wasn't a place for the fourth man to stand, and he often sat on the sand box that was situated in the tender. C.M. Conley was probably sitting there when the tender broke away. How it happened no one can understand to this day, but after that tender made a somersault in the air to land upside down on the engine cab, killing Minor Bazley, John Duncan, and H.P. Cummings, somehow C.M. Conley dropped in between the tender and the engine and landed on the road, half unconscious, with that hot black oil pouring all over him. Somehow, he kept possession of part of his senses. Timbers were falling all around him and the oil was pouring, but he started to crawl away into the darkness and rain. How he crawled away from that engine and didn't roll into the Fraser River, God only knows. But he left a trail of oil as he crawled, over the bottom of the bridge stringers and part way up the bank.

By this time Frank Conway, the train conductor, knew that something was wrong, and he came up on the low side of the train with his lantern, trying to make out what had happened. He couldn't see any lights. He couldn't see any engine. He couldn't see anything, as the rain continued coming down in torrents, but he heard C.M. Conley calling for help. So he worked his way down the bank, carrying his lantern, helped the injured brakeman up to the track, and managed to get him along to the baggage car. Then he went back out with his field telephone. This emergency unit was made up with a long slender pole in two sections that came apart for storage and hooked together for use. One end was a copper hook and the telephone instrument attached to the bottom end. Standing beside the track, in the rain and swaying in the wind, he fished around until he got the pole hooked onto the railway telephone line that ran alongside of the track, and got through to the dispatcher at Squamish to report the accident.

The people at Lillooet were alerted immediately, and they came out in their cars and trucks. There was road access—actually, it was really more of a gravelly goat path—around the hillsides right up to the fallen engine. In fact, the engine lay almost right on that road, because the roadway passed under the trestle at that very place. A train was sent up immediately from Lillooet to pick up the injured brakeman. They put him in a caboose and headed as fast as possible for Squamish and the hospital in Vancouver. In the meantime, people had gotten into the cab and taken out the bodies of the engineer, the fireman, and the other brakeman. They were hardly recognizable, their bodies covered with sticky black crude oil.

At about six o'clock the following morning, I was called by my superior officer to be told that there was a catastrophe up the line, and that the wrecking crew were to get up there as fast as possible. I was wrecking crew foreman, so I gathered up what men I could. We had a very small crew at that time, and there wasn't a wrecking crane on the Pacific Great Eastern Railway. There was a little steam crane that could lift a maximum of seven tons. It might lift a box car truck right beside the line back onto the tracks, but it could not even handle a box car. Our one useful piece of power machinery was the steam Lidgerwood.

The Lidgerwood was a steam-powered winch on a wooden railcar, exactly the same as the logging equipment that was known as a donkey engine. The Lidgerwood Company manufactured their engine for railway use to ballast track. The gravel ballast was pulled off the open-top ballast cars by a steel gravel plough hauled by the Lidgerwood cable, spilling down between the tracks or over to one side, depending on how you set the doors on the ballast cars. We had inch-and-a-quarter steel cable on the cable drum of our Lidgerwood, and the big gear wheel stood seven feet high. You could make a tremendous pull with these machines, and this was our chief mechanical power. Along with it we had slings, cables, and pulleys in detachable blocks, which could be unhooked or opened up to put in or take out a line (hence their nickname "snatch blocks"). We also had timbers and screw jacks for raising and lowering heavy loads, and other jacks, which worked like the bumper jacks on an automobile. When we had a wreck in those days, we had to set up our rigging, haul the derailed cars back to the track, jack them up, put the running trucks underneath them, and rerail them. Most of the getting ready was done by hand, but the big pull came from the Lidgerwood. And how we put it to work is the story of the early days of the P.G.E. wrecking crew.

When we made up the wrecking train there was an additional car, a sleeper, to take Mrs. Duncan, Mrs. Bazley, and her friend Mrs. Graham up to the scene of the accident. On the way up the line, we met the emergency train coming down with the injured brakeman, and we went in to give him our condolences. My God, what a sight! They were afraid to touch him, so they had wrapped him in blankets—just two pink eyes looking at you out of a black mask. He was burnt all over and they didn't want to touch him more than necessary in case his skin would come off. We just had time for a glimpse of him, before the train left for Squamish and we left for Lillooet. When we arrived in Lillooet after dark, it was too late to do anything more that day. We were up before dawn and got to the site at daybreak.

Engine 54 at Fountain Bridge after the tender taken was off the cab. March 25, 1932. Photographer: Artie Phair

As long as I live, I'll never forget the scene of walking out along the track to the end of that broken bridge, swaying back and forth in the wind, and looking down to the mess fifty or sixty feet below. I was young at the time with little experience, and I thought to myself, how in the world do we get a mess like this cleaned up. There was a huge locomotive, weighing in the neighbourhood of 120 tons, over on its side, part of it hanging out over a sheet drop-off into the Fraser River. In fact, you couldn't even walk around it on the river side, as there was no place to walk. And sitting on top of the cab and partially on the boiler of the engine was the tender, balancing precariously. If it ever rolled off, it was lost for good. Our gear was up on the track, south of the bridge, high above the mess. There was no place to pull from and no way to lift. We couldn't bring the little seven-ton crane out on that bridge for a lift, because the crane and the bridge would be pulled down instead. While I was still trying to absorb the situation, my superior said, "Get that tender off the cab of the engine, Eric, or we'll lose it for sure". So that was where we started.

Engine 54 in the ditch at Fountain Bridge, March 1932. Photographer: Artie Phair

And this is how. When you pull with a cable, you pull in a straight line. Our Lidgerwood was on the south end of the bridge. We wanted to pull that tender off up the hill slightly north. To do that, we had to run our cable all the way over to the north side, through a pulley block on the north side, and down to the tender. But there was no rock, no trees, nothing to hang a pulley block on north of the accident. So we had to manufacture a tail hold, a place to put our snatch block, by making what we called a "deadman". A deadman is a long trench, about six to eight feet deep, dug into the hillside (it was soil in this particular spot). This was in the days before Cats or mechanical diggers, so we did the digging by hand. Into the trench we put the biggest timbers we could get and some steel rail. Then we dug a notch in the centre of the trench, towards the wrecked engine, making a kind of T-shape. We fed a heavy choker cable through that notch, around the timbers and steel rail, and back on the ends of that choker sling. Then we threw all the dirt back in on top of the timbers, and tamped everything down really firm, so that the deadman would not shift or pull out.

Then we hauled the end of the Lidgerwood cable down through the gulley by hand, through the brush and the roaring stream, up the other side to the snatch block that was hanging from the deadhead, and back down to Engine 54. We only had six men, plus what section hands we could get hold of, and we had about a thousand feet of cable, reeled off the Lidgerwood drum. While we were pulling cable, we were getting wood ticks on our clothing off the brush, as this was the time of year when ticks are virulent. Ticks have pincerlike locking jaws. They burrow under your skin, locking their jaws into the flesh; with their bodies still outside, they engorge themselves on your blood until their bodies become the size of a grape. They can cause serious infection. Each night in the bunk car, we had to strip down to the skin and examine each other for pests. Even the engineer of the work train, who wouldn't leave his cab, found one on himself, evidently blown in by the wind as we disturbed them, pushing through the scrub and bush.

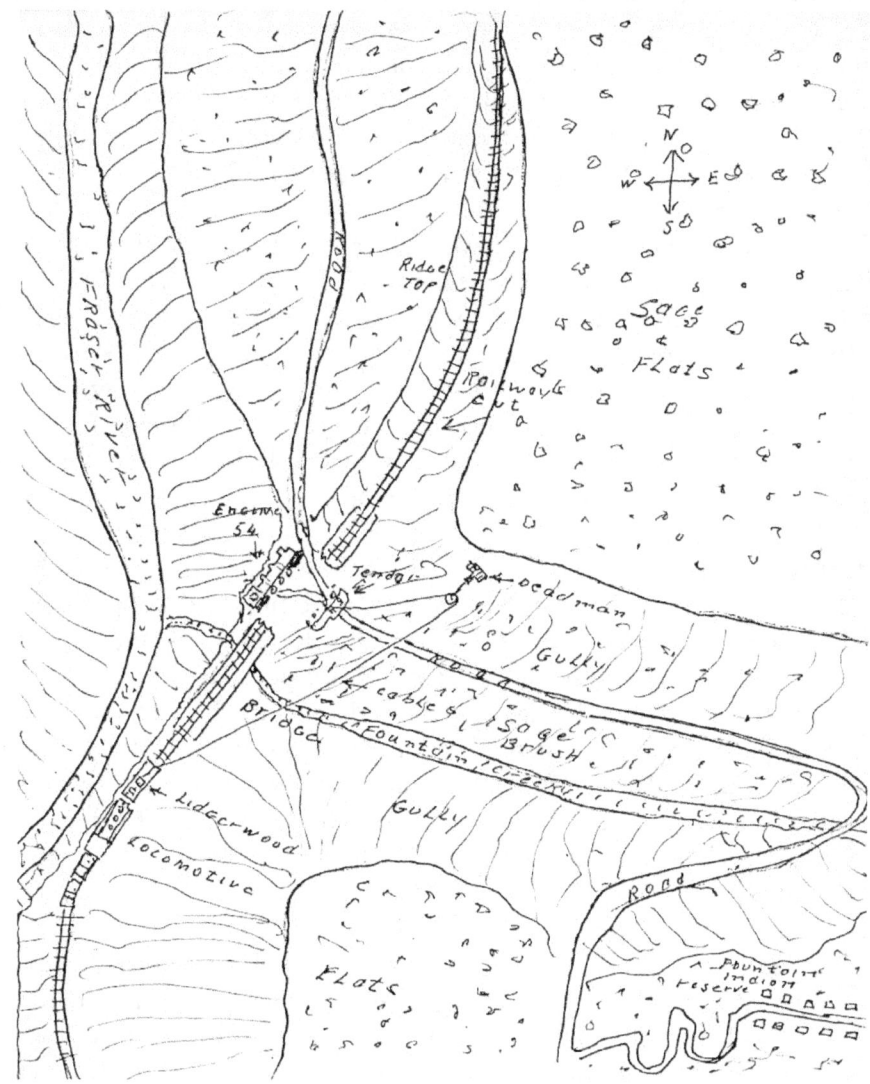

Map diagram of the Engine 54 derailing at Fountain Bridge. Hand-drawn by Eric P. Stathers.

We got the cable down to the tender, but then we were faced with the problem of how to fasten it onto the tender. Someone had to get up there in order to attach it. The only way this could be done was to push the end of the cable, which had a loop in it, through the water tank hole, and then push a long steel pin through the loop and hold it there while the Lidgerwood took up the strain on the cable until the pin jammed up against the tender. All that time we were hoping to God that the tender wouldn't be pulled off until we could slide down and get the hell out of the way. Since I was the wrecking crew foreman, it was up to me to get the job done. My father was an old sea captain who had commanded men for many years, and I remember what he had told me. He said, "Son, if you ever get in a position where you're commanding men, never send anyone where you're afraid to go yourself". I took a look at that tender and I knew what it was like on the far side—one slip or misstep, and down you went into the muddy torrent of the Fraser River, far below. So I said, "Who'll go with me and help me fasten that cable up on the tender?" We had a couple of young fellows in the group, but no one came forth. So I said, "Well, I'm going, and I'd sure like to have some company to hold this cable, because I need one hand to hold the pin and the other hand to hang on with". The man who answered was an older, slow-moving, gentle sort of fellow, whom I had at least expected to say, "I'll go with you, Eric". So he took the cable and I took the pin, and we climbed up onto the tender. Hanging on with one hand, he shoved the cable through the hole, while I also held on with one hand and shoved the pin through the eye in the cable and then yelled to the master mechanic to take up the slack. By this time, with both hands busy, I was keeping my toes crossed that he didn't pull too hard and pull the tender and all of us down below. However, the operator of the Lidgerwood was very skilled, and he eased the cable tight enough so it would hold. We clambered down from there very quickly, I can tell you, and got out of the way. Then they took up on the Lidgerwood cable and flipped the tender off the top of the engine cab and onto the solid part of the bank. While the cable was attached, we moved that tender right off the road and out of the way, so that repairs to the bridge could begin.

Then the bridge and building crews went to work to repair the bridge and get traffic moving over the line again. Meanwhile, the master mechanic consulted with the company officials about taking out Engine 54. Our crew was so small, and we had so few men working during the March of 1932, that we had to strip the railway shops at Squamish in order to have a team of men for wreck work. So it was decided that we would not try to recover the engine, but would contract the job out. Our Lidgerwood cable was old, worn and frayed, and our other cables were not strong enough to handle a locomotive. Instead, it was decided that we would return to the Squamish shops and put a new fourteen-hundred foot cable on the Lidgerwood and have slings made up to the size required to take the engine out.

So back we went to Squamish and the preparation of the equipment for the job of taking the engine out. It was a sad day for the town. There were only about three hundred people there at the time and we all knew each other. To have three men killed at once was a terrible loss. There was no compensation to speak of, although the widows did get some sort of pension. But a popular man like Minor Bazley was missed by everyone, and the others the same. It was just fate that Mike Powell picked that day for his trip to Vancouver and asked Minor Bazley to come up and take the run for him. The same applied for John Duncan, who took the run in place of the other man. Instead of Minor Bazley and John Duncan going down the hole, it would have been Mike Powell and his fireman. This is something that is hard to understand—how one man on this particular occasion took the place of the other man, and met his death when he was not scheduled to do so.

As I said before, when we went out on wrecks we had to strip the shop crew to such an extent that it crippled the shop. We had to work until the line was reopened before getting back to the shop. But Engine 54 had to be recovered. A locomotive engineer named Angus McRae and a brakeman by the name of Harry Brightbill took the contract. To take that engine out of the hole without a crane was an interesting piece of engineering. We supplied our Lidgerwood with the new cable on it, the new slings, and our tool car, which were all sent up to Lillooet. The locomotive foreman there agreed to operate the Lidgerwood for them. Here is how they went to work:

First, they had to get track down to Engine 54. They got a steam ditcher and cut away the sides of the cut on the line north of the bridge, worked the ditcher down to make a roadbed down the side hill to where the wrecked locomotive lay, and laid track all the way down. At that time there were no Caterpillar tractors at all in the valley, so all the earth and material had to be dug and pushed by the steam ditcher and manpower. It was hard going. Underneath the locomotive they built a solid bed of ties and timbers, but with no rails on it. They set the Lidgerwood in the same spot where we had used it at the south end of the bridge, anchored it with the work train locomotive, and tied it down to the rails. They ran the Lidgerwood cable through a snatch block hanging from our deadhead on the far side of the gulley and back down to Engine 54. There they made a rolling hitch by passing the cable over the engine and down and under it, and back up to tie on to the top side of the engine frame. That way, as they took the strain on the cable the engine would roll uphill like a barrel. If they had done it by what looked like the easy way—by attaching the line to one of the steam chests (the round domes on the top of the engine) and pulling the engine upright, the wheels might have dug the ground away underneath and the whole works could have slipped down into the river. So they rolled it uphill.

Engine 54 rolled upright below Fountain Bridge

The other trick was to chain rails to each set of wheels on the locomotive. They chained them on tight to the lower wheels and to the topside wheels, so that when the engine came over onto its feet, so to speak, the wheels would already be sitting on rails on a solid bed of ties. Then all that would remain was to couple up these rails to the track they had laid down in the temporary spur line they had built with the steam ditcher. They had hired extra men to take the cable across the gulley like we had done, and everyone was standing by holding their breath as Angus McRae gave the signal to the Lidgerwood engineer to start the pull. The timbers creaked and groaned, and slowly, slowly, the engine started to turn. They watched the lower side with great apprehension, to see that it didn't slip and cut the bank away. Slowly, slowly… and then over it came with a thump onto the solid bed of ties, with the wheels sitting chained onto the two rails. Then by shifting the chains, they were able to connect those rails to the temporary spur line rails, and they had a route up the hill. It was then safe to disconnect the Lidgerwood cable.

The Lidgerwood had to be reset in order to pull Engine 54 up the grade. The cable was reeled in from across the gulley, all the slings and gear were picked up, and the work train went back to Lillooet, where they turned the Lidgerwood around so that it was facing south behind the engine. When they brought it back to the scene, they placed it north of the temporary line on the north side of Fountain Bridge. Again they anchored the engine and the Lidgerwood down to the rails and fed the Lidgerwood cable down the grade to hook onto Engine 54. When they had the strain on the Lidgerwood cable, the chains were taken off the wheel on the engine. A man with wedges and a hammer took a place behind each one of the driver wheels, four on each side. If the engine slipped or the cable broke, the whole works would have tried to roll down the track towards the Fraser River. So as the cable was slowly reeled in by the Lidgerwood, the wedging men followed closely, resetting wedges in sequence and watching like hawks. Up she came, slow and steady, until they had gotten to the top of the temporary grade, right next to the main line. The track gang cut the main line, connected it with the spur line, and with a short pull, Engine 54 was sitting on the main line. Then the track gang cut loose the spur and restored the main line and they were able to push the damaged engine back down into Lillooet. The front coupler was still okay, but the back end, where the tender had torn off, was unserviceable.

Lidgerwood winch taking Engine 54 out. Note the Lidgerwood cable and pulley block on the front of the engine.

Then the work train went back up above Fountain Bridge and, using the same techniques, they pulled the tender and the trucks up onto the main line, restored the main line, chained the tender to the Lidgerwood, and pushed back into Lillooet again. At Lillooet, they checked the bearings and moving parts so that the engine and the tender were safe to roll, connected everything together, and pulled Engine 54 and the tender back down to Squamish. Within a few weeks, the shop men had gone over it and fully repaired it, and it was out again back on the job with a new coat of paint, pulling trains up the mountains. It took a lot longer than that before we were able to accept the loss of those men. C.M. Conley made a slow recovery and was able to come back to work; gradually, the episode faded from our memories. There were a great many wrecking calls and other incidents and stories that came with the passing years.

In those days, the P.G.E. had very little equipment, but wages were low, and time and labour were cheap. We had no wrecking cranes, no big D8 Cats, no pipe-layers, and no automatic machinery for servicing trains like they have today. A lot of grunting and sweating went into the job of keeping the railroad running, and even more into re-railing equipment when it came off the track. We needed a great deal of ingenuity to get out of the kind of trouble we were running into, operating a railway through the mountains of British Columbia. Our Lidgerwood, being a cable haul machine, could exert a powerful pull, but only in straight lines from pulley block to whatever we were pulling. We could not pull sideways from the machine itself, only straight ahead; otherwise the Lidgerwood would roll off the track. Bars, levers, spikes, hammers, ties, timbers, and hand-operated jacks provided most of the lifting power. Repairs were made from the scrap pile. Still, the line kept operating and conditions started to improve. Twelve years went by.

By 1944, Mike Powell had enough seniority to hold the day freight or night freight runs out of Squamish. This time he was working the regular day freight run out of Squamish to Lillooet, with F.J. Mulhern as his fireman on Engine 56 (the same class of engine as Engine 54). Both men were very experienced and accustomed to the sharp curves and mountain grades of the line as it was in those days. I had learned by this time to admire the knowledge and judgment of all our locomotive men, especially in the wintertime and in bad weather. It's a difficult thing when you're coming down the grade and you see a big ball of snow in front of you and you don't know whether it is really a snowball or a big rock encrusted with snow. I've been sitting in the locomotive coming down with our wrecking train, taking the fireman's place while he's getting his meal on the run, and I've hollered to the engineer, "Look out! There's a rock on the track!" and somehow or another they have an uncanny instinct. They say, "No, I think that's a ball of snow, maybe a little rock inside, and we'll keep going". And sure enough we'd hit that snow and it would disintegrate; maybe you'd hear a thump and a rock would go flying up against the front of the steam engine. Those crews seemed to know exactly what to expect at each stretch of the line—every rock, every tree, and where to expect hazards—so they were prepared, even with changes in the weather.

The big rainfall and snowfall sections of the line are down at the bottom end from Squamish, up through the severe grades through the Cheakamus Canyon, through the Alta Lake area (where the Whistler ski facilities are today) and down steep grades into Pemberton. Along the 28-mile stretch of Anderson and Seton Lakes (known as the lake district) the line is almost flat, but in those days was very twisty and curvy. After that is the dry belt going into Lillooet and up the big grades onto the Interior plateau of British Columbia, where there is not nearly so much rain and snow as in the coastal rainforest areas. The railway crews knew about all this because they worked with it all year round, in severe heat and severe cold. They were used to the changes in the weather, and generally they could read the storms and be ready at any trouble spot along the line.

This particular day, August 12th of 1944, when Mike Powell and F.J. Mulhern got to the lake district, it was a bit windy along Anderson Lake, but it was not raining much, so they were taking the train along at a pretty good clip on the flat. What they did not know was the state of the weather on the mountain tops over the line. It was a cloudburst storm, pouring water onto the high elevation hillsides, just like the rain that flooded out of Fountain Lake, the trip that Mike Powell had booked off in 1932. With a pretty fair-sized load of freight behind them, they came around a curve in the line… and there was a huge mudslide coming down a small gully, moving across the path of the train. As the engine met the slide, it was pushed up onto the mound of rolling mud by the momentum of the freight cars behind, rolled a bit, tipped over on its side, and was carried right out into Anderson Lake. The engineer and fireman were both trapped inside the cab as the engine and tender disappeared into the water and pulled away from the rest of the train. They never had a chance.

No trace was ever found of Mike Powell, or of his fireman, F.J. Mulhern. We hired divers, who went out and searched the wreck—all around it, underneath it, as far as they could go with their diving suits. Scuba gear was just coming into use at that time. From the raft which the divers were using, we could peer down through the crystal-clear waters of Anderson Lake, and about thirty feet down you could see the back end of the tender, so the engine would have been no more than forty or fifty feet under the water. It was not possible to recover the engine. You might wonder why we didn't bring the engine out. When a working engine, which is very hot, hits the ice cold water in those very deep lakes, the metal contracts too quickly and everything cracks, making the engine worthless. Engine 56 was a steam engine, and although diesels had started to appear by 1944, we had not gotten any by that time. We didn't have the equipment to recover Engine 56 from Anderson Lake and the costs to have it done were beyond our reach, so it was abandoned there.

Divers searching for the bodies of Mike Powell and F.J. Mulhern in Anderson Lake, August 1944.

Evidently, fate had determined the end of Mike Powell. Even though he missed going through the Fountain Creek Bridge after a mountain storm flood, he was carried off into Anderson Lake by a mudslide from a mountain storm. He was a fine man and he and his wife were very nice people, although like the Bazleys they had no children. Once again it was a tragedy for our little town. But he and F.J. Mulhern had absolutely no chance. The mudslide picked them up and carried them right into the water, rolling the engine so they couldn't get out. So today, Engine 56 lies in Anderson Lake, a coffin for the two men who went down on that date. If you get a boat and ride out about fifty yards from the shoreline near Mile board 135 (today's mileage on the new railway) and look down, you may yet still see the rusty and encrusted outlines of the tender and the engine, far below the surface of the lake.

This was an episode in the early days of the Pacific Great Eastern Railway. Everything has changed since then. All of the track, trestles, bridges, and old temporary wooden construction have since been replaced with concrete abutments, steel spans, and heavier rail. The line has been shifted and straightened and slide areas have been protected by groins, which are big ditches on the uphill side of run-off areas. Today, a speeder patrolman runs just ahead of the trains, scouting for rocks on the track or any trouble. He is in immediate radio contact with the dispatcher and can talk directly to the engineer and the train crew following. So conditions today are altogether different from those that faced the crew of the old pioneer Pacific Great Eastern Railway. Today, the British Columbia Railway is a modern, well-equipped operation, protected against the kinds of accidents that this book is about. But how we got ourselves out of trouble is the story of our wrecking crew operations in the early days. Just up the line from Anderson Lake, there is another engine resting in the depths of Seton Lake. But that is a story for a future chapter.

3 THE BIG SNOW

January 1935

Since June 1934, my wife Mary and I had been busy in the new house we were building in Squamish. As soon as the shell was completed, with outside walls, doors and windows, and the roof on, we moved in. Since it was the depths of the Depression, we were building it bit by bit, when we could save enough money out of the pay cheque to buy some more material. The cold weather came early that fall, and we were not at all prepared for it. In those days there was no insulation used in the houses in Squamish; we just had shiplap lumber on the inside walls and ceiling, so there was not much between us and the weather. However, we had a wood stove in the kitchen and a wood-burning heater in the living room, and by keeping them going full blast we were able to keep going even during a couple of Squamish winds that fall. Squamish is at the head of Howe Sound. Along the Pacific Coast, under certain weather conditions, cold air pours out from the Interior, over the top of glaciers and permanent snow fields on the Coast Mountains, and down to the inlets of the sea. Sometimes, with gales and storms, the winds blow off the ocean the other way. That fall, it blew so hard that the curtains were moving from the drafts around the windows and we had to put blankets over the windows to stay warm. On a couple of occasions we closed off the bedrooms and put mattresses on the floor in the living room to keep warm at night. There was a bit of snow as well.

However, in January we started to get snow that stayed and it gradually piled up in different snowfalls, until the afternoon of Sunday, January 20th. Up the line, it had been snowing all day, so the snowplow gang had been sent out to keep the track open up to Lillooet and to come down again to Squamish by Monday afternoon, when the mixed passenger train was due to go north. The snow belt went all the way from Cheakamus Canyon, up past Alta Lake, down past Pemberton, and up to the top of the hill at Birken. That heavy snow belt combined with severe grades, which averaged 2.2 percent on most part of the line, and created problems most winters.

We had some visitors that night and they left early on account of the snow, which kept coming down in great heavy flakes. I remember looking out of our piano window and outside, underneath the light from the street lamp right in front of the house, snowflakes were coming down like leaves almost as big as the palm of your hand. They continued to come down all night. I got up once or twice during the night and peered out the window and that snow was getting deeper and deeper. It came time to get up in the morning and go to work. As I was making my breakfast, I looked out of the back door and realized just what I was going to have to walk through in order to get to the shop. I got out my hip waders, which are rubber boots with tops that come right up to the top of your legs, and a long rubber coat which came over top of the hip waders and kept me pretty dry in wet situations. After having my breakfast, I went out onto the back porch of our house on Wilson Crescent and set off for work.

Now before this storm had started, there was already about eighteen inches of snow on the ground. You couldn't walk on it, but it was harder snow. The back steps of the house were completely covered. When I stepped off the porch, I was above my waist in soft fluffy snow and it was still snowing very hard. I had to force my way through the snow right to the corner of Wilson Crescent and Cleveland Avenue, where the master mechanic, Harold Bailey, lived. I made my way up the driveway to his house and knocked on the back door. When Harold Bailey had seen the snow coming down on Sunday evening, he had telephoned the shop; the engine watchman and another man had been running the engine back and forth between the shop and the station all night long to keep the track open. So all we had to do was make our way to Castle's Crossing, which is now just to the side of the Overwaitea store. Harold Bailey was quite a bit older than I was (I was in my twenties at that time), so I had to break trail, and believe me, it took all I had to push my way through that snow. It was chest high and flowed almost like water around you. Harold Bailey followed in my tracks, and even at that we had to stop and rest two or three times before we got to Castle's Crossing, where we waited for the engine to come down.

As soon as the engine arrived, we climbed into the cab and proceeded down towards the station. On the way down we picked up two or three fellows, and when we got to the station we blew the engine whistle to let the men living in town know that there was transportation waiting to take them up to the shop. It was about two miles from the station up to the shop. We waited until a few men showed up, then went back up to Castle's Crossing, which was about at the end of town in those days, picked up about a dozen men, continued up the line to the shop, and backed the engine from the yards into the roundhouse tracks. The first thing we had to do when we got to the shop was to shovel communication paths between various shops and buildings. All thought of ordinary work was forgotten, until we had some way to reach the stores, the car shop, the roundhouse, the blacksmith shop and the other buildings. So every man we had was busy shoveling snow.

Some time before ten o'clock, Harold Bailey came out with the news that somewhere on the hill between Birken and Pemberton, the snow plow had hit a slide on its way back from Lillooet and was off the track buried in the slide. The train crew had managed to get their engine out of the slide and the engine crew and train crew fought their way back to Pemberton, and were tied up there waiting for instructions. So there was no hope of the snow plow getting back and clearing the line or clearing our part of the yards, and until we cleared the yards, we could not move. So the yard crew was called. Harold Bailey went with them on the engine that had been running back and forth all night, and they headed back to town to fetch another train crew, and somewhere they found a section crew and he came back with the whole bunch. Somehow, by noon they had managed with their shovels to clear enough switches that they could get the engine over to the repair track, which was ahead of the car shop, and pick up the Jordan Spreader.

The Jordan Spreader has a movable front plow about two feet high that can be lowered down to the track to clean out snow or gravel for about two inches below the top of the rail. It was designed for spreading gravel as track ballast. The moveable front section is called the nose. It also has side wings that are about fourteen feet long, so when you run down one track, the wing will reach across and clear off the next track as well. The nose is put down to plow snow off the tracks, and when it comes to a switch or a crossing, the nose is lifted as the spreader crosses, so the switch points do not get damaged. This machine is operated by compressed air supplied from the locomotive and by a man at the controls of the spreader itself. So once the crew coupled up to the Jordan Spreader, they operated it like a snow plow, cleared the switches in the yard, and made their way back onto the main line.

Now our only source of heat and power at the shop was a steam boiler that operated on crude fuel oil, which was brought up from Vancouver to a big storage tank down near the docks, and then brought up to us in a tank car, which coupled onto the boiler feed system. And on this day, the damned tank car had run out of oil. So the engine and train crew coupled up to the tank car, took the section crew with them, ploughed their way down to the oil storage, and managed to fill up the tank car and bring it back up to the shop. By this time, it was about two o'clock in the afternoon and we had another engine under steam. We also had about five feet of snow on the ground; it started to rain, and the snow started to sink. The yard crew went out to plow the main line some more.

While they were busy on the main line, we tried to get the tank car into place to be hooked up to our steam boiler, and the car went off the track. So we had to call the yard crew back to help us re-rail the car. By this time, the snow was getting very wet, especially where it had been plowed and compressed. As the rain came down, the space between the rails was filling with water. We had to get down under this tank car to put down our re-railing equipment in order to put the car back on the tracks. It was after three o'clock before we got the tank car into position and hooked up to deliver fuel oil to the steam boiler, to keep the shop going. It had stopped raining, but that didn't help much, because it was starting to freeze and the men were wet through from kneeling and lying down in the wet snow to get the rerailers under the tank car trucks.

The only way to get home was by the engine that the yard crew had. So around 4:30 pm, the men were called together and we all climbed aboard the engine with the Jordan Spreader on the front. Only so many could get into the engine cab, so there were quite a few on the spreader, and I stood on the front of the spreader. By this time, the snow was frozen hard. So as we travelled up the yard to where the switch connects onto the main line. I had my hand on the emergency cord, so that in case the spreader jumped the track, I could pull the cord and stop the engine. The engine headlight was on, of course, but with the spreader in front, the light was prevented from hitting the track, and so it was hard to see anything ahead. As we neared the highway crossing—the road is still there today, going across the track just north of the shops—I could see a big pile of ice and snow looming up about sixty feet on the other side of the crossing, and I thought, My God, that's frozen ice. Here I am on the front of this spreader, and we're going to hit that pile and that huge chunk of ice is going to crush me against this machine like meat in a sandwich. The locomotive engineer saw it and knew he'd have to hit it in order to get through, so he didn't slow down at all. We were going pretty fast. I couldn't move fast enough to get over to one side. I had just made up my mind to take a chance and jump into the snow, when we hit the crossing, derailed the Jordan Spreader, and went sliding down the bank. The engineer brought everything to a sudden halt. The way to the main line was blocked by the derailed spreader.

It was pitch black by this time. We were all cold, tired, and soaking wet. The master mechanic ordered the engine back to the shop and said, "That's all we're going to do today, boys. We might as well go home". The only way to get home was to walk down the track, and of course it had been several hours since the engine had been over it. Almost a foot of snow sat between the rails, covered by this time with a thin, breakable crust of ice that let you drop every step of the way. The younger and stronger fellows went ahead to break the way. One of our crew was an older chap named Henry Smith, who was a labourer in the shop. He was a fine man, getting along in years, and as we walked home he was getting farther and further behind. George Nesbitt and I were walking together, and we both kept an eye on Henry as he was stumbling along and dropping back, and finally we both agreed that we'd better go help Henry, because if he lays out in this snow all night, he's had it. So we each took one of Henry's arms and put them over our shoulders and we walked Henry Smith right down the track to his home. Then I had another quarter mile to walk back to my own home.

Now in order to put in a garden or do anything in your yard, you had to put a fence around the place to keep out the cattle, which roamed free in those days. So by this time, I had got hold of some split cedar posts and put in a rough four-foot high fence with page wire around a portion of the property. It was freezing hard now after a freezing rain. The trees were coated with ice and branches were hanging down lower and lower. By the time I got home from Henry's house, the ice on top of the snow was frozen so hard

I could walk on it, and it was so deep that I walked right over that fence. There wasn't even a sign of those four-foot fence posts. I walked through our front yard to the back door and stepped through the kitchen door, right off the snow. Tree branches were breaking and tree tops were snapping, which sounded like rifle and cannon shots. My wife was very glad to see me arrive home safe and sound. She was keeping the home fires burning, but it was nice to have somebody bring in some more wood from the back shed. It was wonderful to get into that warm house and get my rubber clothes off, because I was soaked with perspiration from working so hard in that rubber gear. I had a hot supper and a bath and went to bed.

When we got up early the next morning and looked the situation over, it had not improved at all—everything was still frozen solid. However, I made my way over to Harold Bailey's house, and we walked out to the track again. Of course, this time there was no transportation up to the shop, so we had to walk. By this time, we had a bigger crew because some of the people had spent Monday digging them out instead of coming to work. The town was in a sorry state. There was no machinery in those days—no bulldozers to move snow or clear roads. We had horses, of course, but you couldn't use them in those conditions because the ice would cut the horses' legs and injure them. So everybody spent the day digging paths from store to store and house to house, just the way we had done up at the shops, trying to regain communication. Everything had completely stopped. But the storm was passing, and it started to lighten up and the temperature started to rise. There was a hard crust on top of all the snow.

The kids were having a ball, since the school was closed. All the kids put on their skates and skated up and down the school grounds and over the fields, on top of this ice-covered snow. As it warmed up, the thaw started and the crust got mushy. Right after lunch, my wife decided that we needed some groceries. Since I would likely be tied up at the shop for a long time, she thought that she should get to the store. We had two young children and we were running out of milk. So she donned her heavy clothes and made her way down to the nearest grocery store, which was about half a mile downtown. The crust was still holding the kids, who were lighter, but adults were breaking through, and by the time Mary got the store she was pretty well exhausted from struggling through the breakable crust. Mrs. Adams at the store said, "Don't worry about carrying these things back home, I'll send the boy up to deliver your groceries. You just get back home and look after those two little boys". So she got back home, and had black and blue bruises on her legs for some days, where she had broken through that ice crust on the top of the snow. At about four o'clock she sees this young fellow coming with a cardboard box full of groceries. He was crawling on his hands and knees, pushing the box ahead of him on the ice, and every once in a while he would fall though and disappear from sight. Poor kid, he must have been exhausted too, since it was the end of his work day. Nothing much could be done about the roads in town until the road foreman managed to get to the grader, which was an old type gasoline-powered machine. It took a couple more days before he had made much impression on the town. However, I only learned of these things afterward, because at that time I was too busy attending to my duties at the shop.

By eight o'clock, the crew had assembled at the shops. The engine crew, like the rest of us, had to walk up the line. The first job was to get the spreader back up on the railway line, and we got the rerailers down and put it back on the rails. Then we pushed through the wall of snow up at the north end switch onto the main line, and the yard crew set to work to clear the yard, using the Jordan Spreader as a plow. The rest of us went back to the shops and took stock of the situation.

The line was snowed in. The only snow plow we had was off the track somewhere between Pemberton and Birken. The engine and crew were sitting back at Pemberton. We could not look to the C.P.R. or the C.N.R. for help either, because they were battling the same conditions as we were and had no equipment they could lend us. Something would have to be done quickly, because the P.G.E. was the only link for transportation of food and supplies for the people between Squamish and D'Arcy. So our master mechanic telephoned Vancouver to report on the situation, and they asked if we might construct some sort of a plow on the front end of a locomotive. Now at that time Engine 59 was in the shop. Engine 59 was one of the most powerful steam locomotives of the time, a 2-8-2, with smaller diameter drive wheels, for use with the heavier freight trains. So Harold Bailey (the master mechanic), Mr. Johnson (the locomotive foreman), Angus McRae (the senior locomotive engineer), and myself (the car foreman) had a meeting to figure out how to go about building a plow on the front end of Engine 59.

In our enforced economy drive—this was the middle of the Depression—the shop had been working mostly off the scrap pile. We had no money to buy new parts and equipment, so we had to make what we needed in order to make repairs on the rolling stock. One of our treasured sources was a big pile of 5/16th inch steel plates, left over from construction days on the railway, which had been left to us along with the Lidgerwood. Beside that pile of plate steel was the curved top portion of an old gravel plow. The Lidgerwood had been originally designed for ballasting work. Rail cars full of gravel could be emptied by hauling the plow from one end to the other through the cars, with this little gravel plow being pulled through by the Lidgerwood cable. The regular ballast cars, called Hart cars, were specially designed for construction work. When the P.G.E. were short of these cars for a period of time, they converted a bunch of flat cars into gravel cars by using some of the 5/16th inch steel plates as aprons on the end of each flat car. They were hinged onto one car and flopped over to reach the next car. They would put stakes on the sides and boards inside in order to fill up the flatcars at the gravel pit. When they were ready to dump the gravel on the track, they would just pull off the boards with a crowbar, run out the cable to the plow, and pull the plow along the flat cars, spilling the gravel off. When I remembered this little section of curved plate—the top portion of that gravel plow—which was out there with that pile of plates, I mentioned it to Harold Bailey. So it was decided that we would build ourselves a snowplow onto the front end of Engine 59.

There was no sign of that pile of plates, of course, because they were buried in the snow, about halfway between the shop and the north switch. The yard crew and the engine crew were off working to clear the yard, so we had to go after the plates ourselves. I took all the men that were left from the shop and the car shop—there were about six or eight of us—and we managed to break our way through to the pile of plates with some shovels. We were well up above our waists in snow with an icy crust on top. We took turns at being the lead man, smashing the crust and beating the snow down. That man would then step aside, and the next man would lead and break trail, and then the next, until finally we got to the plates and dug them out. Then we had to manhandle a plate loose and slide it over to the old roundhouse. We made three trips to bring in three plates. It was all that the men could do to stumble and slide and shove those plates across the yard. It was 5/16th inch steel plate and they were about ten feet long and about four feet wide. Somehow, we got them into the shop. By this time we had gotten the yard crew to clear the track with the Jordan Spreader so we could get a cable onto the curved plow section. We pulled the plow section up to the main line and back to the roundhouse, where we transported it with rollers to Engine 59.

The design of this plow required some thought. The cutting point was to be the curved portion from the Lidgerwood gravel plow. The three steel plates had to be anchored onto the front end of Engine 59 with angle iron, pipe, and timbers in such a way that when the plow struck snow, the front end of the engine would be forced down onto the track. This was very important. If the nose were forced up, the engine would easily derail and be useless. Also, the shocks had to be transmitted evenly to the front of the locomotive frame, so we needed wooden bracing as well as the steel cladding to throw off ice and snow. After a conference between Harold Bailey, Angus McRae, and myself, we were able to produce a design that our shop crew could fabricate with the materials we had on the spot.

We had a very good blacksmith by the name of Don Kirkwood, who came from the Canadian Pacific Railway. He could shape and work iron the way a child might play with a piece of plasticine. We also had a supply of Australian gumwood, which is one of the toughest woods known to man. So the carpenters went to work to form timbers out of the gumwood, while the boilermakers and the machine shop crew got going with pipe and angle iron and drilling. Meanwhile, the blacksmith kept his forge hot. Everyone in the shop was involved. Work progressed continuously; from Tuesday night until Friday night there were people working around the clock.

One of the most important jobs in converting Engine 59 into a snow plow was to make sure that the men in the cab were going to be safe when they tackled the drifts. We knew that the snow would be fifteen or sixteen feet high up in the canyon and beyond. Without some protection, the front windows and doors of the cab would be smashed in. So using timbers, we laminated two-inch planks across the front of the engine cab in order to make a four-inch wooden wall that could withstand anything short of solid rock. Unfortunately, that meant that the only way the engine crew could see ahead would be to stick their heads out of the side windows…but they were used to doing that sometimes, anyhow.

Plow on Engine 59. On the left side, Harold Bailey, Master Mechanic.
On the right side, Eric P. Stathers, Car Foreman.

By Saturday morning around ten o'clock, the last rivet and bolt were attached on the front of the plow and it was ready to go. Harold Bailey called the head office in Vancouver. Robert Wilson, the General Manager of P.G.E., asked him to keep a place in the cab of Engine 59 for him, and told Harold Bailey that he would be on the next boat to Squamish. Since Robert Wilson was responsible for all of the P.G.E. railroad operations, and the line had already been shut down for five days, he wanted to be there on the spot when the line was cleared. So Harold Bailey told us that Robert Wilson would be up on the Union Steamships boat the next day, at about 1:30 pm. It was decided that they would take a trial run up the line on Sunday morning, as far as Cheakamus, to see how well the plow worked. So Harold Bailey went out Sunday morning with Angus McRae as engineer plus his fireman and crew. They got to Cheakamus and could see that the canyon was fully blocked, so they worked their way back down to Squamish.

The plow worked fine, but there was a problem with ice forming along the sides of the engine. Engine 59 was brought back into the roundhouse for a small modification. All steam engines had a steam line running to the front end of the engine, with a steam hose attached to it. This steam hose was used continually for cleaning off various things, as well as for a connection to supply steam for other machinery, like the Lidgerwood or other track equipment that operated by steam. It was also used for cleaning the engine and for frozen switches. When you came up to a frozen switch, a couple shots of steam would thaw it out very quickly. So in the roundhouse they ran a feed from this line, back along the running board on each side of the locomotive to steam hoses that reached right back to the cab. These steam hoses turned out to be a vital part of the operation.

Side view of the snow plow on Engine 59.

Meanwhile, the assault team was organized for Monday morning. It required three locomotives, each with its own engineer and fireman. First came Engine 59, complete with the plow we had put together in the shop, and extra men in the cab. The second unit was another locomotive. The third unit was a locomotive pulling our auxiliary train as a work train, with sleeping accommodation and cooking facilities, a tool car, a tank car with fuel oil for the locomotives, and the Jordan Spreader. In the work train were all the section men we could gather, as well as the cook. All this because we did not have a mountain snow plow.

Snow plows are very specialized pieces of equipment. Most railroad men on this continent were used to operating in the prairies and over gentle graders in low snowfall areas, and they worked with a wooden plow. Only the mountain divisions had any experience with a mountain plow, which is a different thing altogether. On flat land, wind can drive snow into huge, hard-crusted piles along the track, but you know that when you hit that pile all you're going to find in there is ice and snow. Running a line through the mountains is completely different. When a slide covers the tracks, you have no idea at all what may be in there. Rocks, trees, and mud—everything on the hillside will come down, covered with ice and snow. Rocks will damage the equipment and cause derailments, but in some ways trees are more dangerous, especially when they are lying parallel to the track. There were three or four occasions in the old wooden plow days, on the C.P.R. and the C.N.R., when crews were bucking a slide in the mountains and trees were actually driven right through these wooden plows. In one case, the man who was operating the plow was actually decapitated, his head torn right off. It sounds dramatic, maybe, but the men who had to buck these mountain slides using only the old wooden plows were taking their lives in their hands. It took a lot of guts to wade into a blocked railway line with makeshift equipment, and that is what these men were being asked to do. Rotary plows were also used to some extent on the mountain divisions of the C.P.R. and the C.N.R., but they were not very satisfactory. If there were any rocks in the slide or the cutes, the rotating blades would hit these rocks and break. Then before the plow could go any further, spare blades would have to be bolted on, causing endless delays.

On Monday morning everyone was up early, all the engines were fired up, and the train moved off as soon as daylight came. At the head of the line was Engine 59, with six men in the cab; Angus McRae at the controls, with his fireman, Andy Steele; two special duty men, Scott McDonald and Charlie Midnight; the master mechanic, Harold Bailey; and the general manager, Robert Wilson. Engineer Andy Hutton and fireman Fred Eadie manned the second engine. When they got to the canyon, they stopped and broke up into two units. The work train stayed about half a mile back. The plan was for the first two engines, coupled together, to drive full tilt into the snow until they got stuck. The work train engine would then come up and couple on and help pull the engines free. When they had backed clear, the section crew would shovel away all the snow on the line to give a clear run into the next part of the snowdrifts.

Engine 59, with snowplow stuck in the snow.

So they fired up for a full head of steam, and the two engines took a flying run at the snow, driving everything ahead into a compact wall that piled up until it went right over the top of the smokestack. The force of the impact and the pressure turned snow into ice, which froze immediately all over the locomotives. The whole works was stuck and could not move. Then Scott McDonald and Charlie Midnight took hold of the special steam hoses that we had run from the front of the engine to the cab. They poked their steam hoses out the side windows and melted a hole in the snow, big enough for them to drop down onto the ground. Then they worked their way along the side of the engine, melting the ice and snow to clear off all the side rods, wheels, and the driving gear of the locomotives. The reason they had to do this was that, along with the driving parts, the reversing gear and linkage were clogged with snow and ice and would not operate. They actually burrowed a tunnel along the side of the engines, making a kind of Turkish bath, with clouds of steam and water dripping from the top of the tunnel. When they were done they came back up into the winter cold, and how they didn't catch pneumonia is a mystery to me.

Engine 59 stuck, with a steam cloud behind the smoke stack from the steam hose that the men used to free the engine.

Then the work train came up and hooked onto the two locomotives and helped pull them clear of the slide. When they had backed off, the section crew cleaned off the remaining loose snow. This was uphill work, all right. Cheakamus Canyon is an average grade of 2.2 percent. On most of this stretch, there was no sign of any track. The snow was twelve feet deep on the bank side, and the only markers were the telephone poles that ran alongside of the track about 150 feet apart. The two engines would take a run of maybe three or four pole lengths, driving as hard as they could and as far as they could, which would vary depending on whether it was just drifted snow or slide snow. The front of Engine 59 had been boarded up for safety, and in that deep snow the side windows had to be closed as well, so they were running blind, full tilt straight into the drifts and slide snow, containing God knows what. This was very dangerous for the operating crew. The engineer and fireman, however, sat on raised platforms, one on each side of the cab. The other men had to find a safe place to hold on, and keep out of the way of the footplate. Every engine is supplied with water and fuel from an auxiliary vehicle called the tender, which is coupled immediately behind the engine. A steel plate the width of the tender is bolted to the tender floor and extends across to the floor of the locomotive cab. This footplate, from continual rubbing and shifting with the movement of the engine, develops a razor-sharp front edge. So Harold Bailey and Robert Wilson showed a lot of fortitude being right on the job with the frontline troops, and you have to give them credit. So they bucked through, and bucked through.

P.G.E. grade west of the Cheakamus, after Engine 59 had been pulled back from where it was stuck. Note the depth of the snow compared to the telephone poles alongside track.

At the old Twenty-six Mile, just north of Brandywine, there was a high cut with walls sixteen to twenty-five feet high. This cut was not very long, but it was full of snow. They knew that there was no danger of trees or slide material in this cut, so they decided to try and punch a hole through in one sweep. They cut the locomotive off from the work train and coupled it behind the other two, and these three engines went full tilt into the cut and succeeded in breaking through. Further up the line, coming onto the flats before Alta Lake, they left the work train and the three engines all coupled together and, with the throttles open, had enough power to push steadily along. It was certainly an impressive sight to see three locomotives throwing a huge spume of flying snow off to each side of the track, as they drove through snow that almost covered the engines. By Monday night they had reached Alta Lake, which is known today as Whistler. There was a water tank at Alta Lake where the train crews could fill up the engine tenders, and a siding, so they could get the fuel oil car alongside the engines to refuel. All the men had a hot supper and a chance to rest. Alta Lake is in the heavy snow belt. I wasn't on this trip, but I've been up there another time when we were working in ten feet of snow on the level, and I gather that there was a good ten feet of snow on the ground on this trip. By the time a train hits ten feet of snow on the level, you're throwing snow well up over the top of your engine. The descriptions given here may seem fanciful, but they have been confirmed at the time this chapter was written by Scott McDonald, who was working one of the steam hoses in Engine 59.

The snowplow just punched a hole through the snow, with the shovellers clearing the track behind the engine.

The next day, Tuesday, they pushed on. In this stretch of line there were a lot of short cuts, where the rock and the banks rise up sharply on either side of the line. There is no place for the snow to go when you push it, so it just jams up and compacts, unlike on a slide or a side hill, where it gets pushed off to one side. In a cut, you just have to get in and drive it out of the way. This was very hard on the shovel gang. Shoveling snow is back-breaking work, as anyone will know who has ever tried it. The men worked in terrible conditions, in the rain and snow, sweating and straining to move mountains of soggy wet snow, yard after yard, mile after mile. At night they returned to the bunk cars, which were full of wet clothes, had poor sleeping accommodation, and had no proper heating. Even the food was not all that good. It was pretty damned tough.

Meanwhile, the head office of the railway and the P.G.E. employees came in for a lot of criticism in the newspapers and on the radio—this was long before television, of course. The head of the old CCF party, Dr. Lyle Telford, was making political hay out of our troubles, being very critical of the inept government that could not even do a simple thing like run a provincial railway. There were headlines every day about the inept management and the inadequate employees. Here we were, doing our utmost to get the road open and keep it open, working all the hours that God sent, and becoming exhausted in our efforts to keep things moving. Meanwhile, he sat in his nice warm office in Vancouver and criticized the employees of the Pacific Great Eastern. I'd have liked to see him on the end of a shovel in one of those cuts after the plow had stalled, and see what he could do. Then how much criticism would he have for us at the end of a day's work? When the next election rolled around, that party received very few votes from our district, I can tell you. You don't forget things like that.

By Tuesday night the crew were at Birken, which again had a siding, so they could stop and service the trains, and the men could get some rest. From Birken, it's all downhill into Pemberton. Early Wednesday morning they were on their way. There was only one cut, and a lot of side hill plowing along the Green River, until they managed to reach the snow plow some time around noon on Wednesday. Luckily, the plow was not damaged. It had just been caught in the slide and needed digging out. They managed to pull it out with the engine and got it back on the track, and by Wednesday night they were back in Pemberton. Meanwhile, the road crew from Lillooet had tackled the job of reopening the line from Lillooet going south. Road master Pete Rebegliati rounded up an engine and some flatcars and all the men with shovels he could get, and they started working their way down the line from Lillooet towards Pemberton. The dry belt country in this area does not get much snow, so they were able to make better time than our crew coming from the south. However, their method was much the same, running at the snow with the engine, and then clearing it off with shovels and the steam hose. They would return to Lillooet at night and come back out over the line the following day. So the crew from Squamish and the crew from Lillooet actually arrived into Pemberton at about the same time. Then a snowplow crew was organized to make a run down to Squamish, with the plow and the flanger another track-clearing tool that removes snow between the tracks and at switch points. They cleared out the sidings and the main line, returned north to Lillooet, and then it was business as usual.

So the line reopened after being closed for eleven days, and the regular train—mixed passenger and freight—left Squamish on Friday afternoon, on schedule. But that was not the end of our snow problems for that winter. We were able to keep the line open between Squamish and Lillooet using the original wooden plow, but they were also having problems on the line north of Lillooet. The terrain there is quite different, and the snow is much lighter, but they were getting slides of mixed gravel and snow, which is very heavy stuff to shift. So we did not take the plow off Engine 59, but instead sent it north, to keep the line clear between Lillooet and Clinton. Beyond Clinton, they were up on the plateau, where the snow is just like powder, and the engines and flangers could keep the line open.

That specially fabricated plow remained in service for a number of years after that. Each spring we would remove the framework and plow from the front of Engine 59, and store it away in the Squamish yards. The next winter, as soon as our regular plow began working, we would install our special plow on the front of Engine 59 and send it north for winter service, in order to keep the line open north of Lillooet. Finally one day they tackled a slide that had a little too much gravel in it, and our poor old plow came back to Squamish looking like it had hit a brick wall or a granite cliff. It was buckled up like a concertina. The engine was not damaged much, but that was the end of the Engine 59 plow. It performed remarkable service during its lifetime and there was a lot of credit due to the men who built and the men who operated it.

In those days, there was a great feeling of loyalty among the men towards the railroad. They took pride in seeing that they did the best job possible under the adverse circumstances that they had to work under, when we had no money and lacked the proper equipment to handle so many jobs. I don't think the people of British Columbia had any idea of the devotion that these men gave to their jobs and the service they gave to their province, with their efforts in keeping the P.G.E. railroad operating. It didn't help much to hear people talk about the "Please Go Easy" or the "Prince George Eventually", and other clever jibes, when our men were working their guts out to keep the road open without the proper equipment. Perhaps people reading this story will have some appreciation of what the working man felt towards his job and his loyalty to his company in those bygone days. It seems to me that we've lost that somehow, and I hope that readers will understand why I think we could stand to have a little more of that feeling back in our workforce today.

4 UNDERWATER SALVAGE

1937 and 1943

Early on in my career as a car foreman for the Pacific Great Eastern Railway, one of the things that required fixing was the accommodation provided for our crew during our trips up and down the line picking up derailments. When I say our crew, that included me. When I first arrived in 1929, we traveled and ate and slept in the tool car, along with the cables, slings, jacks, tools, and so forth. The living conditions were terrible, with all the men crowded together like sardines in a can. What we needed was a separate car for the crew, an accommodation car of some kind. Now out in the marshaling yard there were a number of lightweight steel coaches. These had been part of the passenger service on the North Vancouver to Whytecliff line. This service was provided by three or four motor cars, like interurban cars, which pulled these lightweight coaches behind them, like a great big day coach. When the line was closed down in November of 1928, this equipment was brought up to Squamish. So I got permission to convert one of these coaches into a bunk car.

Those coaches were just like tin cans, with one sheet of steel between the car's occupants and the outside elements. There was no insulation in the walls, just a wooden lining inside the steel plate, with big, single-pane glass windows along both sides of the car. We blocked off some of the windows, and scrounged a cook stove to put at one end, along with a dining table and an ice box to keep our meat. We got some old steel beds to make double decker bunks in the car, and put another heater down at the other end of the car from the cook stove. This was a great improvement, as far as it went, and we used this car through the 1930s and 1940s, until we could get something better. Not having insulation was a problem, because the car was very cold in the winter and very hot in the summer. The winter was the worst. I've been out on a call in the winter and had my blankets freeze tight to the wall of the bunk car. The men would hang up their wet clothes when they went to bed, and the moisture from all the bodies and drying clothes used to condense on the metal roof of the car and drip down onto the men in the upper bunks and down onto the floor of the car. But still, it was a great improvement.

This particular time, in the summer of 1937, we got a call to a derailment at Anderson Lake, so we collected a crew together and made up our salvage train, which included the Lidgerwood, the little seven-ton steam pot crane, the tool car, some flat cars, and our converted bunk car, and headed up the line. The 28-mile stretch we call the Lake District was just about the only part of the line which did not climb up or down at maximum grades, so you might think it would be relatively easy to operate trains through this stretch, but this was not the case.

Anderson and Seton Lakes were at one time one long lake, until sometime in the last glacial age when a landslide came down practically at the centre to form a flat strip of land about a mile long. During the gold rush days of 1858, the miners came up from the coast, up the Fraser River and north on the Harrison River, through Harrison Lake and up the Birkenhead River to Anderson Lake. A steamboat at Anderson Lake carried them up to this strip of land, which was called Seton Portage, and here was built the first railway in British Columbia. It consisted of wooden rails with iron straps on them, and the rolling stock was little carts pulled by oxen. Freight was transferred from the steamer to the carts, and then passengers and freight rode the mile to Seton Lake, where everything was transferred to another steamer, which proceeded up to the other end of Seton Lake and the outskirts of Lillooet, which is Mile Zero on the Cariboo Highway.

When the Pacific Great Eastern Railway construction crews came to these lakes, they decided to build along the west side. I have no idea why. It must have been hard to choose between the east side and the west side, as they are both very rugged. The roadbed was built more or less to follow the contours of the rock bluffs, and it was very curvy. There was only one tunnel at Anderson Lake, just after you pass D'Arcy, which is a village at the south end of the lake. The line jumped from outcrop to outcrop, across little gullies at the edge of the lakes. The construction crews just made a crisscross cribbing with timbers and filled in with gravel in order to build up the roadbed. There was no provision for any shoulder between the line and the lake. In other places, they built trestles that were anchored into the sloping rock, with water underneath the line, so if the train became derailed it went right into the lake. In some places the line ran on solid rock right at the lake's edge, with a vertical drop into water so deep you couldn't see bottom. There were plenty of places where if the train jumped the track, all that would have been left would be a few air bubbles to mark where the cars had sunk out of sight. For years and years, the line operated on the original 60-pound steel rails and not very much ballast, because there was never the money to upgrade it from its first construction condition. Today of course, this has all been changed. All the wooden cribbing has been replaced by concrete retaining walls that reach from one rock outcrop to the next, and gravel fill behind the walls provides a good roadbed and plenty of room for a good shoulder between the rails and the walls. Where there used to be wooden trestles there are now steel bridges. The curves have been eased and the line has been straightened out a good deal. The track is 125-pound steel, well ballasted, making a fine modern line—altogether different from the conditions we had to face.

This accident involved a gas-driven electric crane that belonged to the Bridge River Power Company, who had been doing quite a bit of construction work to supply electric power to the Bridge River area mining companies during the little gold rush boom in the mid-1930s. A lot of traffic for the railway had been generated by mining activity—it had been keeping us rolling for quite a few years. They had been using this crane at Shalalth on Seton Portage, and as the work had been completed, arrangements were made to ship it south to Vancouver for delivery to the B.C. Electric Railway Company yards. The crane must have weighed around 60 tons, and it had a long boom, about thirty feet long. As a locomotive crane, it ran on tracks, so it did not need to be loaded, but was just connected onto a southbound freight train. So the B.C. Electric gave the operator at Lillooet orders to have this crane picked up.

Now for some reason, the power company crew did not detach the boom from the crane, which they were definitely supposed to do. Instead, they lowered the boom onto a flatcar and tied it down with telephone guy wire. As it happened, the crane was facing forward down the line, with the boom sitting on a big block on the flatcar in front of it. Since there was no way of turning it around, even if they had thought of it, the freight crew just cut the load into the train. As the crane worked down this curvy stretch of track, with the boom still attached, it was swinging from side to side on the flatcar. It was just a matter of time before it would break loose. They got from Shalalth down to Seton Portage, where the train crew had to stop and phone in to the dispatcher. Then off they went again down the side of Anderson Lake. Somewhere about six miles down the line, the boom worked free, swung over to the bank side of the track and dug into the bank, bringing the crane to an abrupt halt. With all that pressure from the moving crane behind it, the boom buckled and twisted. The coupler between the flatcar and the crane broke, and the rest of the train proceeded down the track while the crane sheared off down the bank and into the lake, piling up the rolling stock behind it in a heap of flatcars and boxcars.

Derailment south of the Bridge River Power Company Crane

By good luck, there happened to be a gentle sloping bank where the derailment occurred, instead of the usual sharp drop-off. It was the site of a very old slide, which provided a smooth area of seven or eight acres, a nice sandy beach out to a gentle slide into the lake, and a shallow rise back from the tracks to the rock bluffs some way inland. Not much damage had been done to the track and there was plenty of room to work, so the line had been restored by the time we arrived. The first thing that needed to be done was to rerail the boxcars and flatcars and get them out of the way. The flatcars had remained upright, as well as some of the boxcars, although they were crosswise to the track. However, several of the boxcars were lying over on their side. Our little crane could not lift them, so we had to use the Lidgerwood cable and turn the cars over with what is called a "rolling hitch". What this amounted to was passing the cable over the top of the boxcar, down the side and underneath, and hooking on to the steel girder or wooden sill of the car. This gave us a wrap around the car, so when we took up on the cable, the car would be rolled over onto its feet and into an upright position. It may sound easy, but doing this is no easy task. Before we could put the cable in place, we had to dig a hole underneath the tipped-over boxcar, and then work the cable through, while another man wriggled into place to put the cable hook onto the sill of the car. The wrap did not form a smooth arc, of course, but angled a bit over the car towards the farthest end away from the Lidgerwood. This way, when we pulled it, it was like unscrewing a screw. The car would turn on its axis as it swung up off the ground. When it was upright, we had to build a skid bed with timbers and rails, and use the Lidgerwood to haul the car over to the main line. We could pull the trucks over to the track, and the little steam crane had enough power to pick up the trucks and put them on the track. Then we had to jack the boxcar up in the air over the track, roll the trucks underneath, drop the car back onto its trucks, and the locomotive would pull it back to the nearest siding. That siding was at Marne, south of the derailment. That was the effort required to deal with one car. Then we'd start all over again on the next car.

I should explain about these trucks. When the first railway cars were built, they were quite short, with two wheels on a fixed axle at each end. These did not travel very well around curves, because the front and rear wheels tried to stay in line. When the length of the car increased, more wheels were necessary to carry the load. Separate "trucks" or "bogies" were developed, consisting of two axles and four wheels in a unit, with heavy springs to reduce running shock to the car. These trucks have a steel frame, four steel wheels, two axles, and springs; they are heavy. On top of the trucks is a heavy round casting like a round dish. This casting is made to match a casting on the underside frame of the railcar. When one casting is inserted into the other, the car is not rigidly attached. The car casting sits about two inches down into the truck casting, and there is a two-inch round steel pin that sticks up in the centre to hold the car and the trucks in place. The swivel mounting permits the trucks to follow the track with their wheels, and allows some lateral movement between the trucks and the car. The steel pin is not keyed to the castings, but just sits there. In the shock of a derailment, the cars will be forced up off the tracks. Sometimes the cars will ride up on those pins or slide right off and away from the line, while the trucks, which are heavier and lower, generally remain close to the rails. Of course, when a boxcar turned over, it generally separated from the trucks, which would then be recovered and hauled back to the tracks separately.

That summer of 1937 was a really hot one. On the site it was maybe 110 or 112 degrees Fahrenheit in the shade—but there was no shade. Everyone was working and sweating. We were sweating when we were standing and doing nothing, but the sun kept us dried off until dinnertime, when we had to go into the bunk car to eat. I don't know how the poor cook survived, working over his hot stove in that tin can of a car, with no air stirring. We were all hungry, of course, but the minute we got into that car we started to sweat, and the hot soup and meat and potatoes didn't help cool us down any. We just bolted our dinners and got out of there fast. The hot weather always took a lot out of us. Some years later a man we had cooking for us made up a drink of oatmeal water or iced tea with lots of salt in it, which helped considerably to relieve our thirst. We had never heard of salt tablets in those days.

Picking up all those cars took several days. There were only two regular trains a week, so we had the line to ourselves for long periods of time, but we needed it since we could only handle one car at a time. We had to recover the trucks, right the car, skid it up to the line, jack it up over the rails, rerail the trucks, slide them under the car, jack the car down, and then haul it back to Marne siding. When we had recovered all the cars, it was time to go after the Bridge River Power Company crane.

Bridge River Power Company crane in Anderson Lake.

The crane was some way from the tracks, and it was going to be a heavy pull, so we had to rig up the strongest straight pull we could get with our Lidgerwood cable. That meant using pulley blocks, and since there was nowhere to hand a block—no trees or bluff handy—we had to put in a "deadman". The section crew brought us some bridge timbers that were lying alongside the track, and we dug a long trench about seven or eight feet deep into the slide up the hill, parallel to the track. We put timbers and rail into the trench, and dug a slot in the middle from the ditch towards the track. Then we wrapped a heavy choker cable around those timbers, fed it through the slot, and filled in the whole T-shaped trench, tamping it down hard so nothing would slide or shift. The Lidgerwood was brought along the line, with the locomotive and the work train behind it, and we put on our Lidgerwood stops.

Close-up of the crane in the water of Anderson Lake.

For normal work, railroad men had developed some stops that clamped to the track to help tie down their cranes. But when we tried these, the Lidgerwood, which was an extremely powerful steam donkey engine, had just pulled the stops right off. So we got to work in the Squamish shops and made our own Lidgerwood stops. These were shaped like the old oxen yokes, in an upside-down capital "Y" shape, with slots across the two forks of the Y. We set the stops down on the track were we wanted them and drove wedges with a hammer in order to force the stop hard against the rail, grabbing it tight. Then with ordinary railroad ties across the tracks against the two stops, we could stop a regular train wheel, three foot diameter. For a simple pull, the engineer set all brakes on emergency, which made the whole train act like an anchor. If the load did not move, the train would slide along the tracks as cable wound in, until it hit the Lidgerwood stops. If we kept on pulling, either the load would shift or the Lidgerwood climbed right over the stops. That happened more than once on different jobs, and it was a real mess. We had to stop and jack the Lidgerwood up, pull everything back, and start over again.

The little steam crane also had rail clamps in order to make it more stable. Braces welded to the crane body extended down towards the track. We could put the clamps under the rail and connect them to the brace with a turnbuckle. The turnbuckles have a right-hand thread on one end and a left-hand thread on the other, so by turning the centre we could take up on both end-rods at the same time and cinch the crane down to the track. This added perhaps five or ten percent more capacity to the limit of the lift before the tracks started to come up in the air and the crane tipped over. We watched the tracks to see when we were at the limit of our lift.

Trying to pull the crane out, before digging out the track.

Turnbuckles are also used to secure the cab of locomotive cranes. The Bridge River Power Company crane had some that were designed to keep the cab locked in place, so that it did not turn while traveling up or down the line. When the crane derailed these turnbuckles had been broken, and the cab was swung around across the bed of the crane. Before we could move the crane, it was necessary to somehow get the cab, which had all of the machinery in it, swung back parallel to the bed of the crane. Otherwise, it would be lopsided and fall over. This meant getting into the water with jacks and cables. We jacked and pulled until the cab was turned around parallel to the bed and then tied it in place with cables. We did not have any diving gear, but it was very hot weather and the lake front was shallow there, so with just our pants and shirts and boots on, we managed that part of it okay.

Then it was time to hook up for a pull. We had extended a cable from our deadman hold down to the middle of the track, to secure a pulley block. The Lidgerwood cable ran through that block, straight down to a block on the big crane, and back to the anchor block, to give a mechanical advantage on the pull. The little steam pot was rigged to try and lift the corner of the crane as the pull was made. There was a terrific weight involved here. When they construct locomotive cranes, they fill up the bed with round steel punching to make it very heavy and stable, in order to act as a counterweight for any load which the crane will lift. Now between the cab and machinery, the bed, and the steel punchings, there was maybe 40 tons, and with the trucks, almost 60 tons of dead weight to pull up out of the water and back to the track. So with everything set, we took a pull. The crane did not budge, but we broke a block.

While we got another block into place, some of the men went under the lower corner of the crane with a big jack, dug a hole underwater in the sand under the corner and managed to get some lift on the corner of the crane, which would ease the strain on the rigging and allow a better pull for the little steam pot. There was no way to get any timber underneath the crane in that soft sand and dirt bottom. So with a replacement block, and the whole pull rigged, we tried again. And broke some more rigging. So we stopped and picked up the pieces, repaired and spliced what we could and decided to give it one more try. Out we went into deeper water to put down some more jacks, and succeeded in getting a bit of lift on both sides of the crane. Then we gave it another try—and everything flew to pieces. The mainline on the Lidgerwood was still good, but we had smashed all our blocks and our rigging was all used up. By this time we had been out quite a while, so it was decided that we would go back down to Squamish and see about getting some more equipment while the boys had a couple of days off.

This break also gave us a chance to think about the job. First, Harold Bailey, the master mechanic, went to the logging companies in Squamish and borrowed some big heavy high-rigging blocks. Mr. Keely was the general manager of the logging company, which later became Empire Mills. These were huge blocks—it took two men to lift them—and along with the blocks he got some very heavy cables, chokers, and lengths of cable that we could use for pulling. Our Lidgerwood cable was fine, as it was an inch-and-a-quarter cable. We got all this gear into the tool car and figured out the timetable. It was obvious that even with the new heavy rigging we could never pull the crane up the bank, because the ground was just too soft. The answer was to pull the crane right through the roadbed. This meant we had to pick our time to open up the line; the best time would be after a passenger train went south on Saturday morning. That would give us the rest of Saturday, all Sunday, and Monday until the evening, when the up train was due. That was the plan; so we headed north on Friday, back to Anderson Lake.

Pete Rebegliati, who was the road master from Lillooet, got extra section men down from the sections on each side of the accident site, and as soon as the train cleared through Saturday morning they got to work. They cut the rails right opposite where the crane lay and dug all the dirt out of the roadbed, clearing it right out, in order to make a ditch from the roadbed to the crane. Then we hooked up all of the heavy-duty rigging, putting the big blocks on so we could get a double purchase by using a diamond hitch. We didn't bother with the jacks this time, because we didn't intend to lift, just to pull. So I took up my spot for giving the go-ahead signals, with a flag in my right hand to control the Lidgerwood operator, and using my other hand to control the little steam pot crane operator, and gave them the go-ahead sign. We took up all the slack and then, sure enough the load started to shift. We kept winding in line and pulling and pulling, and as the crane dragged through the ditch, the Lidgerwood was sliding slowly down the track until it hit the Lidgerwood stops. We didn't stop—we kept on pulling—and the Lidgerwood climbed up on the stops, and we kept pulling, and the crane kept sliding, and why I don't know, but the Lidgerwood held at those stops and didn't go over. We didn't stop pulling until the Bridge River Power Company crane was sitting in that ditch right across the P.G.E. grade, and the bed of the crane was level with the grade. If it hadn't been for the rotating part of the crane, we could have laid rail right over the bed and no one would have known it was there.

The next job was to get the crane turned around parallel with the track, which was not difficult. We were able to anchor the bank end with cables to a rock outcropping, and then got a purchase on the other end with the Lidgerwood cable, and by pulling and dragging we swung it around in line with the track. Luckily, there was no trouble with the cab portion, which stayed in line with the bed of the crane. But it was now necessary to jack the crane out of the ditch, back up to line level. We had our heaviest jacks, but in that soft sand we seemed to go down two inches for every inch the load was lifted. It was jack, and block, and jack, and block for the better part of the day. Finally we got the whole crane onto blocks, and then as we jacked it up in the air, the section crews were filling in with gravel, in case the jacks slipped. They actually built a roadbed under the crane as we kept jacking it up. After a whole day of this, we had the crane up high enough for Pete's crew to slide ties and rails in underneath. The steam pot pulled the trucks onto the line, and they were put on the rails under the crane. We eased off with the jacks, and the crane was back together again. By this time it was Sunday night. We called it a day, had supper, and a swim in the lake to cool off and then went right to our bunks. The work train just stayed there on the line overnight.

Next morning was Monday. The passenger train would be coming through that evening, so we started picking up all our equipment and cables, when somebody said, "I see a big piece of something out there in the water". It was a very calm morning, not a ripple in the water, and Anderson Lake was so clear at that time that you could see fifty feet or more down into the water. We could see a dark, round object about twenty-five or thirty feet out in the lake. Harold Bailey and I went to have a look, and he said, "My God! That's the big drive, the bull wheel off the crane. We've got to get that!" I replied, "Well, how in hell are we going to get it?" He said, "We'll have to go in the water and get it". I said, "Who?" "Well," says Harold, "you're the foreman. I guess it's up to you to get it out".

I was young, in my twenties, and could swim, and I knew that none of the men were much on swimming. I had done some underwater swimming while I was a kid. We put together a raft out of railway line, with boards for paddles and a couple of long poles, and three of us poled over to this object. Sure enough, it was a big geared bullwheel, about two feet in diameter and about eight inches across. So I dove underwater in my shorts—we had no bathing suits along, of course—to where this bullwheel was resting on the sandy bottom. The bank started to shelve there, and when I took hold of the bullwheel, it started to roll down into deeper water. I dropped it quickly and came up for air. While I caught my breath, hanging onto the raft, I figured that the only way to get it was for me to swim down, tip the gear up, roll it up towards the bank until I ran out of breath, then drop it and come up for air. When it was close enough to the bank, we could get a line through it and haul it in. There was a big hole in the middle of the bullwheel.

So that was how I did it: Dive down, tip it up, roll it as far as I could, then re-surface. It was a heavy casting, 200 pounds or more, and even in the water where it would weigh less, it was quite a heavy lift. The only way I could hold it was to put my hands under the gear teeth and roll it up so far then hold it with my legs and knees while I got a new grip, roll it a few more inches, and hold it—and then I'd have to come up for air. I don't know how long I could stay down—more than a minute, anyway—but after a number of tries, I managed to get it into shallower water, where I could hold it with my knees and stick my nose and mouth out of the water to breathe, and still hold it from rolling back into the lake.

The rast crew passed me a chain to hook onto the bullwheel. It was a very heavy chain with a slip-hook on the end, and it was hard work trying to wrestle with that bullwheel while using both hands to pass the chain through the hole and hooking onto the chain with the slip-hook, telling the men on the raft to give me some slack, and taking up the slack. They couldn't see what I was doing, and neither could I, because moving around on the lake bottom stirred up all the sand and mud. I got the chain hooked on, and while they hung onto the other end of the chain from the raft, I went towards the shore and they threw me a coil of light rope. I swam back to the raft with one end of the rope, and then we pulled out a length of light cable and shackled it to the chain. With the Lidgerwood and a system of pulley blocks rigged up on the Bridge River Power Company crane, they pulled the bullwheel up and onto the bank, while I followed behind, in case anything let go or broke, to prevent it from slipping back into the lake.

Finally, when we got it on shore, I came out of the lake and started shaking off the water, when one of the men said, "My God, Eric, what's happened to you?" I looked down to see what he was talking about. I was a mess of blood and grease, all the way from my calves right up to the inside of my groin, and my hands and the inside of my arms had a myriad of little razor-like cuts. What with all the grease on the gearwheel, and in the excitement of being underwater and fighting the weight, I had not felt the cuts being inflicted on me by the gear edges. But as soon as I stepped out of the water, the blood started to ooze out of them. None of the cuts were very deep, but with the whole combination of them, I guess I was quite a gory sight. So they took me over to the bunk car, and laid me on the bed with a clean sheet, and then they went to work on me with coal oil—it was all they had to get the grease off. When they had removed all the grease they could, they used iodine on the cuts, and oh boy!—If you have ever had a bunch of iodine on you, you know that it hurt like hell. There was no use trying to bandage me up, because I had so many cuts, I'd have been wrapped up like a mummy. I just had to lie still on the sheet, while Harold Bailey took over and organized the rest of the pick-up and got us moving home. It only took an hour or so before the cuts started to heal up and stop bleeding, because they weren't very deep, but there were so many of them that it was very painful, I can assure you. After that, I got dressed, and was careful not to move around too much. When we got to Squamish, I went right home to bed, called the doctor, and stayed in bed for a couple of days until the cuts had healed up enough so there wasn't any more bleeding.

That ended our experience with the crane, but this accident was the cause of serious litigation between the Bridge River Power Company (which was actually part of B.C. Electric) and the old Pacific Great Eastern Railway. The power company blamed us for the wreck, and we blamed them for not taking the boom off the crane. The onus, of course, is on the carrier; as soon as the carrier picks up any piece of equipment, or accepts it, then they are responsible. At the same time, anybody who offers such equipment for shipment is supposed to see that it is crated or lashed in such a manner that it will not be damaged in transit. So both parties were responsible, and the matter went to the courts, and it dragged on for a long time. In the meantime, the P.G.E. wouldn't pick up any piece of equipment from Shalalth, outside of material going into a closed car, unless an inspector was sent down from Lillooet, which is about twelve miles away. The shipper had to pay the cost of this inspector's wages and his traveling time there and back, and of course they did not like this. However, we would not pick up a thing until this had been done. Finally, the case went to the highest court in the province, and there was a settlement. It was a saw-off, I think; we were held responsible, but were able to offset with the costs of picking up and delivering the crane. If it had not been for the help of the logging company, we would have taken a lot longer to recover that crane. The company that supplied the heavy rigging was Keely Brothers, which became Empire Mills, with Mr. Keely as manager, and eventually became part of Weldwood Company. By the time the case was finished, the court costs were more than that whole business was worth.

In later years, we had other incidents at Anderson Lake; two of them were boxcars that went into the lake, loaded with lumber. The first one was soon after the Second World War. Three loaded cars went into the water, and the trucks stayed with these cars, tied by the brake rods. When one of these boxcars is loaded full of lumber, the car will float about fourteen inches out of the water. So we got hold of an Indian at D'Arcy who owned a fourteen-foot boat with a 15-horsepower outboard engine, and he and his helper put a tow rope on these cars and towed all three of them down the lake to the beach at D'Arcy, where we had a better chance of fishing them out. One of our crew had been with the submarine service during the war and decided that he'd like to go for a sail down the lake, so he jumped aboard the top of a boxcar, and proceeded to enjoy himself. However, all of a sudden, the wind got up and the lake got rough, and there he was on top of the boxcar, with the waves splashing around him, soaking wet with spray and nothing he could do about it, because they couldn't land the boxcars and he couldn't get off. It took a good two hours to haul the boxcars down to the end of the lake where the beach was, and even then he had to jump off and swim to shore, because the beach was so shallow that the trucks grounded long before it got anywhere near where we could reach it. So this was another water salvage operation.

However, by this time we had better equipment and more practice. If you go by D'Arcy, you will see at the south end of the lake a huge round boulder on the left-hand side of the track, which is where we were able to anchor our pulley blocks and haul the cars up onto the beach. Actually, the lumber was unloaded first, and then they were hauled out with the Lidgerwood onto the bank and re-railed in the usual way. In another wreck after that, we cut the trucks off the boxcars before floating them up the lake, and recovered the lumber and cars as before.

Both Seton and Anderson lakes were the scene of so many accidents in those early days that many of them were not worth recalling. Only the really bad ones left any impression on my mind. There were a number of very difficult areas there, where there was no room to work. In a later chapter I will recount stories of wrecks where we were working up against sheer rock walls, with no room to swing the crane around and no way to pick up anything, because the back of the crane would hit the rock wall. The lake district might have been flat, but it was anything but easy to operate through. Of course, that was all in the past. The line is completely different now, without the conditions that we had to face in those early years.

5 SAVED BY THE SWITCH

1943

Pavilion is a station up on the railroad about twenty miles north of Lillooet. When they were building the Pacific Great Eastern line, they had to find a route that would carry them from Lillooet, which is right on the Fraser River, up onto the high plateau of the Cariboo. Pavilion is right on the old gold rush trail. It is situated between two ranges of hills, part way up Kelly Lake, which is at the top of the grade. Long before there was any railroad or any gold rush, the different Indian bands from the Coast and the Interior traveled and traded through this area, living mostly on fish and game. Horses came in with the fur brigade people, and cows came in after the gold rush. In the gold rush days, there were two ways to get into the Cariboo from the coast. One was to follow the mountain pack trail up the side of the Fraser Canyon from Hope to Lytton, and then up the Thompson River, and north through Cache Creek and 100 Mile House, to Barkerville. The other route turned off the Fraser River at the junction of the Harrison River, through Harrison Lake, Anderson Lake, Seton Lake, to Lillooet, then up the side of the Fraser River through Pavilion, and over Pavilion Mountain to Kelly Lake and Clinton, where the route joined the other way from Cache Creek north. There was another pass from Pavilion through the Pavilion Lake valley, which the Indians used, but that came out at Cache Creek and was a roundabout way to the goldfields that few people took. They did not spend much time looking around, but headed straight for the pay dirt.

There is more than one kind of pay dirt. An enterprising young man named Robert Carson had joined the rush for riches, but for some reason, when he got high up on the road over the Kelly Lake hill, he stopped to look at the view. At the edge of the plateau, where the terrain flattens out, it is beautiful lush rolling grasslands, dotted with little lakes and sparse bush. What he saw was a vision of beef cattle, grazing on the thick range grass. So he staked a claim on an area of land for cattle ranching, and filed a pre-emption claim to homestead there. This was the beginning of one of the first ranches in British Columbia. The Carson family is well known among our earliest settlers, and were an important part of the community. They even took their name and the ranch as a kind of basis for the farm broadcasts on the CBC, and in my time Ernie Carson was the Member of the Provincial Legislative Assembly for our constituency, and a fine man he was, too. Anyway, there was a demand for beef to supply the mining camps, and people on their way back and forth required supplies, so the Carson family established a little general store at Pavilion and did their freighting of beef over the road from there. This so-called "road" was really something to experience.

Let me give you an idea of what the people during the gold rush had to conquer with their wagon trains. The hills were so steep going down from the plateau into Kelly Lake that the wagons needed to have their back wheels chained to act as a brake as they went down into the bottom of the valley. Even this was not enough on the steep trail, so they would cut down the biggest trees they could get and chain two or three of them behind the wagon to act as a drag. The road from Lillooet to the base of Kelly Lake hill is all rolling hills, so the old wagon road dipped up and down with the contours of the land. The oxen were powerful enough to handle the pulling and pushing, but when horses and mules came in, they would rest at the top of a hill, hold back the best they could on the downhill part, and then rush through the dip at the bottom to get momentum for the hill. The road was not much better when I first came into that country. In the 1940's I was a passenger in a big Oldsmobile and the man who was driving had no idea what he was doing. He was a city driver and he scared the devil out of me, going much too fast around those sharp corners on the switchbacks. Four or five times, I figured for sure we were going over the bank. Hairpin bends and a rollercoaster—that was the old highway.

When they came to construct the railroad up this stretch of country, trying to service the established communities, it was some problem. The line climbs from an altitude of 740 feet above sea level at Lillooet, up to an altitude of 3510 feet at Kelly Lake, in a distance of 35 miles. This means grades between 2.2 percent and 2.5 percent all the way up the mountain. In one spot it's a good 1500 feet from the railroad track down into the Fraser River, and it gives you a funny feeling if you're on the front end of a train coming around some of these corners and look out over the edge of nothing—almost as if you're flying down between the mountains. To get through Pavilion, the line makes a big horseshoe bend around the two ranges of hill and goes around the little bench of land where the Carsons built their store.

At this time, in 1943 or thereabouts, there was a general store, a little gas pump, and a place where you could put up for the night. There was a slaughterhouse opposite the store, and quite a long siding, with a loading platform at the slaughterhouse. Halfway down the siding was a crossover track onto the main line. There was also a dead siding, which was a great place for outfit cars when the section crews were working up or down the line; with those grades and curves we pretty nearly always had an outfit car parked there in the summer months, maintaining the line either side of Pavilion station. A few Indians lived there, but most were up at the village and the reservation farther up the hillside in the Marble Canyon, on the way to Cache Creek. Marble Canyon gets its name from the curious rock formations—beautiful old Indian glyphs and stonework in the huge limestone deposits along Pavilion Lake. The Indians were always traveling back and forth between Pavilion and Lillooet, especially going down on the Wednesday train and back up on the Thursday night train. We were still running just the two mixed trains a week then. Anyway, the passenger trains always stopped at Pavilion.

This particular mishap involved Engine 54, coming south with a mixed train. They had order to pick up a refrigerator car from the siding at the slaughterhouse. I don't know whether it had been used for supplies for the store or for beef going down to Vancouver. Anyhow, the train was stopped north of the crossover switch. The front end brakeman cut the engine off from the train, turned the switch into the crossover, rode in onto the siding past the siding crossover switch, threw it back to the siding, and backed up to hook onto the refrigerator car. Then the engine returned out past the siding crossover switch, and the brakeman threw that switch back over to the crossover, ready to back up to his train again. Something made him look up—and the train, passengers and all, was rolling down the line, onto the crossover and right at him! I don't know where he jumped to, but the train crashed into the refrigerator car and drove it and the engine right down the siding to the mainline switch at the south end. The whole works could have gone right onto the main line. Locomotives will very often roll right through a switch whether it is set for them or not. I guess the engineer had all brakes locked on his engine. Anyway, it got hung up and derailed right beside the switch, and everything came to a stop. Nobody was hurt. The train was traveling very slowly when it slammed into the refrigerator car, so there was not much damage to equipment. But the engine was lying across the main line, by the south siding switch.

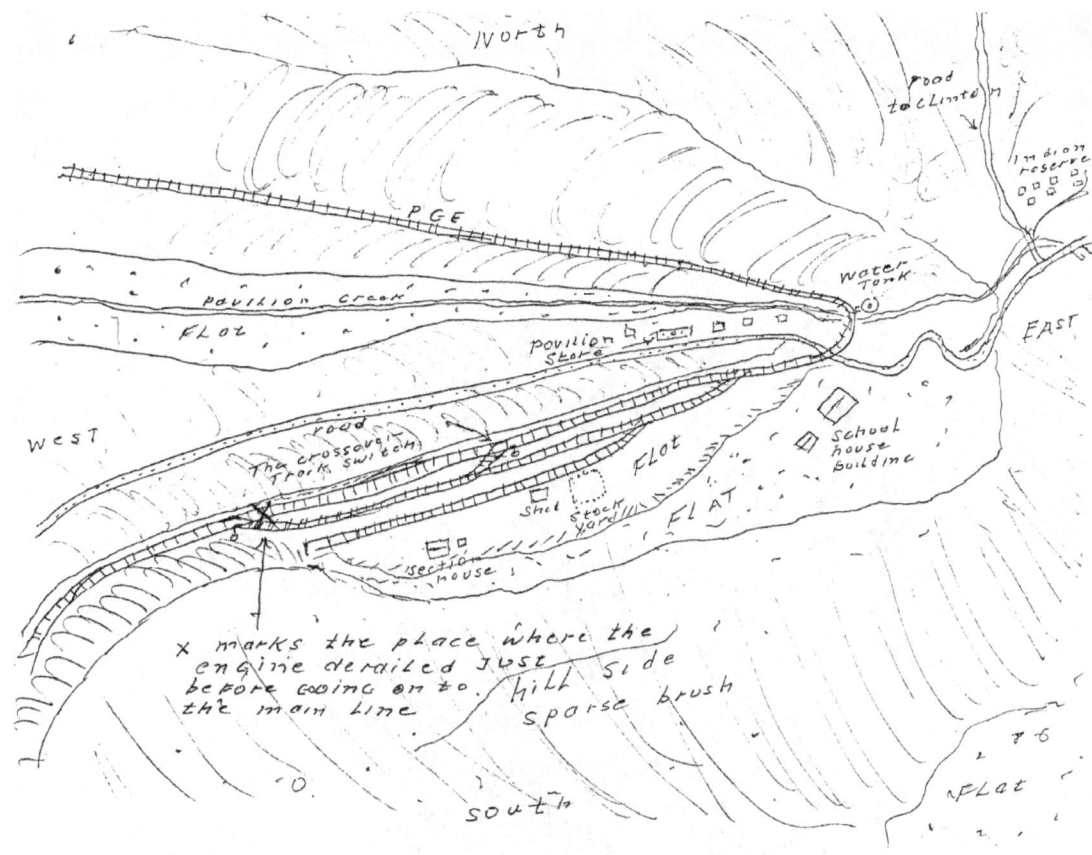

Map diagram of the Engine 54 derailment at Pavilion.
Hand-drawn by Eric P. Stathers.

There was an investigation, of course. The reason the train started to roll down the hill was because the brakes failed. Either they had not been set in the emergency position, or they leaked off enough air to move after the engine had been cut off from the train. We all knew that the entire line in that area was on a 2.2 percent or higher grade, except for the siding, and anytime our wrecking train was working in that area we had the handbrakes set on every car, so that even if the airbrakes had been set and went off, our train could not get started moving. But no handbrakes were set on that passenger train. I don't know the outcome of the investigation, of course, because when it took place we were out cleaning up the mess. I did hear that the brakeman left the service shortly afterwards.

This accident took place at about three o'clock in the afternoon, and we got called out in Squamish around 4:30, just before we left work to go home. We made up our usual train, with the Lidgerwood and the seven-ton steam pot crane, and worked our way up to the scene. By the time we arrived, they had brought an engine down from Williams Lake to haul the train away to a siding somewhere. There was no way to get past the derailed Engine 54. On one side of the line was a high bank going up, and on the other side the bank fell off sharply down to the highway, and from there down into the creek bed below at the bottom of a steep gully. These were the days before bulldozers, too; we had no way to cut into that uphill bank.

View from the bank side, looking across the gully to the other side of Pavilion Valley. The white line on the other hillside is the P.G.E. grade. Photographer: (Assumed) Artie Phair.

By this time, the section crews under Pete Rebegliati had started to construct what is known as a "shoefly"—a short bypass line around the wreck, on the edge of the bank. There was always a good big pile of railroad ties sitting on the flat somewhere along a siding. In fact, some of the farmers in that area earned extra cash by cutting ties and delivering them to the railway, at different points along the line. So the section crew dug rows of these ties into the bank below the line, made a crisscross, and the weight of any load passing over them was supposed to keep the ties in position and not make them shift. So by about ten o'clock at night, they had this shoefly built.

As soon as they had the rails in place, we very cautiously took our wrecking train over the shoefly. It was only a short train, consisting of the engine, tender, four cars, and a caboose. All the ties and timbers creaked and groaned as they were compressed into place under our load, as we inched past the fallen Engine 54 and the refrigerator car, up to the north end of the siding, and backed our work train into the siding. Then we got out our tools and got ready to tackle Engine 54. There was not much we could do, really, until daylight the next morning, but there was a freight train on its way up the line, which was expected to reach us sometime between midnight and one o'clock in the morning. So we had to get out and see that the freight got safely over the shoefly.

It started to rain and it was quite a miserable night. Eventually, the freight train came puffing up the valley, and stopped at the edge of the shoefly. Now in order to get the train safely across, we had to keep an eye on the wheels of every car as it crossed over the timbers on the temporary tracking. All we had was coal oil lamps and it was hard to see. The cribbing reached too high up off the ground for us to see anything from the ground, so we had to stand up on the cribbing, hanging onto the timbers right underneath the rails. It was not a very happy position to be in. However, there was no other way to do it, so our crew—there were six or seven of us—was distributed along the lower side of the shoefly, with the hillside below us and the track above us.

So the engine started across, and made it without any difficulty, and about half the train was safely over when I saw a wheel come off the track right onto these ties, coming bump, bump, and bump, towards me. I thought, My God, if he goes off the end of these ties, it's going to topple right over on me, and I hollered as loud as I could. The conductor was Frank Peveril, and he stopped the train right away. Then we had to fetch the replacers. These are big pieces of steel, specially shaped, that come in pairs, and have to be spiked onto the ties. When a wheel comes off, we set these replacers and then pull ahead, so that the wheel climbs back up onto the rail and slips back into the right position. They have to be put in just right, or they don't always work. So the crews had to climb in under the car, hanging onto these ties and cribwork, and spike these replacers onto the ties. Well, we succeeded in getting that car back on the track. Then the conductor went up to the engineer and told him: "Go very slowly, and be looking at me all the time. Don't look ahead, but watch my lantern. If you see me swing the signal to stop, stop right now!" Then he came back down to the shoefly, and said, "We'll try here again, fellows". So we started up again, and went another ten feet, and damned if this wheel didn't jump the track again, and this time the flange of the wheel was right on the edge of the tie. If it had gone another four inches it would have dropped off the edge of the tie, and the truck would have toppled over out of the train and on top of us, which would have been a hell of a mess and possibly hurt or killed somebody. Well, it stopped, right on the edge. So once again we had to crawl in under the cars amidst the timbers, spiking these replacers down, and finally we got it back on the rails once more.

This is where I got my first experience of how to use (and how not to use) grease, when you're replacing cars. Frank Peveril was an old conductor. He said, "Have you got any grease in the tool car?" "Yeah," I said, "yeah, we've got a bucket of grease in there," "Well," he says, "get me some grease here, get a rag and tie it on the end of a stick, and give me the pot of grease". So I went to the tool car, and we got this bucket of grease and a rag, and tied the rag onto a nice long stick, and Frank proceeded to slap grease on both of those rails like there was no tomorrow. When he had done the job to his liking, he gave the signal to start up again. He'd greased the pair of wheels that went off before, but he hadn't done some of the others, and by golly, within ten feet one of the other wheels was off the track. By this time, everything was greasy. No matter, we still had to crawl up on those greasy rails, and set the replacers next to the track and the derailed wheels. Meanwhile, the conductor took the rest of that bucket of grease and greased that shoefly track from one end to the other.

When we were ready to go again, he handed me the grease pot and said, "You take the bucket of grease on the low side, and where it climbs, you just keep that grease going ahead of the wheels. Grease the inside of that rail so that it's slippery, and the wheels can't climb". So he gave the engineer the high sign, and I worked my way along as the wheels were going over the lower side of the rail, and - this was on the fourth try. We got the train over. And we were a sight. Our coveralls were just covered with sticky damned grease, covered in it, and of course no change of clothes along. Nevertheless, we were very pleased to have gotten that train over the shoefly. It was not a happy position to be in, underneath those cars as they squeaked and slid over the cribbing, to think that any minute one of the boxcars could come right down on top of you. After the train passed, there was nothing much more could be done until daybreak, so we went to bed.

The train crew hauled our Lidgerwood up the line to the nearest "Y", which was at Kelly Lake, to turn it around so it was facing south, and brought it back down. In the meantime, Pete got his section crew out, and they went to work to lengthen the shoefly out. Before the next train came, they had time to put in a lot more ties, and put a little more elevation on the cribbing (that is, tip the line up a little so the wheels would not climb the rail) and they made the curvature a lot easier, a more gentle bend. Our gang got the Lidgerwood line set onto the refrigerator car, pulled it away from the engine, and set it over on the little blind siding. Then we hooked on to the engine tender.

The tender was lying over, still connected to the engine by two huge steel bars, and these had to be cut in order to get the tender away. The problem was that those same bars were actually holding the tender up, and when we cut the bars it would probably fall. But to cut those bars, we had to crawl in between the engine and the tender. So we blocked up the tender, and got our Lidgerwood rigging set with a good purchase on the tender, before starting to cut through those bars with a cutting torch. When the bars were letting go, we took up on the Lidgerwood line, and pulled the tender away from the engine and up the bank. Then we got it onto the track and using the rerailers pulled it up to the north end and set it in front of the refrigerator car. That left the engine.

View of Engine 54 from the south end. Note the main line switch that was not lined up, which possibly caused the engine to derail. Photographer: (Assumed) Artie Phair.

All we had at that time was the seven-ton crane, which was not useful for hauling out derailed locomotives. We could not lift the engine, so it had to be jacked up. So the section crew joined with us, to dig out underneath the wheels of 54, and put in a solid bed of ties. This gave us a bed to set the jacks, and we jacked the engine up in the air. On the uphill side we set steel plates against the wheels of the 54, to hold it while we jacked on the downhill side. Then it was a matter of jacking, setting ties, jacking, setting steel plates, jacking, setting ties, until finally we had steel plates under all of the wheels, and ties under the plates. We couldn't put the timbers right through of course; there were two sets of them. We jacked and moved plates, and jacked again.

These were all manpowered jacks. You had to chin yourself on those levers each time you pulled the jack up one notch. All the blocking had to be built and set solid to take the pressure of the jacks and the weight of the locomotive. It would take an hour or more to get everything into place, before you could start jacking. Then there was another hour or two of jacking, jacking, jacking, and you'd run out of lift on the jacks, and have to re-block, and build the base up higher. It was very hard work, and we were all tired, exhausted by it. Fortunately the weather was good, and it was not too hot, but it took two days of hard work to get this engine back. Finally, we had the engine sitting upright across the tracks, on a solid bed of timbers, with steel plates under the locomotive wheels.

View from the bank side of the engine. Note the tender driven into the cab of the engine.
Photographer: Artie Phair.

Then we greased the plates, rigged the Lidgerwood to pull on the far side of the engine, and gave it a strong pull so it would skid, moving sideways over the steel plates, until it jammed against the solid timbers. Then it was a matter of jacking up the back end of the engine, moving the timbers around, putting the plates down farther over, setting it back down, greasing, and another pull with the Lidgerwood. The engine slid a little nearer to the siding, and we did the whole business yet again.

In the meantime, trains were going by over the shoefly. As we eased the engine clear of the mainline, the section gang were able to ease the shoefly in close and closer to the grade, so there was less danger. We didn't have to stop and watch every train as it went through. Also by this time, we were running out of food. We always carried a good supply when we came up from Squamish, but this was during the war, and many things were rationed. Our cook could bake bread, but he wasn't very good at it. The men ate substantial meals, but they were all rationed, and we were running short of meat, sugar and jams, all of which were rationed. We had to feed the wrecking crew, and the train crew, as many as 12, 14, 16 persons at a sitting; quite often we were providing four meals a day instead of three because of the long hours, so it took quite a bit of food to keep the crew going. We were tied up at Pavilion siding all this while; we just stayed there until we got the job done.

Well, one night Harold Bailey and I wandered down to the Pavilion store after supper, and there was a light in the back. We had been by several times, but the store had not been open. The local people of course knew that it was only open on certain days, when someone came down from the Carson Ranch, but we didn't know that. So when we saw the light on, we knocked on the door. A woman came and looked through the glass, and we motioned, if we could come inside, so she unlocked the door and let us in. Harold Bailey introduced himself as the master mechanic of the railway, in charge of our wrecking crew, and introduced me as the wrecking foreman, and explained that we were running short of food, and wondered if she might possibly help us. So the woman said, "Certainly, anything I've got in here, you're welcome to it". So Harold Bailey made some purchases. There was only one can of jam available, and not very much sugar, but we got that, and handed over the ration tickets for it, and got some bread as well. And then we caught sight of a beautiful whole smoked ham, behind the glass case in the counter, so Harold Bailey said, "Could we get some meat? We're right out of meat. Do you suppose we could buy some ham?" "Certainly," she replied, "how much would you like?" "Well", he said, "there's that big piece of ham. How much could I get?" "Oh, you can have the whole thing, if you want it". "Fine. We'll take it". And we got that beautiful ham, home smoked on the ranch. As I mentioned, they had their slaughterhouse and their smokehouse, and they killed and smoked their meats from the Pavilion Ranch. So Harold Bailey said, "By any chance, could we get any beef?" "Yes," she said, "but I can't give you any right now, because I haven't any in the store. It's all in the ice-house, up there by the water tank, keeping cool. I'll have to wait until my husband comes home. We have to keep it locked, and he's got the key, and anyway it's too heavy for me to carry. How much would you like?" Harold Bailey said, "Well, how much can we have?" "Oh," she said, "you can have as much as you want". "Well," he said, "we've got sixteen men to feed, and we'd sure like a big roast, or whatever you've got, but I don't know how much I can afford to get, because I've only got so many meat ration tickets". "Oh, forget those things," she replied, "we don't bother with those things up here. We've got cattle roaming all over the woods here, why on earth would we bother about stupid ration tickets? Forget about that, just tell me how much meat you want, and we'll let you have it". So Harold Bailey said, "If you've got a hindquarter, give me that, but I want a great big roast anyway". "Okay," she said, "I'll tell my husband when he comes home". So back we went to the crew car, and went to bed, and about three o'clock in the morning I heard a clump, clump, clump up the back of the stairs on our car, and something went thump, down onto the platform. I got up out of my bunk and went out to see, and there was a huge box of meat. So I picked it up and brought it in, and set it on top of the ice box.

The cook got up in the morning, saw this big box, and wondered what was in it, and I said, "There's a hell of a good roast in there, you can cook that for dinner". That roast must have weighed well over thirty pounds, because it completely filled our huge single-oven camp stove. I think he had to pare it down to get it in. There was no roasting pan that big, he just put it in there on a big flat cookie tin, and at dinnertime he produced this roast. I tell you, I have never tasted any beef like that. It wasn't grain fed, it was Cariboo Range beef, just straight meat, and not marbled with fat like you see today. This huge roast was done to perfection, brown on the outside and just a little red in the middle, juicy red meat, a bit bloody on the inside, and did we ever tuck into that meat! We hadn't seen a roast of beef like that for years, nor ever had a chance to eat that much beef. After dinner, when we'd all had our fill, the men went back to work. The cook didn't put that roast away. He stuck it out on top of the icebox along with a sharp butcher knife. Anybody who went into the car just sliced off a piece of this meat, and ate it, just like candy. Boy, it tasted good, and no matter how much we ate, there was lots more left. And for supper that night, we had the ham. Well, I tell you, after being on short rations, we weren't exactly starving, but we'd been cutting it fine. To be able to eat all the meat you wanted, was the greatest luxury in the world.

We still had to re-set the steel plates a couple more times, and pull the engine around a couple of times, before we finally got the 54 lined up with the siding track. Then by putting down the replacers, and pulling with the Lidgerwood, we got the engine back on the line and pulled clear of the switch and the damaged rail. While the section gang restored the main line, we brought the tender back down and hooked it back up to the engine. This was tricky, because we had no replacement couplings. So we made some buffers out of wooden beams, chained the tender tightly to the Engine, and coupled it together into our wrecking train to be hauled back down to Squamish for repairs. This is that Engine 54 which went through the bridge at Fountain. Once more, we had recovered it and brought it in for repairs.

And that's the story, of a simple little incident which very nearly became a major accident. If the engine had run through the south switch onto the mainline, unconnected with that runaway passenger train, and no way to supply air for the brakes, they would have gotten up such a speed on that steep grade that inside of another mile they'd have peeled off over the bank into the Fraser Canyon. With the people being killed and injured, and the rolling stock gone, a catastrophe like that could have wiped out the railroad. So this was a case where a derailment actually saved a lot of lives.

Today, the grasslands are still there. But the transportation system is all changed. All the roller-coaster dips of the old highway have been filled in, it's paved now, and one day will form part of Highway 99. The railroad is vastly different, with the curvatures eased, new heavy mainline rail, the money for proper ballasting and maintenance, and modern rolling stock and equipment. The rail yard is still there at Pavilion, but the old water tank is long gone. But it still gets hold of you, that country, you can see how a person would be drawn to it, riding horseback over those rolling hills and pasture lands with the cows. It's a bit more difficult, when you're hanging on to a pile of railroad ties in the pouring rain while a freight train rumbles and squeals over your head, and you're wondering if one of those boxcars is going to fall on you. But as we learned, it's cattle country. Sure, I remember the backbreaking toil, and the short rations. But we came back to Squamish with Engine 54, and a lifetime memory of Cariboo beef.

6 MUTINY AT MILE 65

1948

It was February 11th, 1948. We thought winter had just about run its course when, once more, down came the big flakes in Squamish, drifting as big as saucers. By nightfall, there was almost two feet of fresh snow on the ground. That evening the Operating Department of the P.G.E. decided to send out the plow for a run, up to Lillooet and back, so that the track would be cleared for the passenger and freight train the next day. The train consisted of the snow plow coupled to an engine, then a caboose, then a second engine. The second engine was along to pull the first engine out of drifts, if it got stuck. It would have been dangerous to push with the second engine, into that caboose, which would not have survived such pressure. And off they went, heading up into the canyon.

Mile 65 is located on a natural cut in the valley, between Brandywine Falls and Maguire siding. There's a high bank running up on the left hand side, where the snow rolls down onto the track. It is avalanche situation, except that it's not high enough for an avalanche, but the snow piles up deeper here than on either side of that spot. Well, they got here, and the snow plow hit the heavier snow and got stuck, I think, so they pulled back to make another run at it. Snow plows are not really designed for backing up much, and when they backed they caused ice to form on the rails. When they moved forward again, the plow jumped off the track. The front end rolled and swung over the bank, while the back end was still up by the rails, so the plow was actually standing on its nose, down on the flat part of the valley floor.

The engine crew knew that there was nothing more to be done, and it was snowing harder than ever, so they decided to run back down into Squamish. They worked their way cautiously around the curves, but they weren't more than a mile and a half from the plow when the tender of the south-end engine went off the track, right alongside of a big rock bluff that was a slide area. Snow was piling up, and for all they knew could come down on the train as it sat. And the way to the south was blocked. After looking the situation over, the crew decided to move the north-end engine and caboose back up the line about 100 yards, to an open area. There was also a little stream running alongside of the track there, which would serve as an emergency water supply to keep that steam engine in service. Snow is no use at all; you can throw snow into the tender until you're exhausted, but you get so little water out of it that you're actually working for nothing. When they tried to contact the dispatcher, they discovered that the snow took down the line. So we did not get notification until the next morning.

So, about eight o'clock the next morning, we got the call to put the wrecking train together. We rounded up our crew and our crew car, and we also took along an old wooden coach, with whatever section men we could find, and their snow shovels, to go to the rescue of this stranded crew and the snow plow. It happened that the Jamieson Construction Company had started work building one of the shops, and they had a D6 Cat and an operator, so we included the Cat in our wrecking train. We did not have any loading ramp, so it was a bit tricky to load a Cat onto the flatcar. What we did was to make a set of steps out of railroad ties, against the end coupling of the flatcar, up to the height of the coupler. Then the operator would back his machine up onto these steps, and start to climb up the ties. If he was lucky, on the first attempt the machine would climb high enough for the cleated caterpillar tracks to get a purchase on the deck of the flatcar, before the ties rolled under his machine and it slid down. If he was not lucky, we set the ties up again, and he made another run at it. Once the cleats grabbed, he could pull himself up on the end of the flatcar, balance, tip down onto the flatcar deck, and move the machine into the middle of the car. Then we piled the ties on to that car.

We made up our train with the engine at the front, the Cat on its flatcar next, then our crew car, the old wooden coach with the shovelers, and the caboose. All we had to clear off the snow in front of us was the pilot of the engine, also known as the "cowcatcher". There was quite a lot of snow on the line, as much as three feet in places, so it took us a long time to get as far as Garibaldi Station. At Garibaldi there was a siding, so we stopped to let the shovelers jump out and clear the switch, and we moved the flatcar with the Cat up to the front of the train. The weight of that car helped the wheels to cut through the snow, so the flatcar stayed on the track okay, but we started to have trouble with the light wooden coach. As we left Garibaldi and got past the water tank there, we came through a side hill where the snow was rolling down. The cowcatcher on the engine would push this snow aside, but it rolled back in underneath the wheels of the coach, and we were off the track with that coach three times. Each time we had to get out and dig right down through the snow, down to the rails and the ties, and set our replacers in, and then move that coach forward or back to get it back on the track again. In one of these attempts, after we got the coach back on, we had pushed the caboose at the back end off the track - it was pretty light, too, and it couldn't buck that snow backing up. So before we knew it, it was dusk, and we had only traveled a little way, practically to Brandywine. Brandywine is a public park now, but at that time there were a lot of little houses there on a flat spot, and when you turned right on the track, there's a big rock cut there. This rock cut was absolutely plugged with snow. There was no way in the world that we could ever try to buck that snow with our engine. So off come the ties, and the Cat gets unloaded and starts pushing its way through the cut.

This was a fairly long cut, it was getting dark, and we realized that we were not going to be able to do very much more that day. But in the meantime, there are seven men up ahead of us somewhere—we've lost communication with them, but they're up ahead of us somewhere. This is their second day, and they must be getting pretty hungry. The train crew and the engine crew just carry enough for themselves for a one-day trip, so they would be getting hungry for sure. The snow in the cut was too soft to walk on. I tried it, and sank up to my armpits. But the Cat kept on working, and I stayed behind him, and I guess it got colder. Anyway, I got past the Cat, and out the end of the cut, and went on until I got to this big fill that turned to the left there. At the far end of this fill I could make out the outline of an engine, and as I got closer I saw a man walking down the hill towards me. When we were close enough I saw that it was Harry Nicholls, the engineer of the engine that was on the south end. So I stuck my hand out to Harry, and said, "Dr. Livingstone, I presume". He said, "Cut out that sort of stuff," or words to that effect, "never mind that— have you got any ham and eggs in your cook car?" "We sure have," says I, and Harry turns around and hollers, "C'mon, you guys, let's go get something to eat". So back they came, trooping back across the fill, and followed me back down the line, through the cut and past the Cat, and into the cook car, where we fed them. It kept on snowing but the Cat continued working, and got the cut cleared. This allowed us to move into a spot where we were clear of cuts, because we certainly did not want to get snowed in.

So that was it, for that day. We fed what shovelers we had, and we fed our whole crew, and then we turned in for the night. And that was a real bad night. It kept on snowing and snowing and snowing - I guess it snowed another eighteen inches. That heavy snow sat on the roof of our bunk car, just a tin roof as

I told you earlier, and all the moisture in the bunk car condensed on that roof. The men sleeping in the upper bunks were actually getting wet from that dripping water, produced from the heat of the car and the bodies and the wet clothes. There was a lot of coughing and hacking. One man in that crew, it turned out later, actually had tuberculosis - he was coughing continuously, and afterwards had to go to the sanatorium. I guess it was lucky we didn't most of us catch tuberculosis. Well, we got through the night, and the cook called us for breakfast (before daylight, of course), and we rolled out after breakfast in the dawn light to start again.

The Cat driver started his engine, and as soon as his machine was warmed up he went on towards the remaining small cuts, clearing the line. Then Harold Bailey, who was in charge, said, "Now it's time to move on up to the other engines". Our engine had steam up, and the work train engineer, Andy Hutton, swung the control bar over to move the locomotive –nothing moved. There was so much snow around the engine and the wheels of the work train, that he couldn't shift the train. So everybody turned out with shovels to clear away snow from all the wheels on the train. Then Andy freed it up by going back a bit, ahead a bit, back a bit, ahead a bit. I think he must have been partially frozen to the rails. Well, this took some time. When we finally caught up to the Cat driver, he had just finished clearing a small cut in front of the derailed tender on the south end engine. Our immediate problem was how to get that tender back on the track. It was in such a position that we couldn't push it from the south end, because that would only push it further off the track. And we couldn't very well pull it, either, because we had not put the Lidgerwood in front of our train, and only had our engine and the Cat to pull the tender and engine. It was still snowing, but by this time the snow was getting wet and heavy, and starting to turn to rain. And it looked as if we were stymied.

While we were talking, the Cat driver came over to Harold Bailey and myself, and said, "I can get around that engine, if it will do any good". "What?" we said, "there's no way to get by there. There's no bank—it drops down 150, 200 feet into that creek below—and there's no place to get by, only a tiny outcropping of rock. No way we're a asking you to try that! You'll tip over, and roll right into the canyon. "Oh, no," he said, "I think I can make it all right". So he started. And I've got to give that man the greatest credit and praise for the guts he had. He'd take a scoop of that heavy snow and push it up alongside of the engine, and then roll over it with his pat treads until it started to squeak and groan, and then it would settle. Then he'd lift his blade, back up, get another blade full of snow, and push it on top of what he had done, and go a little further until the Cat started to tip, and he'd drop his blade to prevent going over, then back up, and fetch more snow. He kept on doing this, building a little bridge with the snow over this rock outcropping, pushing out until the machine was in danger of tipping, then lowering his blade to keep control, and backing up. Actually, he was turning the snow to ice, and anchoring it to the rock. By this time it had stopped snowing, but there was well over three feet on the level ground, all over. He kept on working, extending this road of ice, until finally he was able to get around the front of the engine, and get onto the track again.

South Engine off the track. Note the Cat still working at the roadway built along side of the engine.
Photographer: Unknown.

Then it was no problem at all to clear off the line between the south end engine and the caboose on the rear of the north engine. The north engine was brought down and coupled onto the south engine. Our crew put down the replacers, and spiked them in place. It took several pulls, because we slipped a couple of times, but finally we had that second engine back on the track. This was Harry Nicholls' engine, and the first thing he did was to check the water level in his tender. It was away down, and Harry insisted that he had to get water right away, he was not going to risk moving that engine without more water. So there was nothing for it but to pull up ahead again to that little creek, where the north engine had stopped to wait for us.

Engine now coupled to the north end crew. Note Harry Nicholls indicating the depth of water in the tender. Photographer: Unknown.

We dug down through the snow to the little creek bed until we found a pool, and dug out the pool with shovels, until we had a place to fill some buckets. Then the whole crew formed a bucket brigade, like so many coolies, a human chain from the creek to the tender. We passed full buckets up to the tender, and the man on top of the tender had a rope with a hook on it. He'd haul up a bucket full of water, empty it, throw it down, and haul up the next one. This may not sound like much, but do you know how many buckets of water it takes to fill a locomotive tender? Harry wouldn't let us stop until he figured he had enough water to get him back to Squamish. I guess we had the tank half full, and it was hard work.

By the time we had that done, it was getting near dark, and time to head back to Garibaldi siding. So we pulled ahead to let the Cat move to the south end of us. By now it was raining steadily, and conditions were changing.. The Cat operator just walked his machine down the track and cleaned off the rails ahead of us all the way to the siding, and we were able to back down safely to Garibaldi station. By this time communications had been restored, and we received the news that a steel snow plow had been borrowed from the C.N.R. and had been shipped up that day on the barge. This was great news for us, because we hadn't even been able to reach our wooden plow yet, to see what had happened to it. So we were to sit at Garibaldi waiting until the snow plow arrived. Meanwhile we got to a water tank, and all the engines had their tenders filled with water, and the oil supply topped up from the fuel car we had brought along with us.

Now the only locomotive left in Squamish was Engine 52, and she was in the shops. Three engines and three engine crews, which was all we had, were at Garibaldi siding, along with the Master Mechanic, Harold Bailey, the car shop foreman, which was me, and half the crew from the shops. We knew that the men at the shop would somehow have to get 52 in shape to drive this C.N.R. steel snow plow, and we wondered who they would find for an engine crew. Somewhere about noon of the following day, we saw a column of smoke from a steam engine coming up the line. Well our wooden plow had come up that line, and our wrecking train had come up that line, and even so, the snow on the track reached half way up the nose on that steel plow, which gives you some idea of how much snow had fallen in this storm. The engine was being run by our locomotive foreman, Jack Frost, who had never run behind a snow plow in his life before, with a machinist from the shops working as his fireman. We were glad to see them, and they were glad to see us. The sidings were cleared off, and we reorganized the train.

C.N.R. Plow to the rescue, with Jack Frost (locomotive foreman) at the throttle. Photographer: Unknown.

The strategy was for Engine 52 and the steel plow to clear the line up to where our Russell plow was in the ditch, with a second engine following up to pull 52 out of trouble, bringing the wooden coach with the shovelers and the caboose. Well, I thought, I want to see what this steel plow can do when it hits all the snow we've been bucking up the line. The best place to do that is in the cab of the lead engine. I'd be just as well off there as riding in that light wooden coach, because this plow is going to throw snow up onto the banks, and it will roll back in big snowballs onto the coach and the caboose. I don't want to be in there. I'll take my chances, and enjoy the view, so I got into the cab of Engine 52 just ahead of the engineer, who was a Scotchman named Fred Eadie.

Like all machinery, steam engines use oil for lubrication. To get inside the cylinders and lubricate the drive pistons, oil must be fed into the steam. A special kind of oil is used, which runs thin under the heat and pressure of steam, but which is very sticky and thick at ordinary temperatures. This steam oil is supplied from a lubricator in the cab of the locomotive, connected directly to the steam chest. The other moving parts of the engine, which operate at more normal temperatures, are connected to a second lubricator that holds light thin oil. The control valves and the reservoirs for both lubricators are in the engine cab.

The C.N.R. plow clearing the siding and main line at Garibaldi. Photographer: Unknown

Engineer Fred Eadie was standing up there, getting the signal to go ahead, and just as we were starting up he turned on the lubricators. My God! Somebody had put the steam oil into the light oil reservoir, and light oil into the steam section, and with all that pressure, as soon as the valve was opened, it blew light oil all over everything inside the cab. Well, you should have heard those Scottish curses. That man was just bellowing. He was jumping up and down, cursing all the men in the shop. The fireman started to laugh, so he began cursing his fireman, and I thought, well, Stathers, this is no place for you, and I climbed up and stood on top of the tender. I could still hear him cursing.

A big heavy bar, called the Johnson Bar, controls the direction of a steam locomotive. You push it ahead to go forward, pull it back to back up, and put it dead centre to stop. There is a geared ratchet mechanism that holds it in the setting you want. But the teeth were not sticking properly in the ratchet, so he had to drive the engine with one foot on the Johnson Bar, and one hand on the throttle, and the other on the air brake, with the other engine whistling behind him. He had to keep going, with oil all over him, and the fireman laughing at him.

The train assembled, ready to clear the line to the derailed wooden plow at Mile 65. Photographer: Unknown

How we didn't go off the track, I don't know, but we plowed ahead and never stopped until we came right up to the snow plow. I got out and took a look. That wooden plow was standing right on its nose. You couldn't see the lower portion of the nose at all as it was buried in snow, which came right up to the cupola. The top of that cupola is a good twelve feet from the rail, so there was at least fourteen feet of snow down to the nose of that plow. If we had been equipped with a wrecking crane, we could easily have put a cable across the top of the plow and around the nose, lifted it, and pulled it back up on the track. But we had no crane, and no way of doing that. This was going to be a digging job.

So we backed the whole works all the way back down to Garibaldi siding, and set the C.N.R. plow back out of the way. We reorganized the wrecking train, with the flatcar ahead and then our crew car, and up the line we went, leaving the section crew at Garibaldi Lodge. By this time it was dark again, so we tied up behind the derailed plow. We had to spend another night in this crew car, with the men soaking wet and their clothes steaming, and the water dripping from the roof, and the guy with T.B. coughing. Oh Boy! It was pretty bad. By morning the men were starting to get a little down in the mouth, but we were up and eating breakfast by daylight. Damned if the train wasn't stuck again! It had snowed another foot during the night. So the first thing we had to do was shovel out all the wheels on the train, and then run back and forth, back and forth, and shovel some more, until finally we got moving.

Then it was time to tackle the snow plow. I said, "C'mon, fellows, there's only one thing to be done. We've got to get right down under the nose of that plow, and get a jack under there. We'll have to jack up the front end, and block it, and then we can pull it back up on the track with our engine". So we started to shovel.

The derailed wooden snow plow. Note the depth of the snow we had to shovel, from the top of the front to the hole where the men were working. Photographer: Unknown

And we shoveled, and we shoveled, and we shoveled. It was raining, and the snow was heavy, each shovelful seemed to weigh more than thirty pounds, and we could only throw so far. And we shoveled, and we shoveled, and about eleven o'clock, when we were about two-thirds of the way down to the nose of the plow, one man said, "To Hell with this. I've had all I can take". And he threw his shovel up out of the hole, narrowly missing my ear. The rest of the gang said "I'm with you" and they threw their shovels up onto the bank. "To hell with this. We're not going to do any more". They clambered up the bank, and climbed into the cab of the snow plow to have a smoke.

Well, there I stood on the snow bank. This was the first time I'd faced a situation where my crew had actually refused to work. I had to sympathize with them, because I was just as tired as they were. My left arm was so tired from throwing the snow up that it was aching, just like a toothache. Well, I thought, we've got to do something. We'll try a little psychology. So I walked back through the snow to the cook car, and said to the cook, "Get me two good big pots of coffee, and make a big plate of sandwiches, and give me your helper and a bucketful of cups to come along with me". It took about half an hour to get all this stuff ready, the cook's helper came back with me, and we climbed up inside the tilted cab of the snowplow. The floor was over at an angle, and the men were sitting on the back side in a row, all wet and bedraggled, with their feet up. "How would you like some coffee, boys?" I said, "There's some sandwiches, too". "Oh boy, that's great". So the cook's helper dished out the coffee and I sat down in the middle of the men. We all got our coffee, and a sandwich or two. It was dry inside the snowplow, and with two or three cups of coffee and something in their bellies, the men started to warm up. We smoked a couple more cigarettes. The cook's helper gathered up all the crockery, and I said, "Well, boys, I'm going out and start shoveling. Anybody coming with me?" And they all said, "Well, yeah…I guess so". So I climbed out and got a shovel, and the others followed, and much to my relief everyone went back to their accustomed places.

I've got to admire those fellows for their fortitude and their guts. They went down in that hole, and they shoveled and shoveled, until finally we hit gravel, under a little shallow running stream. In order to get a foot jack under the nose of our plow, we had to dig a hole in the gravel right in the middle of this stream. The men were working in about 10 inches of running water, and some of them did not have high rubber boots, and that water was damned chilly, I can tell you. These foot jacks were big engine jacks, with a foot on them. In order to set them, it was necessary to dig out enough space to get some kind of blocks or timbers into the gravel below the nose of the plow, with enough room to set the jacks in. Well, finally we got the jacks into place. Then of course, it was jack and block, jack and block, and jack and block, until we managed to get the plow back up on an even keel.

The steel plow had been busy all this time, working to clear the line and sidings south of us, and they had worked their way up to our wrecking train. Our engine had run low on water, and since the line was now cleared down to Garibaldi they followed the steel plow and the section gang back down. Pete Rebegliati, the Roadmaster, stayed behind with a few men to give our crew a hand. We were now ready to try a pull with our engine, but the engine had not returned. We waited a little while, and I said, "They should have been back long ago, Pete. We'd better go back and see what's happened". So the two of us started walking back toward Brandywine. I hadn't thought of it before we started, but as we were walking along the track, there was a fourteen-foot wall of hard-packed snow on each side of us built up by the wings of the plow. If that snow plow had come roaring around any of those bends, throwing up snow, we'd have been caught right between the two walls of snow and ice, and chopped into pieces. Believe me, I was thoroughly relieved when we got to Brandywine bridge. Then My God, there's the steel snow plow, off the track, right on the middle of the bridge! Our plow operator was not accustomed to the C.N.R. plow, which was a drop-nosed plow. He remembered to lift it when he came to switches, but he forgot that there is double-tracking in the inside on bridges, and the drop nose caught and derailed the front trucks.

This was an ugly situation. In order to get that plow back on the tracks, somebody had to fetch the pair of heavy steel replacers that are carried on the front of every engine. These replacers weigh 130 to 140 pounds. There was no room to walk along side of the snow plow on that bridge. If you tried to get around the side and fell off the bridge, you'd have fallen into the water all right, but about thirty feet downstream was a straight drop of about sixty feet into a great big pool. The creek pours over the lip of a chasm, straight down sixty feet into a big basin. So nobody wanted to bring any replacers around the side of the plow. I don't blame them a damned bit, either. They were happy to see me arrive. I was the wrecking foreman, so they all looked to me for the solution to the problem. Well, we got the replacers, put some ropes on them, climbed up on top of the engine, pulled them up with the ropes, carried them across the top of the plow, and lowered them down to the crew in the front of the snow plow. From there we were able to shove them in under the front of the snow plow, from the sides.

Then it was a matter of putting those replacers down next to the derailed front truck wheels, underneath that boxed-in steel plow. Nobody wanted to go in there. The front trucks were right under the nose of the plow. It's all smooth; there is nothing to hang on to. If a man was in there putting the replacer in, and somebody made a mistake and gave a signal to move the engine, he would be minced. Just minced. It was dark by now, difficult to see anything. At the best of times, this would have been a risky situation. My own crew were accustomed to recovering derailments, but they were all back with the wooden plow. So nobody made a move, they waited to see what I would do.

This was one of those times when it's up to the boss, if he's a boss at all, to take the lead. You can't send men in where you won't go yourself, and still keep the respect of the men. So I said, "Who'll come in and give me a hand?" And one of the section hands, a little man named Mike Favaro stepped forward, to crawl in there with me, with a hammer and some spikes. I've always admired Mike for that - he's still around Squamish, I talk to him from time to time.

Now there were doors on the side of the snow plow where you could look in and see what was happening inside. I told the conductor, "You crawl along the side of that bridge, and shine your lantern in at the door, so you can see what we are doing". If he was doing that, I could be sure he was not giving any signals that would catch us under the plow. So the conductor crawled out to the door, and hung on, and shone his lantern in, while Mike and I crawled to the trucks with the replacers and spiked them in place. On bridges they put extra rails down so that if a derailment should take place, the wheels are held from running off the edge of the ties. This makes it more difficult to set replacers, because there is very little room. However, we managed it. First we did one side, and then the other side, and after everything was in place Mike crawled out, I crawled out, and the conductor crawled back. When everybody was well clear, the conductor gave the signal to pull, and we were lucky. On the first pull, the snowplow got back on the track, and it was just a matter of picking up the replacers and repairing the track. It was too dark and too late to do anything more with the wooden plow, so again we had to tie up for the night. That meant another night in that crew car.

It wasn't quite so bad this time, because we weren't getting any more snow. We cleared the snow off the roof (shoveled it off, because there was a lot of it) so we could get away from that drip, drip, drip, off the ceiling. The next day, we brought our engine up to the snow plow and chained the two couplers together for a pull. We had the plow sitting on blocks and timbers in front of the rails, and with a couple of pulls we got it in line with the track. Then it was a matter of crawling in under the plow to set replacers, which was somewhat easier than on Brandywine Bridge. And finally, the plow was back on the track. So we hauled our wooden plow back down to Garibaldi siding, and the C.N.R. plow went right on up the line to Lillooet, while we picked up our scattered equipment. Of course, it had been snowing pretty near every night, and you can't stop after dark to try and find everything. So we had a practice of leaving a bar sticking up alongside of any pile of equipment we took out. After a while, everything had been accounted for, and we picked up the plow and headed back into the shops at Squamish. The C.N.R. plow turned around at Lillooet and came back to Squamish, where it was loaded on the barge and returned to Vancouver, with thanks. And the next day it was business as usual, the first thing in the shop being to put our plow back in shape to fight the next snow storm. Repairing the plow didn't take very long. Over the years we had replaced just about every wooden part of it, and some of the steel as well.

I couldn't sleep on my left hand side, my shoulder was so sore. I went to the doctor two or three times about it, and he told me that I had strained the muscles so badly in my left arm and shoulder that the tissue in the muscles had ruptured, and it would take months for it to heal. I was not to do any heavy lifting at all with that left arm. This of course was impossible for me at that time. I had to keep working, and if I worked, I had to lift. It took actually a year and a half before my shoulder was recovered from that terrific strain of continuous shoveling, moving that heavy snow.

Luckily for us, we didn't have much more snow that winter, and the wooden plow, along with the flangers, were able to control the snowfalls that we did have. A flanger is a car with a small plow under its centre, which is pulled by freight trains. They lift the plow up at switches and intersections, and then drop it again between the tracks. It will handle between six inches and a foot of snow, provided it's not too packed, and throw it a considerable distance away from the track. But flangers are not very good for sidings, that's a job for a plow with wings.

There's a limit to everything. We'd kept going through the Depression, and through the war, and we were still trying to maintain an up-to-date railroad service with a plow designed in 1904, lifting derailed equipment with crowbars and hand jacks, and clearing away twenty feet of snow with hand shovels. I guess I worked the men too hard, but it was a shattering experience to have them actually refuse to take an order, and not being used to such a thing, there was no way I was going to back down. Still, it worked out all right. Company officials were at last convinced, after the line had been tied up for seven or eight days, that the Russell plow was unsuitable for the heavy snowfalls on our line. For the winter of 1949 we had a new mountain type of plow, with little shoes that dropped right on the track, so no snow could get in underneath the nose or back of the trucks. This plow would clean the line right off, and the pressure of the snow forced the nose right down on the track. The wooden plow was no longer needed at the south end, so it was sent up to Lillooet where it derailed a few times cleaning up snow slides, and was used for clearing yards. It came to grief in a gravel slide farther north and eventually wound up at Prince George. Its replacement was part of a change for the railroad, the first time in years we started to see some better equipment. Better days were coming. They just had to. Men could not continue to outwork the machinery, because it was wearing them out.

7 TRAGEDY AT SETON LAKE

1949-1952

Time after time, through the 1940's and into the 50's, our wrecking gang was called out to pick up after derailments up and down the P.G.E. line. It was very frustrating, because most of these mishaps were caused by the condition of the rail and the roadbed. We barely had enough money to keep going during the 1930's, and maintenance fell behind. Then we had low priority during the war, and fell further behind. When the war was over, the company did what it could to catch up, but it took a number of years just to recover lost ground. We needed new rail to replace the worn-down 60 pound rail we had, which was just too light, but steel was in short supply after the war. We needed new ties, because wood won't last forever—it rots out. These were available, and we started to get them. And we desperately needed new equipment, both rolling stock and shop equipment. So when William Rae retired in 1946 ,as Chief Inspector of Boilers for the provincial government, he was appointed on a part-time and advisory basis as a sort of superintendent of motor power and equipment, over our Master Mechanic, Harold Bailey. Like everyone else in the P.G.E., William Rae had a very small amount of money to work with, but he was able to find some second-hand rolling stock, and various tools and equipment. Some of the cars he acquired were in pretty rough shape, and needed a lot of work. But we had worked off the scrap pile through the 1930's, and I guess with the very limited funds he had, William Rae was doing just about the same thing.

In 1948, he heard about a locomotive crane that was in a scrap yard in Washington State. This equipment was a gasoline-driven, battery-started locomotive crane that was made for the U.S. Army and shipped over to Manila in the Philippines during the war, but it was never taken out of the crates. After the war it was shipped back to the U. S., where the scrap dealer obtained it in public auction. He moved it to his scrap yard, set it up, lengthened the boom, and used it to pile scrap. William Rae went down to look at it, made him an offer, bought the crane for a very good price, and had it shipped up to the P.G.E. shop in Squamish.

The capacity of this crane was thirty-five tons, with the boom in the highest position, when you were lifting right in the middle of the track, next to the coupler of the crane. As soon as you lowered the boom away from the centre of gravity of the crane, the lift capacity diminished considerably. By the time you were maybe twenty feet from the track, the capacity was only around ten tons. It had good sets of outriggers on it, which were normally set out manually. These were steel beams that reached out from the side of the crane bed, and wooden blocks that could be set onto the ground, to stabilize the crane and prevent it tipping over under a lift. This was especially important when we were working on a curve on elevated track, where the line is angled so the outside rail is higher than the inside rail. When you lift on the high side the capacity is increased, but when you lift on the low side of the curve the capacity is decreased. Having those outriggers increased our stability, and therefore improved our operating range. This was a wonderful advance over the little seven-ton steam crane we had been using up to that time.

The boom that had been lengthened was too long, so we shortened it in the shop. It had a big hook, and a smaller hook at the far end of the boom, which had a gooseneck on it. Because it was a fixed boom, we had to provide some method of tying it down during transport up and down the line. So we built an idler car in the shop, and mounted a small truck on the idler car that could move back and forth as the boom swung with the direction of the crane. The boom was tied down to this truck.

During this period the railroad was converting from steam to diesel-powered locomotives. That gave us the chance to transfer our two Lidgerwoods onto steel flat cars and change them from steam to diesel. We also upgraded our outfit car, by insulating the ceiling, closing off a lot of the windows, improving the heating, and increasing our kitchen facilities. So thing were a lot better than they had been during the war. We also had our new steel snow plow, and we certainly needed it. And we had acquired a number of diesel units, 660 HP apiece, which we operated in pairs, coupled together so they could be controlled from either diesel units in the pair. Since we still operated our steam fleet, the diesel units were often tied into the middle of a freight train as an auxiliary engine, which allowed us to haul longer trains and more freight.

This was the way that the morning freight train was made up in Squamish yards on the morning of January 23, 1950. At the front was Engine 53, a steam engine, with engineer Alex Munroe and fireman Harry Seymour. In the middle of the train was a diesel pair, with engineer Charlie Midnight. Alex was married, with two boys and a girl. Harry, who had been away at the war, was recently married, with one very young boy. The weather was very poor in Squamish. It was snowing hard, and the wind was blowing from the north. As the train went north they hit more snow, and it got steadily worse. At Darcy, at the start of Anderson Lake, they reported in, Engine Number 53 at Darcy. The dispatcher released them to proceed down Anderson Lake to the next check-in point, at Seton Portage. With the amount of snow coming down, they were on the lookout for snow and possible rocks on the tracks. This was in the days before there was any patrolman in front of the train.

In those days, the communication was all done by telephone. The dispatcher's office was in Squamish, and the telephone line ran parallel to the track all the way up the line. There were a number of points along the way where it was compulsory for the train crew to stop, and the conductor would report in to the dispatcher. There were telephone boxes at the stations, and also at all sidings. Even if there was no station there, there was a pole with a telephone box. These were often used when there was a meet between trains. The conductors called in, so the dispatcher knew where everybody was along the line. Also, if it was required, there was a portable telephone carried on the caboose, and the conductor hooked it onto the phone wire and reached the dispatcher that way. It was compulsory to call in from Darcy, that at Seton Portage between Anderson and Seton Lakes, and then again at Lillooet, past the north end of Seton Lake.

So the crew called in from Seton Portage, reporting that the snow was falling and the wind was blowing. The temperature was low, which caused the relatively warm water of the lake to form rolling clouds of fog. All this reduced the visibility, which they reported as only 100 to 150 feet. They were familiar, of course, with the running conditions along Seton Lake. The track was laid through vertical rock cuts and shelves of rock on the west side of the lake, and in many places it is vertical rock right into the water from the edge of the track. There were also a number of slide areas, pitches of 30 degrees or steeper, some of them running right up to the plateau on the top of the mountain; a direct slide down a thousand feet or more, into the lake. No vegetation would grow in these slide areas, because periodically, as the snow built up on the top and was released by changing weather conditions, the slides would come down. Most of these slides carried a great amount of rock with them, covered and embedded in the snow. The weathering of wind and hot temperatures during the summer months loosened this rock.

It had been very cold for a long time, but it also had been so windy and so rough that the lake was not frozen over. This is a big lake, fourteen miles long, and more than a mile wide in spots, and waves will form up to six feet high during a storm. In the thirty-six years of my working life, I only saw Seton Lake frozen over solid twice. But although the lake was not frozen, ice had formed up to two feet thick all along the sloping banks and the rocks of the edge of the lake, and it was slippery and icy. And it was snowing harder than ever.

Well, the dispatcher released them, gave the go-ahead to proceed with caution, so they carried on. About a mile and a half from the end of the lake, as they were rounding a curve, the fireman could see that something was wrong ahead, so he shouted "PLUG IT!" (meaning put the emergency brakes on), which the engineer immediately did. But it was too late. The locomotive, with the men inside it, was carried up onto a moving slide, along with a boxcar of coal and a tank car loaded with crude oil. The men in the diesel units did not hear any whistle, and of course that was the only communication they had between the front engine and the pusher diesels. Perhaps it would have been masked by the noise of the train and the howling wind and the roar of the slide. But the engineer sensed that something was wrong, because the train was stopping even though his units were under power. So he cut his throttle immediately, peered ahead through the blizzard, and could see nothing. He and the fireman put on their slickers, and walked up alongside the track to see what had happened, and the crew from the caboose also came up quickly.

The engine was gone. Disappeared. There was a tank car in the lake, with just the coupler sticking out. There was a boxcar sitting partially on the grade, clear of the track. And the track ahead of their train was totally buried by a giant slide, eight feet deep and about 300 feet across. The men ran along the shoreline of the lake in the dark, calling out the names of the men who had been in the engine. They worked right across the slide, and right back, in case one of them had somehow jumped clear or escaped in the water. The blizzard kept on, coating them with snow as they scrambled along the icy edge of the lake, searching, calling. But there was not a trace of either man. Finally, when it was obvious that they must have perished, the conductor went back down to the caboose and pulled out his emergency telephone. The slide had carried away several hundred feet of telephone line and access to Lillooet, but he was able to contact the dispatcher at Squamish and tell him what had happened. The wrecking crew was called early next morning.

The dispatcher, when he received these reports from the freight train about the continuing storm and snow, passed this information on to the company officials, who decided to send the snow plow out about four hours behind the freight train. The freight train crew were told to stay where they were until the snow plow arrived, and it would pull the back end of their train back into Seton Portage. Nothing more could be done to help Alex Munroe and Harry Seymour. We put our train together, including our Lidgerwood (now diesel-powered), the new 35-ton crane, and even the little 7-ton steampot in case it might come in handy, with our tool car and the crew car, and took off for Seton Lake. Meanwhile, the snowstorm continued. Telephone service was interrupted by a number of breaks along the line, and the phone crew was out ahead of us, on the job. They had a huge four-wheel-drive speeder, a very heavy machine, specially built and totally enclosed, with snow plows on it, so they could travel in snow conditions impossible to a regular speeder. It was unheated, of course, but it kept them out of the wind and weather. So they were up the line ahead of our wrecking train, and ahead of them was the snowplow, and up at Seton Lake was the freight train crew waiting in the caboose. We all relied on that telephone line and our dispatcher, to know where we were on the track. Since we did not really know where the others were much of the time, we proceeded very cautiously. We got past the telephone gang, and went on until early evening when we reached Seton Portage, and phoned the dispatcher.

We were told that the lines were down between there and the accident, and the snow plow crew had not reported in; they were somewhere along Seton Lake, or maybe even in it. At least the snow plow crew was working with our new steel plow and not the old wooden one that gave us so much trouble in former years. The dispatcher was very reluctant to let us proceed further, until he had heard from the snow plow crew.

However, time was getting on, and we felt that something should be done. Harold Bailey, our Master Mechanic, had a consultation with the train crew and the dispatcher. It was decided that we would drop the wrecking train at Seton Portage, cut off the engine, and go up the lake with the engine, in search of the snow plow crew.

Again we were lucky, because we had one of the newest steam engines, of the 160 class, the last ones that the P.G.E. bought. It was a big powerful machine, with a vestibule cab and two small doors that opened up on the side, so we were enclosed and protected from the storm to a large extent. There was the disadvantage that, in case of an accident, you only had those two small doors to get out, instead of just pushing aside the canvas hanging between you and the tender, as it did on the older steam engines. And I had plenty of reason to think about this. The engineer on that engine was Jack Cooper. He was a wildman at the throttle, was Jack, fearless, and he would go through anything. He was really a good engineer, kind of rough, but he didn't hesitate about any of the bad weather; that didn't faze him one bit. I don't recall who the fireman was. Besides the crew there was Harold Bailey, the Master Mechanic, Mr. Valde, the Chief Engineer, and myself.

Now I don't mind saying that I was damned scared. The storm was so bad that you couldn't even see the distance to one telephone pole. The wind was howling down that lake, and the mist was boiling off in clouds and blowing along in billows over the surface of the water, making a mist. We couldn't see any distance ahead at all, and all along the line were little slides that had come down after the snow plow had gone through. Jack Cooper was really in his element. He would holler out, "Look out, here's another one", and he would open the throttle wide and the engine would hit the slide, maybe four feet, maybe six feet deep, and the snow and whatever else was on the track would come flying over the top of the engine. You couldn't see, you were running absolutely blind for a period of time. I don't mind telling you that I was keeping pretty close to that side door, farthest away from the lake, so that if anything happened and we were to go off the track, I was ready to head right out of that door and jump onto the bank, and take my chances. I didn't enjoy it for one minute. I was scared. However, we kept on going, and hitting these slides, and running blind, with the snow blowing down the lake and piling up on the front of the vestibule cab. After about half an hour we were all peering ahead, standing up and straining our eyes trying to see through the snow and around the bends, with the engineer and the fireman. Finally we could see two red lights ahead of us, and as we slowed down and came up closer we could make out the caboose of the snowplow train.

Stuck somewhere south of Darcy. Photographer: Unknown.

The snowplow crew had made it to the derailed train, all right, but in the course of bucking through the various slides they had iced up on the front of the plow so badly that they couldn't get the knuckle open on the coupler. It was frozen and plugged solid with snow and ice. They were trying to thaw it out with some of the oily waste from the journal boxes of the train, which they put on a shovel and lit, to make a flame. But the wind was blowing so hard it kept blowing out the flame, and they couldn't get enough heat to melt anything. Fortunately, I knew how to disconnect the knuckle and get the pin out, even though it was full of ice. We fetched a hammer and some other equipment from the caboose, and chipped out the ice, and managed to get the coupler working, so the front end of the snowplow could couple onto the rear end of the freight train. Then we coupled our engine onto the caboose of the snowplow train.

Typical type of slide on Anderson Lake. This slide has come from a long way up the hill. Note how little snow there is on the lower side hill. Photographer: Unknown.

By this time we were pretty well frozen, and right close to us was the home of Mr. and Mrs. Jack Cooper, who lived there right beside the track. They were watching us work, out in the storm, through their windows, and when we got finished they came out and hollered, "'Come on in, and get a cup of coffee!" So we all trooped in, the whole bunch of us, and sat down to hot coffee and biscuits and cookies, and it was really welcome, and put new heart into us. The Coopers were wonderful people. Then back we went into the night, and with all that power at the back end we pulled all of the freight train that was on the track, back down to Seton Portage, and set it off on the siding. By this time it was early in the morning of January 25th, and we took the wrecking train right back up to the slide.

A slide at the north end of Seton Lake, similar to the one Engine 53 ran in to. Photographer: Unknown.

When we got to the slide, the crew from Lillooet had already offloaded a D6 Cat, which was working on the slide at the north end. In the daylight, you could see that the slide had come all the way from the top of the mountain, more than a thousand feet, and varied between six feet and eight feet deep. I was wearing overshoes and felt boots, and this slide was so hard and icy, we had to kick heel holes into the surface in order to stand safely. If you weren't careful, you'd slide, and slide right into the lake. It was very hard-packed snow, full of rocks, and the little D6 Cat was not making much impression on it. Somewhere they got hold of another Cat, a D8 (which is bigger), and brought it up, and it was able to work across the slide to the south end. By the late afternoon they had cleared off the track and pushed the rubble and snow over into the lake. Luckily the track was not damaged too much, and the section crew was able to fix it up enough for our train to run over it.

The boxcar was closest to the track. It was an old C.P.R. boxcar, full of Vancouver Island coal destined for Lillooet, which was why it had been right behind the engine. The coal was not very valuable, so they managed to get the boxcar doors opened and shoveled a lot of it out. Then with the two cranes we were able to pick up and drag the partly emptied car onto the track, pick up its trucks and put them on the track, and set the boxcar back onto its trucks. They took it into Lillooet and got rid of it.

The tank car was next. It was full of Bunker C, the heavy oil that they burned in the locomotives. This car was completely in the lake, having been carried out with the slide, and only the coupler was sticking out of the water. We managed to get a heavy cable around the coupler without getting wet. We knew it was going to be a heavy pull. The little seven-ton crane was set on the north side and the 35-ton crane was set on the south side. We backed up with the Lidgerwood, which would supply the chief pull, and set it farther up the line. There was a huge boulder a short distance up the mountain, the size of a small house, pretty near. We put a big long cable around that rock, and ran a lead down from there to the track, where we rigged up a three-block hold. The rigging was set so that the cranes would give some lift and some pull. The Lidgerwood cable, which was set to run clear of the cranes, would provide the chief pull. This was going to be a very hard pull, so I had a man up on the mountainside, Jimmy Nutton, watching that the cable on the huge boulder did not hang up and get cut and frayed on the boulder. If that tail hold cable had let go, with the cables and the blocks whipping around, the crane operators and the signal man would have been in grave danger. I was the signal man. Harold Bailey was running the show, and I was one of the crew.

I was standing on the little steam crane on the north end, to give signals to both cranes and to the Lidgerwood. Actually, I needed three hands, so we worked out a system where I was giving flag signals to the Lidgerwood operator and hand signals to the crane operators. In an operation like this, one man and one man alone has to give the signals, otherwise you can get in a terrible mix-up and cause an accident. The machine operators have to keep their eyes on the man who gives the signals, and they obey his instructions to the letter. The signal man has to be in position where all of the machine operators can see him. In this case, it was also necessary to keep an eye on the tail hold man up at the boulder, and listen for any caution call from him.

Harold Bailey called for everybody to be ready, and then called for a pull. So I signaled all operators, and we pulled. The cables tightened…and nothing moved. We slacked off. Harold Bailey said, "Try 'er again!" So I waved up to Jimmy that we were going to try again, shouting, "Okay, Jimmy?" and gave the signal to pull. Again the cables tightened, and then I heard a holler from Jimmy, "Hold it! Hold it!" The rock's moving!!" So I stopped everything right away, and went up to have a look. And sure enough it had moved, about a couple of inches, maybe, this huge boulder on the mountainside. So I went back and told Harold Bailey that the rock did not look very safe. "Well," he said, "give it another pull". I climbed back up onto the end of the steampot checked everyone, and gave the signal to try another pull. Suddenly Jimmy yelled, "Hold it! For God's sake, hold it! The rock's coming down!" So we stopped the pull, and I climbed back up the mountain again. Sure enough, that rock had moved again, about a foot this time.

I reported to Harold Bailey that we couldn't pull on that rock any more. He reacted with his favourite word. "B—S—!!" he said, "give it another pull". "No sir, I don't think so," I said, "that rock is going to come down on us. That's the second pull we've made, and that tank car didn't move an inch". He was quite a volatile person, and short tempered, and he said, "I told you to give that car another pull, and I want another pull taken on that line". I said, "Harold Bailey, if you want another pull taken on that rock, you can give the signals yourself, and I advise you first to climb up there and take a look at that rock, and see how far it's moved". So he said, "I'm not going up there". And I said, "Well, I'm not going to give another pull". I ought to explain that Harold Bailey had lost most of his left hand in an accident. He was working on an overhead crane in the big Winnipeg shops when someone moved the crane, and his hand was caught between the wheel of the crane and the track while he was up in the air. All he had was one finger left on this hand, and he was afraid of heights from this time. He wouldn't even climb up a ladder, more than about two steps, so there was no way he would climb up that mountain to take a look. So after we argued some more, and I told him it was too risky and I was not going to take a chance, I suggested that we find another hold. Finally, grudgingly, he agreed.

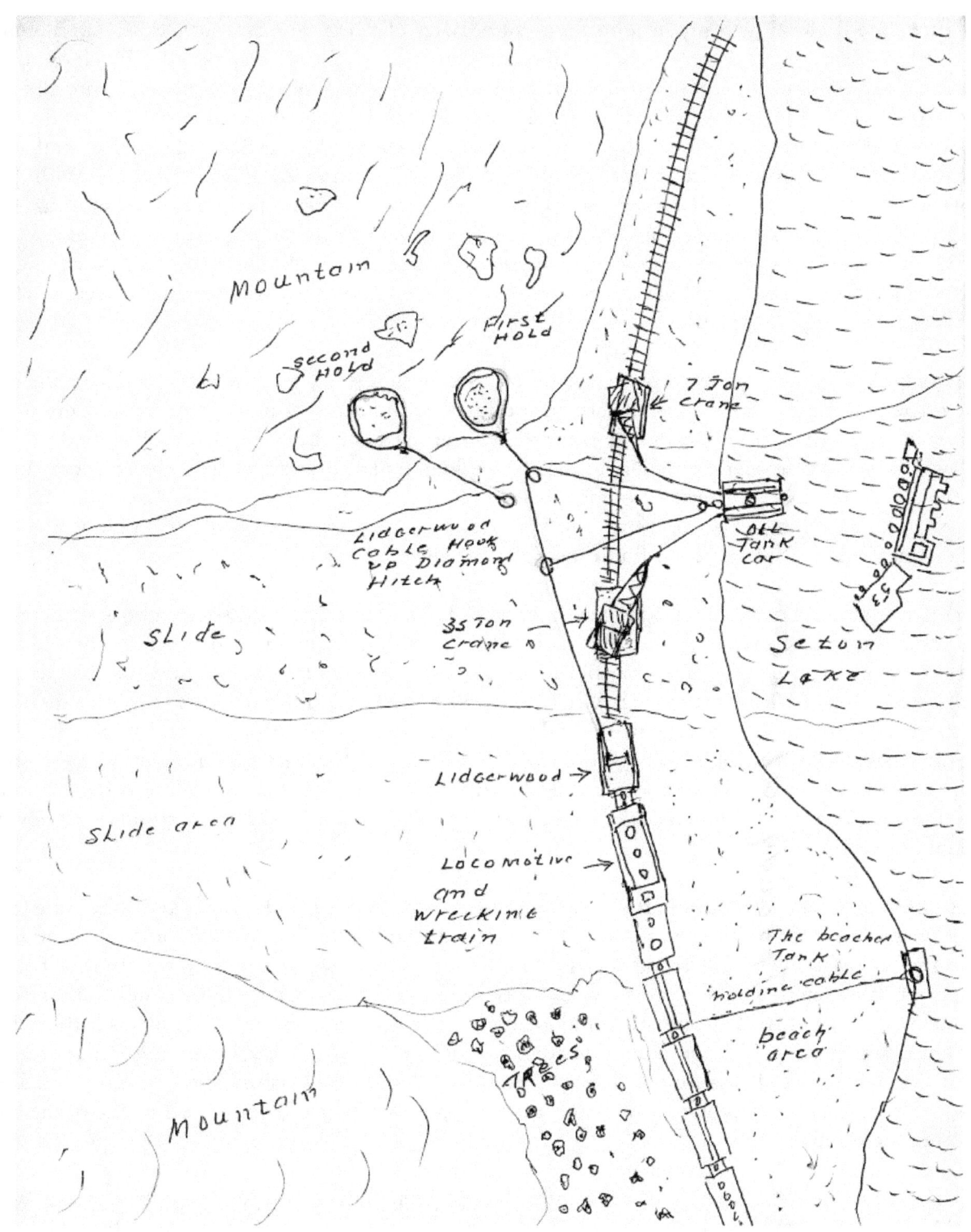

Map diagram of Engine 53 derailment at Seton Lake.　E.P. Stathers

So we had to find a tail hold farther up the mountain. I went back up the mountain again with Jimmy, and took with me two young apprentice lads, Barry Hunt and Tom Fowler. We went up past the huge boulder, and clambered on higher to a solid outcropping that would hold anything, it was part of the mountain. But in order to get our cable set we had to reach up the face of the rock, which was a good sixteen feet above where we were standing. There was a fissure in the rock. All we had to do was climb up, using this fissure. We went back to the outfit car and got all the picks we had. Then we proceeded to climb that rock face. I stood with my nose in the fissure, Barry climbed onto my shoulders, and Tommy handed up a pick so Barry could drive it right into the crack in the rock face. Barry tested it by chinning himself. It was in there good and solid. So then Tommy took another pick, climbed over me, and onto Barry, who was hanging by the first pick, and Tommy drove the second pick into the crack as far as he could, and tested it, and it held him. One more step would do it. So we got another pick, and Barry climbed up and stood on the first pick, and Tommy climbed up onto the second pick, and we passed up the third one. With that securely in place, Tommy scrambled to the top. So we made it up there by using picks as climbing irons. It took up a good couple of hours to haul our cable up there, extend our rigging, and reset everything, and Tommy stayed up there. He was a big skookum husky young man, and could climb up and down like a monkey. This was another reason why I always liked to have active young men on the wrecking crew. He could get up and down using those picks.

So, with all the new rigging in place, I climbed back onto the front of the crane and gave the signals. The little crane and the big crane took the strain, the Lidgerwood cable twanged, and the Lidgerwood, with the train anchored behind it, began sliding slowly down the track, and by golly, that tank started to come out of the lake. So we kept everything going, lifting and pulling, pulling and lifting, and the tank car kind of oozed up through the snow and mud, moving towards the track, and we just about had it at the track when SPANGG!! Something let go, and the tank slid right back into the water, only this time it was bobbing up and down. We had hold of the car frame, all right, but the tank was off.

This was an old tank car, not built like those of today, which are riveted solid right onto the frame of the car. The old type had a separate tank that sat in a bucket seat in the centre of the car and on saddles over the bolsters of the car, with wooden stop blocks on the ends, and a big strap around the tank at each saddle. Those straps held the tank on the car. What we didn't know (and didn't think of) was that the far end strap had been broken during the derailment, and the near end strap had been cut and weakened. The car had been underwater, of course, so we were not able to inspect it before we pulled. So with the strain of our pull, the front end strap popped and the tank slid free. On top of that, in sliding off the frame the tank outlet was broken (the four-inch outlet pipe), and there was a trail of dirty black crude oil all down the bank and into the lake.

In those days, they had just started the salmon hatchery at Seton Lake. They used the water right out of the lake and ran it through their hatchery. There we were with a broken oil tank, only a mile and a half away from the end of the lake. The wind was starting to get up, the lake was getting rough, and if we didn't act fast, the fish hatchery would be covered in sticky black oil. So as quickly as we could, we threw together a raft made out of ties, tied a rope on it, and a couple of fellows got on the raft and paddled out to the tank. Luckily it was floating with the dome up, sticking out of the water like the conning tower of a submarine. There was what we call "grab irons" on the side of the dome, so we could get a cable on it and snug it up good and tight. Then by pulling it out on a rope, we got our light cable attached to the dome and hooked onto our locomotive.

There was a little flat beach area just south of the derailment site, and some big trees there. We figured it would be easier to roll that tank up on a flat beach, where we could get a tail hold from the trees. So by backing slowly up the track with the engine, we got the tank to move down the shoreline to this beach, and it bobbed along, parallel to the beach. The trouble was, as soon as we stopped pulling the tank would roll over towards the lake, more oil would escape, and the tank wanted to escape as well. So we rigged a line on a tree, came back with the Lidgerwood cable, and managed to pull the tank up out of the lake, sideways, so it could not float away. But again, when we slacked off that tank rolled over, and more oil oozed out. In that cold water, the oil was pretty thick and almost solid, but it still tried to ooze out where the four inch pipe had broken off. We were tired, it was pitch dark, we wanted our supper, and this was the fourth day we'd been out, without very much sleep. So we tied a line from the dome right to the railway track, so we could leave it for the night.

Why I did it I don't know, but as the engine moved ahead towards Lillooet, I stopped to watch that cable, and as the tender left the spot where the cable was tied, damned if that track didn't start coming up in the air! The tank was trying to roll back into the lake, and pulling the truck with it. So I hollered to the engineer to stop, and he ran his engine back over the track, to hold it down. By this time we were so dead beat, we just had to quit. So we left that engine sitting there on the track, and went in for our supper. Everyone was exhausted and it was not practical to keep working, so we all turned in to get some sleep.

I remember, when I got into my bunk after supper I was knotted up and tense; wrought up, really, with all the worry and strain of the day. In order to have control of everything during a big pull, the signal man has to be right in the midst of things. I kept thinking about that damned big rock, moving while I was standing out there on the edge of the crane, right in line if anything had let go, for the blocks and cables to come piling down on me. The crane operators had some protection, but I was right in the bight. Then there was that demon tank trying to escape and spill oil all over the hatchery. I tossed and twitched, and dozed off, then jumped right out of my bunk, banging my head and part of my shoulder against the bottom of the upper bunk, waking myself up. That broke the tension, and I relaxed and went to sleep. That was the kind of stress we were under, on those long wrecks. The tension would build up and build up, and you'd just jump, because of your nerves.

When we woke up the next morning, the tank was waiting for us. Now the trucks and the frame of the tank car were not in too bad shape, and we were able to fix them up. Then we had to get the tank back onto the car, but first we had to plug the broken hole in the four inch drain pipe. So we picked out a tree about the right diameter, cut it down, shaved the bark off it, and made a long plug which tapered slightly. The thin end was small enough to go into the broken outlet. I stood by with the plug and two men with sledge hammers, and the Lidgerwood engineer gave a little pull to roll the tank over on its side. The oil started to gush out, but we stuffed our plug into the hole, and the two men with the sledge hammers began pounding. Well, what a sight! Bang! Squirt! We couldn't stop, because that oil was just a-gushing out, so we kept driving and driving in that plug, until the metal cut grooves into the wood, the plug seated right in, and the flow of oil stopped. The three of us were just covered in oil. Even then, after losing quite a bit of oil, that tank was a very heavy pull through the sand, up to the edge of the track. We left it there, and picked up the rest of our rigging, and the wrecking train headed back down to Squamish. Later on, the Lillooet crew came down with an empty tank car and pumped out this damaged tank, and it was finally picked up and re-railed some days later.

It was disheartening, really. Even with our new thirty-five ton crane, we could do very little when cars were off the track beyond the reach of the boom. With the boom right down, the capacity of the thirty-five ton crane dropped to something like only seven tons, and the seven-ton crane could pull maybe two tons. So we had to rely on the tremendous pulling power of our Lidgerwood but that required very tedious and time-consuming exercises in rigging and setting up blocks and cables. That's what took so long, when we were picking up after a wreck.

A couple of days later, Mr. Bailey went back up there with some divers. I didn't go along with them. They made a big raft at Lillooet so they would have a place to work off, with their pumps and their air compressors. The raft was towed out and anchored over the lost engine, and they dived down to search for the bodies of the two men. The divers reported that the engine was sitting on the edge of the slide. On the lake side, it dropped off very quickly. They could not get under the engine. They managed to get in the cab, and there was nobody in the cab. As far as they could see, there was nobody under or around the engine at all. The engine was deserted and the men were missing. They also searched all around the lake. So nothing further could be done, as they reported to the coroner and the authorities. There was no further sign of the men until early spring, when a section crew working along the lake discovered the body of Alex Munroe, washed up on the snore by the wind. Preserved by the icy cold water, the body was in very good condition, and was brought back to Squamish for burial. But of Harry Seymour, no sign was ever found.

This was one of our biggest wrecks, and I've never forgotten it. There was very, very little to joke about, that time. I did not take any pictures, and up to the present time have been unable to discover any. The lost crew were well liked, and it was a very distressing accident. But it was this wreck that convinced the railroad to send patrol cars out ahead of freight trains in the dangerous districts. There had been patrols ahead of passenger trains by that time, but after this they instituted safety patrols ahead of freight trains as well. Today of course there is a completely new communication system, and the delays and mix-ups we experienced can no longer happen. The patrolmen are safer as well, because they have radio contact with the dispatcher and with the engineer in the train behind them. But none of this was available when Engine 53 carried poor Alex Munroe and Harry Seymour into Seton Lake.

8 CHEAKAMUS TO THE LAKE DISTRICT

1929-1960

This is a chapter about derailments that took place over a long period of time, in that stretch of the railroad between the Cheakamus Canyon and the Lake District. I would not want the reader to get the idea that there was generally something exciting or dangerous about derailment incidents. Probably the exciting ones are the ones we remember best. There are lots of others that we might tend to overlook, in telling stories about how we went about picking up wrecks. Some years ago I read a book by Bruce Ramsay on the history of the Pacific Great Eastern Railway. He explained how there had been a lot of money troubles right from the start, and the line had been forced to operate under more than average difficulties. When I arrived in Squamish in 1929, things looked pretty good. There were plans to upgrade the line and the equipment, and to advance beyond the original construction. But as it turned out, with the Depression we hardly had enough money to keep operating, let alone maintain and improve the line. So it was not surprising that we encountered a lot of minor difficulties.

In order to get from the valley bottom on the Squamish River, up to the high point at Alta Lake, the railway must rise from just above sea level to an altitude of 2050 feet. The grade crosses over to the west side of the Cheakamus River and climbs up a very steep rise, following the Cheakamus Canyon. The Cheakamus River is a tumult of rushing white water and small falls, and it has created a spectacular canyon. This is very nice to look at, but extremely challenging to build through. When the line was constructed, there were places where the grade was up to 2.5 percent, and the average over this section was 2.2 percent. There were many deep rock cuts, and many ravines to be spanned. The construction crews could get unlimited supplies of Douglas Fir and Western Red Cedar, which is what they used to crib their way along the side of the canyon. When they lay down the original light steel 60 pound rails, and ran through the very sharp curves, it provide quite a hazardous ride.

Just north of the bridge spanning the Cheakamus River is a big rock cut, called Cunningham's Cut. It is very large and very steep; the walls are fifty or sixty vertical feet, which was quite an engineering challenge for the builders of the line. When the track gangs worked through these rock cuts, they put ties down right onto the rock, and ran their rail through, curves and all. The ballast cars dumped gravel between the ties. In a heavy rain storm, the water would fill up the shallow ditches on both sides and then flood through the rock cut, washing away some gravel from under the ties. Then a train coming over the line would derail, tearing up a portion of the line, and the derailed cars would push into the cut and jam it up. There would be cars off the track on both sides of the line, across the line, piled up, practically standing on end sometimes. In the early days, all we had was the little seven-ton crane and our Lidgerwood, so each car had to be dragged out one at a time. There was nothing spectacular about this work, just long hours, and hard work.

There were many pile-ups in Cunningham's Cut. Just south of there, between the bridge and the Cut, was a flat area where we could set aside the stuff we had dragged out of a pile-up, including the railcars, trucks from the cars, and loads especially logs.

Beyond Cunningham's Cut the line ran very close beside the Cheakamus River, which would get very turbulent and rise very high after heavy storms. This is in the days before there was a dam at Cheakamus Lake. Many times there would be a cold front and a storm, with snow piling up, and then the temperature would rise, the snow would turn to rain, and everything would come down the watercourses at once, in a flood. This would often have a bad effect on our track ballast, as well. In the Thirty's there was an incident north of Cunningham's Cut, where the ballast washed out and a freight train derailed at the back end. An empty baggage car left the tracks and pitched right over into the river, standing on end, over the bank. The caboose, which was immediately behind, left the track as well, but hung up on a big rock on the edge of the bank, teetering precariously. The crew was pitched around inside of the caboose, felt the car rocking, and scrambled up to the high end of the car to weigh it down. But it was so near to slipping that when three of them jumped off the track side, that caboose slipped a little further over the bank.

Harold Bailey was in charge of the wrecking crew then, as I was on holiday. When the crew arrived at the scene, they found that there was not room to work, with a high rock wall on one side and the river bank on the other side. Even if we had had a crane, there was no room to swing it; the rock wall was so close to the line. The little steam pot was on the job, but all it could do was lift trucks and move them back. So the Lidgerwood was called into play. The problem was where to hang a tailblock. We could get a cable onto the cars at the edge of the river, and pull them up with the power of the Ledgewood, but the only place to hang our tailblock was right on the rock wall itself. So Harold Bailey got hold of the rock crew and showed them where we wanted to put our slings, which was some way off the ground up the rock face. We needed two different places, because the derailed cars were some distance apart.

While the rock crew drilled out the holes, we got busy at the blacksmith's shop and made a pair of huge eyebolts out of two-inch steel rod. Each bolt had a slot in the end, and a split, and we made a wedge to go into each split. This gave us a pair of rock anchors. Then it was a matter of two men hoisting themselves up on rope slings, one with a sledgehammer and the other carrying an anchor bolt and a pair of blacksmith tongs. The split end of the anchor bolt, with the wedge in it, was pushed into the hole drilled by the rock crew. Then one man held the top of the eyebolt shank with the blacksmith's tongs, and the other man swung the sledge onto the top of the eyebolt to drive the whole thing into the hole. Dangling on the ropes made both men unsteady, so there were a few misses, when that hammer would pound the rock instead of the bolt.

Eventually, the wedge hit the bottom of the hole, and the bolt was driven harder onto the wedge, which expanded the split and tightened it in there. Then they plastered cement in, so it would set hard. After much dangling and hammering, both bolts were anchored into the rock, and the crew got out of the way for regular traffic up the line.

When the cement was really set, they brought up the Lidgerwood at the front of the wrecking train, passed a sling through the eye of the anchor bolt, and hung a snatch block on it. Then it was simply a matter of attaching a line to the caboose using a diamond hitch, and we were rigged to pull. Both the caboose and the baggage car were light rail cars, and both of them came up quite easily. As I say, there was no room at all for a crane to work, smack along side of that rock face with the river on the other side.

At the top of the Cheakamus Canyon is Garibaldi Station. During the Second World War, a logging operation was set up at Garibaldi to work on both sides of the river. They built a log bridge to get their trucks across the Cheakamus, and cleared out quite an area right up into Rubble Creek and beyond, bringing their logs down over the log bridge, to a railway siding we put in for them. By around 1950 the siding was not being used very much, and it had been let go without any particular maintenance. One of our engines entered the siding, and as the front wheels pulled onto the siding, the track just rolled over on its side and spilled the engine onto the ground. The engine was moving slowly, so the engineer was able to stop immediately. But they could not use re-railers, with the track turned over like that. So they sent for the wrecking train.

This incident happened just after we had gotten our 35-ton crane, and we were still trying out what it could do. We looked over the situation. The ties were too rotten to hold spikes, if we tried to use replacers. However, if we could lift the front end of that engine, the section men would be able to run the rail back up, under the wheels, and we could back the engine onto the main line again. I did some quick calculating in my head. When you lift one end of a locomotive, you have to lift more than half of the total weight. The bigger locomotives at that time weighed 120 tons, so lifting the front end we'd be looking at 70 tons, including the front trucks. Our new crane was rated at 35 tons lift, and you always figure a three-to-one ratio for the cables on cranes. I had figured out the tensile strength of the crane cables, and their breaking strain was about 95 tons. If we could get the crane right up to the front of the engine, we might get a capacity lift.

Now actually I was beyond my jurisdiction in trying out an unproven method, beyond the designed limits of the equipment. But the operating superintendent was there with me. I outlined the idea to him and said, "I'm willing to take a chance, if you'll back me on the responsibility, in case anything happens to the crane". Well, the main line was blocked, and he could see that there was not much alternative, so he said, "It's a good idea, Eric. Do it". So the section gang cut the rails in front of the derailed engine, and put in some new ties on the spur. We switched our wrecking train around so the crane came in from the far end of the siding, moving right up until the crane boom was practically vertical, and the couplers of the derailed engine and the crane were almost touching. We put two special cables onto the front end of the engine frame and hooked them on to our crane hook, set out all the outriggers on the crane, and drove the wedges in firmly. I stationed a man at every wheel so I could stop the lift before the crane started to tip over. We were all set to make a 70 ton lift with a 35 ton crane.

I was not especially worried about the cables, but I had some concern about the possibility of the boom on the crane collapsing. There had been two occasions, on former wrecks, where we had overloaded the steam crane on lifts. One time the steam pot boom just buckled. Luckily it was deflected away by the equipment it had been lifting, so it did not come down onto the crane operator or me. But lifting double its capacity, when we had very little experience with the 35 tonner, I was apprehensive about the boom coming down. I had to stand on the deck of the crane, of course, to see what was happening and to give the orders for the lift. So I checked to see that everybody was ready, and swallowed a bit, and then gave the crane operator the sign to go ahead slowly. He eased it very slowly, and the cables tightened. All the slack was taken up, and he kept lifting, a bit at a time. Those cables were so taut, they were singing. You could have twanged them and played a tune. And sure enough, the engine lifted. Then we needed to swing it over a little, but there was no way now for the crane to handle this. So I signaled the operator to set it down slowly, which he did.

There was a D6 or D8 Cat down by the sawmill, and the owner of the mill was standing watching us work, so I asked him if he could bring his Cat around the train at the far end of the siding to come over on the low side of the engine and give it a little push. It was asking too much for the crane to lift and to swing, but if the crane lifted and the Cat eased the derailed engine's nose over with a little push, we would be able to swing it. So the mill owner brought his Cat into place. We lifted the nose of the engine up a few inches, and the Cat pushed it over a few inches, above the rail, and we held it here. The section gang quickly turned the rails back up, slid some new ties in, and spiked the rails back together. The section crew were working right underneath that engine, but it was only a couple of inches above the rails, and they were okay so long as they kept their heads down. When the track was secure, we lowered the engine down onto the rails. Everything seemed secure, so we took off the slings, and the engine backed out slowly, onto the main line again. So we had gotten away with that method, even though the equipment was used beyond the capacity that it had been designed for.

Along the line going up through Cheakamus Canyon there are dozens of little ravines that empty down into the Cheakamus River. The railway runs through vertical rock cuts, then over trestles and bridges, and into the next rock cut. This area was all built with wood originally, and as time went by the trestles were replaced by steel bridges and concrete abutments which are anchored right into the rock, and rise up almost to the roadbed. If a derailment occurred, the cars would run onto the gravel ballast, and sometimes fetch up against a retaining wall. There was one incident, right on a curve where a derailment occurred, and the train jack-knifed, forcing a boxcar loaded with two-by-six lumber down to the retaining wall and squeezing it over the wall. Of course it plunged down into the canyon and landed in the river. It was more than 150 feet below the track, and too awkward to get a line on, so the decision was made to abandon it. We just picked up the rest of the wreck, and got the line open again.

However, some of the men on the wrecking crew looked down a that car full of lumber, lying there at the edge of the Cheakamus River, and thought they saw an opportunity to get some good lumber for nothing more than a bit of their own labour So, on their own time, they drove up from Squamish one weekend to a spot they had picked out, where the river came close to the road about five miles downstream from the wrecked boxcar. They set out a little catchment boom across the river, and a couple of men stayed there while the others made their way upstream to the boxcar. They enjoyed themselves, unloading that car and tossing the two-by-six lumber into the river, so it could float down and be picked up at the collecting boom. When they had the car unloaded, they returned downstream with high hopes. Alas, or words to that effect, the lumber was so smashed and splintered and banged up by the river current hurling it against the rocks, that there were simply not enough boards left to bother with. So they gave up on it. After that, we did not hear much talk about waste, when we were forced to abandon cars after a wreck.

Farther up the line, in the early days, the old wooden plow was working along the side of Green Lake, in about 18 inches of freshly fallen wet snow. On the side of the line away from the lake was a steep side hill about thirty or forty feet high. There was no way to detect it by looking along the line, but a sizeable rock had rolled down the bank onto the track and had been covered with snow. When the plow struck this rock it was derailed, and veered, fortunately for the men inside, towards the bank side. Before the locomotive engineer could stop, he had pushed the plow along the track and up into a sloping cleft in the rocky bank. The plow came to rest with its nose shoved up this cleft, standing on its rear end, with the men in the cupola lying on their backs in the seats. This upset them considerably.

It was a simple matter to recover the plow, by pulling it back onto the line with the Lidgerwood and using the rerailers to set it back on the track. There was very little damage to the plow, but the plow operators got after us to make some modifications, to make things easier and safer for them. We installed controls to the whistle and to the emergency brake, from the cupola to the roof of the plow. This way, the men could operate the plow either from inside the cupola or from on the roof of the cupola, and still operate signals and brakes. This gave them the choice, in dangerous areas, of staying with the plow or jumping off to the side of the track and risk breaking bones or getting run over. Some choice! A lot of improvements that we were able to make to operating and recovery equipment, over the years, was originally suggested by incidents like this one.

Just the other side of Parkhurst, where a fast mountain stream joins the Green River heading north from Green Lake, there used to be a logging camp and a siding. What happened to cause it, I don't recall, but a north-bound freight had a spectacular derailment there. We got the usual call, and the first thing we could smell when the wrecking train arrived was gasoline. That freight was hauling three tank cars full of gasoline, and after the derailment happened all three were leaking. One had sprung a few rivets, one was leaking at most of its seams, and the third had gasoline pouring out of the bottom, actually running along the ditches on both sides of the track. The gravel had become saturated with gasoline, and the whole area was liable to blow up any second. No smoking was permitted, of course, but it was much more serious than that. One little spark would have set the whole area into one giant explosion.

The first thing to be done was to try and stop the tank cars from leaking any further. So we cut small wooden plugs from some cedar ties, and drove those cedar plugs into all the puncture points we could find on the tanker shells. This greatly reduced the leaking. The next thing was to pull those cars out of the way, to get the line open. During the derailment the tank cars had become separated from their trucks, and there were several pairs of trucks piled up on one another, still on or over the main line. One tank car straddled that pile. It was too far away to be lifted by our crane, so we were going to have to pull it out of the pile with our Lidgerwood, which was sitting just in front of it on the main line. The 35-ton crane was set onto the siding parallel to the wreck.

By this time the Operating Superintendent and other officials had arrived, and they sent back to Squamish for all the fire extinguishers that could be gathered from the offices and shops, especially those from the locomotives. We had not yet acquired so many diesel engines by that time, so most of the fire extinguishers that arrived were small ones. While we were waiting, I instructed the men to hook up the Lidgerwood to that tank car. Then the crew went along the side of the grade, to places where the gravel had not been saturated by gasoline. They brought back this fresh gravel, and covered up the trucks that this tank car was sitting on, completely, and there was a small pile of gravel left over. The ideas were to prevent metal from striking metal during the pull, to prevent causing a spark. One spark would have blown us into another world. This took quite a while, and the fire extinguishers arrived.

When the time came to make the pull, everyone got well out of the way, leaving just our wrecking crew. Luckily it was raining at the time, and not a warm day. So we worked it out, that when the pull started one man on each side of the tank car would spray away with the carbon dioxide extinguishers, and the foam would damp any spark.

Cheakamus Canyon looking South. P.G.E. track is the white line middle left of the picture.
Photograph: E.P. Stathers

Nineteen Mile Bridge across the canyon. Cunnington's Cut just over the bridge to the right.
Photograph: E.P. Stathers

Derailment at Mile 82. Spring of 1952. Photograph: E.P. Stathers

Some of the crew. Left to right, George Devine, Bill Gedge, Mike Stillwell. Photograph: E.P. Stathers

East side looking north. Shoveling gravel over gasoline saturated tracks. Photograph: E.P. Stathers

All ready for the pull. Photograph: E.P. Stathers

Everyone took a deep breath, and I gave the signal to start the pull. On went the fire extinguishers, spraying a blanket of foam over the trucks. In slid the shovels with a little gravel blanket. The Lidgerwood cable tightened up, and that tank car slid along the gravel, clear of the pile, down to the Lidgerwood. And we all breathed easier.

After that, it was a matter of hooking onto the second car with the Lidgerwood, and taking a bit of a lift at the same time with the 35-ton crane, which could reach from the siding to the main line. We got that second car down the bank and into the clear. Inside of another six hours we had picked up the boxcars with our crane and set them back onto their own trucks, and they were out of the way. The problem still remained that those three tank cars were leaking gasoline, and they could not be handled as they were. What had to be done was to run some empty tank cars up from Squamish, and pump the gasoline out of the damaged tanks. These had been ordered. But in the meantime it was dangerous to let any traffic through this area, which was still saturated with gasoline. However, the dispatcher was very anxious to get a train through, and there were steam engines on this train. I told him the site was dangerous, so to instruct the engineer, when he go to the derailment site, to be sure and shut down the firebox, to blank his burners, and coast through past the wreck.

I don't know what happened. It was late evening by this time, and we stood waiting for this freight to pass by so we could spot the empty tank cars in place and begin pumping. The steam engine pulled over the crown of the hill, and we could see the flames shooting out of his firebox. He kept coming, with the train behind him, and the end of the train was over the hill coming down after him. And damned if he didn't keep right on pulling, making steam on the down grade. He didn't shut off his firebox at all, just rode through that whole mess of a derailment, saturated with gasoline with the flames shooting out from under the firebox. If you've ever seen an oil burner steam engine with the firebox going, you've seen those flames, like torches, shooting out from the firebox. Why we didn't explode and go up in smoke on the spot, I don't know, but I was so mad I got right on the phone to the dispatcher and told him what I thought of the whole damned situation, and it was lucky there was any of us left, that we might have all gone up in one big blast. After that, we managed to get one of the tank cars pumped out, and patched up the leaks on the other two, and the line was re-opened. It took about three more days before everything was picked up and out of the way. But we were very fortunate not to have been burnt or blown up.

Just south of Alta Lake was a little lake called Nita Lake, where another fair-sized logging show used to dump its logs and sort them in a booming ground, before loading them for shipment down the line. A mile south of there, the railroad passed through a quite narrow rock cut, with perpendicular sides anywhere between sixteen to thirty feet high. At that time there was a sharp curve on the south end, and we were still operating on the light 60-pound rail. Well, the south-bound freight came humping through that cut, and when the engine hit the curve it jumped the track, piled up in the ties, broke the rails, and stopped dead. The following train kept pushing forward, until the rock cut was jammed completely solid with boxcars loaded with lumber. They were driven in there so tight it was a solid mass. In fact, some of the boxcars pushed out of shape. They were round, instead of square. The pressure of the shifting lumber blew the tops off some of the boxcars. Altogether, there were twelve boxcars and twelve carloads of lumber, most of it smashed to bits in jumbled heaps. What a mess!

We came up with the wrecking train from Squamish, and brought a D6 bulldozer along to work with our 35-ton crane. After we had re-railed the engines, it was largely a matter of getting in and pulling the boxcars apart. They were wedged in so tightly that, in some cases, even the crane could not budge them. We had to feed the Lidgerwood line around the side of the crane, and actually tear the car loose from the cut. Then with the section crews, we would unload what lumber we could. The D6 Cat was able to pull some of them over to one side. We were lucky, because there was an old road quite close by the side of the cut, where we could feed the lumber through, put it onto the lumber truck, and had it transported down to the crossing and reloaded onto other boxcars.

There was no place to set the emptied boxcars, because there was a sheer drop on both sides of the line south of the cut. Those boxcars were all smashed. Some of them were salvageable, some of them were just junk. We brought in some flatcars, and set five of the boxcars onto flatcars to be hauled back to the shops for repairs. The other boxcars were stripped of every bit of useful material. By this time we had taken three days to get the line clear, and were able to move up into the cut. So, using our crane, we hoisted the Cat up onto the top of the cut, on the east side, the Cheakamus River side. We hooked onto the broken up cars, and hoisted them up beside the Cat, which dragged them off in the bush. And today, there are seven boxcars sitting there in the bush beside the Cheakamus River. If you know just where to look, you might see the one boxcar with the end cut out of it, sitting in amongst the trees. It was nicknamed "Stathers' Fishing Camp", although I never had any opportunity to use it. The cut was dubbed Van Horlick's Cut, for the engineer of that freight train.

Another odd incident took place in connection with this wreck. We ran short of water, and the line was open, so we ran up to that little logging camp just up the line to take on water for our crew cars. However, we received an unexpected setback. The railroad had been having a great deal of trouble with log cars that were not cleanly loaded. The problem was that the bark hung down and trailed off the sides of the log cars, falling onto the track, and dangling over the trucks. Coming down the canyon, with the air brakes set on to hold trains down to speed, the brake shoes on those cars would heat up considerably and these bits of bark would catch fire. There were a number of small fires started exactly this way. We got after the logging operators to take care that their cars were clean, before we could pick them up.   Now the man who operated this particular camp had disregarded the requests and instructions about keeping the cars clean, and his operation caused more fires than any other company. It had reached the point where I had to give orders that no loads were to be picked up from this camp until an inspector had been sent up, and of course we charged this to the logging company. Well, this made him pretty angry. After we had sent an inspector up a couple of times, and charged him for it, that straightened him out pretty well. But he was pretty hostile about it. So, when our wrecking train came to his camp for water, he said, "Sure, I've got water in the camp, but I don't have to supply the P.G.E. people with water. You can get your water somewhere else". So the engineer had to run all the way to Alta Lake Station, where the water tank was, to get water for our engine and our cook car. He was a rough and tough logging operator, and I guess I could be pretty tough too, for that matter. As long as we had to bring those log trains down we had problems when cars were not cleaned off, with the trains causing fires. And as long as his cars were dirty, they did not get picked up until an inspector had checked them and go him to clean them off. Those few barrels of water cost him plenty!

Farther up the line, past Parkhurst there is one point where the Green River drops right out of sight close to the track, making a very pretty falls more than 200 feet down into the canyon. At one time there was a bridge there, and trains used to stop, in the very early days, to let passengers see the falls. Close to that spot, there was a derailment where several tank cars and some other equipment went off the tracks. One tank car, loaded with oil, rolled down the hill, tearing out trees, and landed right in the middle of the Green River. This river is a fish spawning tributary, so the fisheries people were after us right away to get it out of there. Well, it was just about 500 feet down, and would take all the rigging we had, and a tremendous amount of time and labour. The tank was smashed, of course, and by this time all of the oil had already poured out into the river, so we couldn't do any more damage to the fish. So we decided to get rid of it by blowing it up, and gave the job to our rock gang.

The foreman came to me and asked, "Eric, how many sticks of dynamite should I use in blowing that tank?" So I said, "I don't know Victor, I don't know how much explosives. But that steel shell on the end is five-eights of an inch thick, and the walls on that particular tank are about three-eighths, and the dome is at least five-eighths, so I guess it will take quite a bit". "Okay", he said. "I'll take care of it". About two weeks later, going back over the line, I looked down at that spot to check the river. There was no sign of a tank. Farther along the track though, I spotted the end of the tank frame. Then I noticed other bits, along side the track. Well, as soon as I got the opportunity, I asked the section man, "How did all those pieces of tank get back up on the track?" "Oh", he said, "that's from the tank that was in the creek". So I got hold of the rock foreman, and said, "Victor, how many sticks did you use to blow that tank up?" "Well sir", he said, "I wanted to make sure, so I put two cases in the tank. It sure blew. It sure blew, in one big boom". Some of the fellows had been hunting in that area, after the blast, and they told me that for a quarter of a mile all around the whole forest was covered with shrapnel, with pieces of the car sticking out of trees. That tank had absolutely disappeared from the creek, and part of it had reappeared back up beside the tracks. That was one of our successful explosions.

This brings to mind the time we had a peculiar derailment in a train going up the line between Pemberton and Darcy. A carload of dynamite in the middle of the train came off the tracks, but it didn't come out of the train, just clipped the rails and hung on, and ran right past a logging camp where a lot of people were working. The train kept moving, nothing happened, nobody was injured. It was very fortunate. There must have been dozens of incidents on this stretch of line that I do not recall any more. But every one was different. Many times, we had a new problem to figure out. And the crew pitched right in with me; they found ways to pick up cars just as fast as I did.

We lost another tank car, an empty one this time, pretty near to where we blew that tank out of the Green River. It was on some rocks, too far away for our crane to touch it, which meant we brought our faithful Lidgerwood out into play once more. So I did what I often did, calling the crew together to discuss ways and means of recovering that tank - what sort of rigging to use, and how to set it up. Some of the young fellows in the crew had been loggers, and were quite knowledgeable, and they disagreed with me as to how it should be done. So I said, "Okay - fine. If that's the way you want to do it, go ahead, "and I won't interfere". Well, you should have seen those fellows go to work. It was their job, it was their idea, they crossed me, and they wanted to show me that by God I was wrong and they were right. You never saw a crew of men work so hard and so fast. They put out all their rigging amongst rocks and trees, with a hitch on each side of that tank car, set two cables underneath, and put timbers up to the track. They slid that tank up on the track so slick and so fast, it was a real pleasure to watch them work. This was the cooperation we got from the men on the wrecking crew.

I was very proud of the men I had to work with. I could talk to them, and get their cooperation. We had some miserable experiences, but when the chips were down they'd do anything for me. Lord knows we had plenty of practice. The worst accident we ever had on this stretch of line is a chapter all by itself, which we will come to later in this book. But all of these incidents took place a long time ago, and those days are long gone. The world, and the railway, are completely different now.

9 LAKE DISTRICT DERAILMENTS

1949

The Lake District is what we called the 28-mile stretch of the Pacific Great Eastern Railway that runs along the west side of Anderson and Seton Lakes. Darcy is at the south end, Seton Portage in the middle, and Craig Lodge, now burned down, was at the top end of Seton Lake, a few miles south of Lillooet. I've already told you about these two lakes in earlier chapters. Over the years, there were a lot of incidents in the Lake District. The stories in this chapter took place after we had acquired our 35-ton crane.

I recall one derailment involving a bunch of log cars, which occurred in 1954. In order to pick up this wreck, we had to shift the logs off the derailed cars, and find some place to put them. With the lake on one side of the line, and a rock wall on the other side, it was not even possible to swing the crane around, because the back end of the crane would have hit the rock wall. Ordinarily it would have been simple enough to pick up logs with the crane, and load them into another log car behind the crane. But we could not do this. Instead, it was a case of picking up a log, backing up with the crane to a place where we had room to put the log on one side, dropping it off, and then running forward to get another log. This took a tremendous amount of time. When the car was empty, we could lift it with the crane and pull it back, and then recover the trucks, and put that car back together again. Then we had to back up to where the logs were, reload the car, and move farther back down the line to a siding to get rid of it. There was no way to set the logs and cars to one side, because there simply was no room there, just rock wall and lake. This was a problem we encountered many times, along the line. But at that time, most of the timbered construction had been replaced with concrete walls, and there was a much safer roadbed, but the rails were still light and would twist like a pretzel under the force of some of those derailments.

There were also occasions where boxcars of lumber went into the lake. I mentioned one in Chapter 6, where we had an Indian crew from Darcy tow three loaded boxcars with an eighteen foot boat down to the beach at Darcy. That time we had left the trucks on those cars, which meant considerable trouble when we tried to haul them over the beach and out of the water. Actually, we did not think of it until we had the Lidgerwood rigged up and were pulling. Then of course it was a real problem to detach those trucks. We tried to work out of a boat, but that was not practical. We could not use a cutting torch under water. So we wound up in the water, under the cars. That taught us a lesson. So the second time we had three boxcars of lumber over the bank from the derailment, we cut the trucks off right where they were, before steering them into the lake and towing them down to that beach near Darcy. Once we got them pulled onto the beach, it was simple enough to unload the cars into another boxcar, and then handle the empty car back onto the line.

South end. Note the sheer rock walls. Photograph: E.P. Stathers

Unloading the logs from the cars. Photograph: E.P. Stathers

Note the concrete retaining wall behind the track. These were originally log cribs when I first came.
Photograph: E.P. Stathers

Getting ready to lift the empty car and take it back to the flat.
Photograph: E.P. Stathers

After you left Darcy there was a tunnel at 83 Mile, and close by was a little cabin right on the lake. We had a heavy derailment there of log cars, right opposite the house, with many cars off the track, and one in the lake. The owner of the cabin was an old bachelor, and he stood there and watched us picking up the pieces, no doubt figuring it was time he left the area. Actually, this derailment was the last straw. It was a nice spot, with quite a bit of flat land beside the lake, where he had lived for a long time. He'd had a lovely garden there for years, which had been wiped out the previous winter. It had been a tough winter, with a lot of snow, and a big slide came down. Just above his cabin and across the railroad track was a rather large rock. That slide had split into two waves, which flowed around that rock and piled up snow and rocks against both ends of his cabin, so tightly that the door was blocked. In order to get out he had to break his window, and then hike into Darcy to get help and grub. He was a very fortunate fellow that he did not get carried into the lake. So I guess when he saw this derailment right above his shack, he figured it was time to get out of there, and he did soon afterwards. At any rate, another car went into the lake during this episode, and once more we practiced our beaching technique. There were many other occasions, including the one with the Bridge River Power Company Crane, which was covered earlier in the story.

But the big one, which I'll never forget as long as I live, took place about a mile and a half down from Seton Portage, at Mile 100.8. There was a very narrow rock cut at this point. It wasn't too high, but it was a long cut, with a curve in it following the contour of the lake. There was very little shoulder to work on on the lake side, and a little more on the bank side. A south-bound freight train of loaded lumber cars derailed in the cut. We were called out on March 31, 1953, and left Squamish about half past two in the afternoon, to arrive at the site before midnight. By this time we had lights, good Coleman lanterns, lots of them, so we could see to work at night. We went to work immediately. It had been very cold for some time, and the ground was frozen solid. The cut was jammed with cars, all loaded with lumber. They were mostly the older smaller type of wooden boxcar, called forty tonners because that was their maximum load. Even fully loaded with trucks on, they weighed only about 45 or 46 tons. That meant we were able to shift them without having to unload them, because our crane was able to pick up one end at a time.

Our procedure was to pull out the trucks, which were piled up underneath the cars, and then pull out the cars. If we could not rerail a car right there, we would pick up one end, run a set of trucks into about the middle of the car, and set the car down practically balanced on the trucks. Then we'd back out of the cut, pulling the balanced car to where we could set it over off the track to one side. Where we were setting these cars over was on an elevation towards the lake, so we were lifting to the high side, which improved our boom elevation. The effect was to increase the amount of load that our crane could safely handle, because the boom angle was higher. Elevation is the amount that the track is "tipped" or angled over, to counteract the sway of train cars going around a curve. The effective lift of a crane is reduced as the boom is lowered. In order to set cars off to one side of the track, it is necessary to extend the boom of the crane by lowering it slightly, which reduces the safe lifting capacity. When we worked on an elevated track, on a curve, you had to add that elevation angle to the boom angle, because the crane base was elevated the same as the track. So it was possible to lift heavier loads farther away from the track on the high side of the curve, and you could not lift as much on the low side.

We extended an outrigger on the back end of the crane, toward the lake side, but we did not wedge it because especially on that frozen ground, it was difficult to set the blocking. We would have had to use a pick and shovel to get a flat base, which would have taken us a long time on each lift. So we had the outrigger out to guard against tipping, but the crane could still move. The first thing was to get the line open, by moving the cars off the track. Of course, we knew that all of the cars would have to be unloaded before we could pick them up properly, for regular use along the railroad. So it was a case of pulling one end of the car over, then the other end, then balancing it on trucks and hauling it back out of the cut. Then we set one end off the track, set the other end over off the track, moved the trucks out of the way, and back to the cut for another boxcar. This went on all night and straight round the clock into the next day, which was April 1st. The Lillooet Lidgerwood had come down with a crew under Stan Malm, and was working from the north end of the cut, pulling cars clear from the north end while we worked with the crane from the south end. The line was still blocked, so although our crew had been on duty since 8:00 am the previous morning, we kept right on working.

There were no problems. It was just a matter of lifting and actually balancing on one truck. When you got them in the clear, you'd lift them high enough so you could set them on a block, and see-sawed them over, like a swing, so the back end was clear of the track, and then pick up the front end, and slide it out of the way. Then take the truck off, to one side, and return to the cut. We did not put out the full outriggers for these lifts, but extended an outrigger on the lake side of the track, in case we tipped. I did have one man assigned to each corner of the crane, to watch a wheel so that if a wheel started to come off the track they were to call out immediately, and we would drop the load.

So we kept on, and we were getting pretty tired. That ground was frozen hard, and the track was hard, but it was April 1st, and a hot day, and everything was thawing pretty fast. It started to get wet and muddy on the track, but I suppose we were a bit tired, and we did not pay particular attention to that. It got to be around 3 o'clock in the afternoon, and we were setting the front end of another car over the line. We had the four men posted, one at each corner of the crane, as usual. I gave the signal to the crane operator, and he swung the load over as usual. The car was just about to clear the line when I heard a shout, "Hold it! The wheel's coming up!" And then without any warning, the deck of the crane started to rise. I was on the bank side, and it was tipping over towards me. To get out from under, I had to run up the full width of the deck, now sloping towards me, and jump. I got there all right, and just as I leaped towards the lake side, something hurtled down onto my head and just about took my ear off. It was the crane operator, coming out of the cab. He landed just about on top of me on the gravel, as the crane turned over onto its side with a terrific crash, on the bank side of the track. My God! We'd turned the crane over, and here we were with the line tied up. I felt sick. I couldn't believe it. I just couldn't believe that I had done such a thing.

Luckily for us, just south of us there was a new little wooden bridge just built, across a gully between the rocks, made of creosoted timbers. All of the old timbers had been pulled up onto the same flat where we were setting out the boxcars, and they were right opposite the body of the crane when it fell. So the crane was not flat on its side, but leaning over about 45 degrees onto these bridge timbers. The cables from the crane boom were still connected to the boxcar we had been lifting, and as the crane tipped the boom just eased gently over and set the load down. There seemed to be very little damage to the boom. Even the crane and the engine did not seem to be much affected, as far as we could tell.

The crane operator and I picked ourselves up off the gravel, and right away I questioned the men who had been watching the wheels of the crane, starting with George Devine who had been on the high side. "What happened, George?" "Well I think the track sank", he said. "The track sank down until the rails were level with the ground". And the man on front said, "Well, I didn't see the front go down, because the boom was in the way, but suddenly the crane went right up in the air and over. We didn't have time to tell you". And the two men at the back said, "Yes, that's what happened with us. The high rail just disappeared into the ground". Well then we could understand it. The heat of the day was thawing out the frost in the ground, and working back and forth over the line, we were helping to thaw out the frost under the track. On this last lift, the rails and ties had pushed through the melting frost, right down into soft dirt. Instead of lifting on an elevation that helped us, the rail had dropped and put the track elevation against us, and that was enough to cause the crane to tip over.

The Assistant Superintendent, who was supposed to be in charge of the whole operation, immediately left to phone in and tell Vancouver what had happened. The train crew and everybody else took off to the caboose or the cook car, leaving my six men, the seven of us, looking at the mess and me. The road was tied up, the crane was in the ditch, we had no other crane - and then a cloud coming down from the north passed over the lake, and it started to snow. April 1, 1954. I think I was the sorriest man in British Columbia. In fact, one of the men came up to me and said, "Don't take it so hard, boss. It wasn't your fault". "Baloney", I said, "I should have thought of this, and had an outrigger out". So we sat there for a while, wondering how the devil we could get that crane back on its feet.

1.5 miles south of Seton Portage on Seton Lake April 1, 1954.
This picture was taken looking south at the crane boom and bank. Photograph: E.P. Stathers

Setting the replacers and rigging on the crane, preparatory to pulling it back on the rails.
Photograph: E.P. Stathers

Just about upright again. Note the cable from the deadman, and the rigging using the power from the Lidgerwood to pull it upright. Photograph: E.P. Stathers

A good picture of a car replacer clamped on to the rail.
Photograph: E.P. Stathers

Inside the cut when the cars bunch up. Paddy Bowman, General Manager, in the foreground.
Photograph: E.P. Stathers

The Lillooet Lidgerwood, still on its old wooden flat car, with a steam engine behind it. We were using it to work from the north end of the cut.   Photograph: E.P. Stathers

After a while I had figured out what to do, so I went back to the caboose where the Assistant

Superintendent was. While we were talking about getting our crane back, a phone call came in. "Oh Lord", he said, "there's another derailment up the far side of Lillooet at Mile 134.7. The line is blocked, and we can't even get into Lillooet". So he decided to send the Lillooet gang with their Lidgerwood away from the north end of our wreck, up the line to this new one, to see what they could do. They got hold of a bulldozer to load on at Lillooet, and off they went up past Fountain, leaving us with only three more cars left in the cut. By this time we were tired out, having been on the job for 36 hours straight without sleep or a break, so we tied up for the night with a call for early next morning.

To recover our crane it was necessary to pull it back onto the line with a tail hold on the lake side of the track. With the section crew we dug a deadman trench right on the shore of the lake, alongside the track. Then we pulled rails into the trench, doubled up an inch-and-a-half cable, and wrapped it around those rails, with a large loop on the end sticking up out of the rock and shale. If you go by on the train today, and look in the right place, that cable is still there sticking up. Then we set a pulley block onto that sling, and went to work to rig up for a pull with the Lidgerwood. By early the next morning the General Manager of the railroad, Paddy Bowman, and the Master Mechanic, Jack Frost, had arrived on the site to take charge of operations. We went ahead as planned with our scheme to get our crane back in action.

The real trick in pulling this crane up was to control the pull so we didn't haul it right over into the lake. It was lying with its wheels right alongside of the rail, which was fine. But when it got up to the balance point, there was a danger that it would have too much momentum as it came down on its feet, and keep on going to tip across the track. We had quite a consultation about this. We had the main rigging in place, with a pull on the crane, and a cable on the boom rigged up with a hitch to protect the boom while we hoisted the crane back up to vertical.

One of my men had been a logger, and he said that he could control the crane by a snub line. He would work a line on the crane from the bank side, opposite to the Lidgerwood pull, keep it taut, and control the crane as it flopped into the upright position, as a protection line. The Assistant Superintendent was very doubtful that such a thing could be managed. He felt that a man would not be able to hold such a weight. The man, Clayton Thorne, said he could do it if he was given enough men, because he would snub around three trees, and he could block the line at the critical time when the crane was coming over on her own. Well, Clayton Thorne and I talked Paddy Bowman into accepting the plan.

So we got ready for the pull. I was busy giving signals to the Lidgerwood operator. Clayton Thorne adjusted his snub line around three trees up the hill, while we took up all the slack on the crane line. Then I gave the go ahead, and the Lidgerwood pulled slowly, and the crane came up. Clayton Thorne kept his line firm, feeding it out just enough to follow the pull, until the crane reached the balance point, and the Lidgerwood line slackened. That was a pretty heavy crane. It weighed 99 tons, and Clayton Thorne did a remarkable job, a very good job indeed. He worked that cable so nicely that it tightened right up like a brake. I'll bet the crane didn't move one inch out of perpendicular, when the wheels came down beside the track. It was a fine piece of work. Then it was a matter of re-railing the crane, which was done. The boom was not too badly damaged, but there was a crack in one of the engine housings so we could not use the crane engine. So it was pulled down the line out of the way.

Then we went to work with our Lidgerwood to pull the three remaining cars out of the cut. That was hard work. We had to jack up the car, put timbers under it, and actually skid the boxcar out of the cut on piles of ties, down the line until there was a space to pull it off the line. Then we re-rigged, using trees for a tailhold, and pulled the car off out of the way. And back we went for the second boxcar, the same thing, and finally the last one was moved, and the line was clear and ready for traffic.

While this was going on, the Lillooet crew had arrived at the wreck north of Fountain with their

Lidgerwood and a bulldozer. There was enough room to build a shoefly around the derailed cars. So they cut the track, and built a shoefly around the wreck, and moved a few cars enough for traffic to get through. Then the whole line was open again, and we were able to take the crane back down to Squamish for repairs. The section crews went to work transferring the lumber out of those boxcars at both ends of the cut. We repaired the crane and were back on site on April 25th to pick up those cars and return them to the shops in Squamish.

That was one of the most disheartening wrecks in my whole career. I don't think I ever felt so low in my life, as the moment when I picked myself up and looked at our crane lying over on its side, and then it started to snow. And there was nobody left but our crews, everyone departed and left us. It was just like we were isolated from the rest of British Columbia. We were cold, and we were tired, and it was a very distressing feeling being left like that.

Later Paddy Bowman came into Squamish to have a little investigation into the accident. He went out and looked at the crane, and then he questioned the men who were with me at the wreck. They all told him that the track had suddenly let go, which helped considerably to support me. But then he started to give me a bit of a rough time about not being careful enough with company equipment, and not putting outriggers when setting the cars over to the side of the track. So I said, "Well, Mr. Bowman, I've written letters telling your officials that you expect me to pick up engines and cars that are much too heavy for this crane, way over the rated capacity. I do work with this crane that it was not intended to do, and I try to do it as quickly as I can. That particular time, I said, "we were not working with outriggers". Fine. You can bet your boots that from now on, I won't make a move without those outriggers set out on this crane, because it's not worth the risk to have it turn over again. So no matter how long it takes, I said, "if you want outriggers out, they'll be out there". And he said, "No, no, no, now don't take it that way, Eric, don't go overboard the other way".

"Well, Mr. Bowman", I said, "in one breath you've asked me to do something, and with the next breath you asked me to do something else. Now if you want to trust my judgment in getting this track cleared as quickly as possible, we have to do things at times without outriggers. Otherwise we're going to spend all day just putting outriggers out, which is just what we would have been doing there, especially with the frozen ground, and we wouldn't have gotten anywhere. You say that we've got to be a lot more careful and if you wish us to do that, and not to do anything without outriggers, that's the way it will be done". And that's the last I heard of the idea, because he knew that if he pressed me too far we would have been two or three times longer in getting the road open. Anyway, I was mad at myself, not at him.

There was another derailment up at Mile 106, just south of Retasket, a few miles down from Lillooet. We left Squamish on June 29th, got there after 7 pm in the evening, worked right through the night and through the next day, June 30th, picking up cars. By that evening, the section gang was able to get a shoefly around the wreck, and the road was open again. Now July 1st is, of course, a holiday, and at Lillooet this was the day of the annual rodeo. And there is no way in the world that the Indian section hands would miss it, so that meant no track work on July 1st. Many of the crew took part in the rodeo, and they all had a whoop-de-do day, I can tell you. It was really something to see a rodeo at Lillooet. They had downhill races the way we have downhill ski races today, with horses just belting down the hill, and when one of the horses lost its footing down would come horse and rider, ass over tea kettle, broken legs, and Lord knows what. Between participating in the rodeo and recovering from it, no work would be done on July 1st and not an awful lot on July 2nd either. So it was a holiday. The boys were getting paid for it, but there was no use going back to Squamish for one day and we couldn't get much work done, so we just stayed where we were. In the afternoon, the crew took off to see the rodeo. I stayed at the work train with Harold Bailey. However, he had friends in town and decided to pay a call on them, so I wandered around town for a while.

About three o'clock in the afternoon, I got a call to say that the motor car had gone off the track at the shoefly around the wreck. This was a gas-powered train car that provided a transfer service over the railway line between Shalalth and Lillooet. There was no road into Bralorne in those days. You drove to Lillooet, and put your car on specially designed flatcars with side rails on them, and our gas car pulled them along the track to Shalalth where they were unloaded on special ramps. Then you drove off the flatcars and took the Mission Mountain Road over the mountain to Bridge River, Bralorne, or wherever you were going. This was the only access into the Bridge River district. As well as cars, trucks, mail, and produce - everything travelled this way. And on the return run from Shalalth, this motor car had gone off the track with these flatcars at the shoefly. I was all by myself there in the bunk car.

So I had to round up the men up at the rodeo, which was nearly two miles up the hill. Some were in the beer parlor, some at the rodeo. I didn't go into the beer parlor, of course. Seeing that I was the boss, I couldn't drink at all and had to stay away from there. But I managed to find some of the boys up at the rodeo and gather them up, and then on the way back they went into the beer parlor and fetched the rest. By this time a train crew was lined up. So off we went to the shoefly. It didn't take very long to get the motor back on the track, and in a couple of hours we had the whole train going. I don't think we were gone from Lillooet more than six hours altogether. We didn't take our whole train, but left the crew car and our other tool car and the crane behind.

The conductor's name was Harry, and I don't want to say too much about Harry, he's dead now. Let's just say that he wasn't the most energetic type of man. He worked his way up from brakeman to conductor. We stopped on the way back to Lillooet to pick up the rest of our work train, and then continued on into Lillooet. Well, I walked back through the train through the end of the motor car, and here was Harry, fast asleep. He was the conductor of the train, responsible for the train, stretched out across the seats with his feet up, fast asleep. Well, look at that, I thought to myself, the man who's supposed to be in charge of the train, and he's fast asleep in the train while we are moving. That's a pretty poor show for a man who is supposed to be responsible for the safe operation of all of this equipment. However, I didn't say anything to him because we were going back.

When we got to Lillooet we needed water for the cook car, so I got hold of Harry and said, "Look, we've got to be spotted over to the water line. It won't take you very long, maybe twenty minutes, half an hour. If you'll just switch us in by the water line, we'll get our hose out and fill the water car, before you put us over on the siding out of the way". "Nothing doing", he said, "I'm in Lillooet now and I'm finished for the day. I'm tied up. As soon as I hit those yards, I'm finished. I'll put in my report and go". And I said, "Look man, you haven't been out that long, it'll only take you another twenty minutes or so to give us our water". "No, not by a damn sight, you're not going to get me to work in the yards when I am here. When I get here, I'm finished, tied up".

Well this was too much. It wasn't very often that I blew my top, but I got really mad. I called that man all the names I could think of, and I can tell you that I have a pretty good vocabulary. I had two vocabularies in those days, one I used for working, and one I used at home. I didn't dare use that working vocabulary at home, or I'd have been thrown out of the house. But the one I used for working had a great deal of emphasis sometimes, for getting things done in a hurry, and I called that man foul names. If anybody had called me those names, there'd have been a fight in a hurry, but he just stood there and looked at me and didn't do anything. Finally, I started to grab him by the collar and I was going to let him have it. He started to run. He ran out along side the train with me after him, and as we ran I got madder and madder. I got to the engine, it was a steam engine. Instead of going around the engine, where I could have caught up with him, he ducked up between the engine and the tender, up the steps and down over the side. I started up the steps after him, but the fireman saw what was happening and heard the noise and goings on. He jumped down into the gangway and put his foot on the steps and planted one foot in my chest and said "Hold it, hold it, Eric! He's not worth it! Don't let yourself get in a mess". "I'm not gonna get in a mess", I said, "That S.O.B. was sleeping on the way up to the wreck, and all the way back from the wreck he did nothing but sleep". "So", I said, "if he wants to start anything, I can finish it. I'll be no worse off than him when I get hold of him". "Well", he said, "You'd better cool off", and he got me calmed down. But if I could have gotten my hands on that man that day, he would have been mighty sorry that he didn't spend a few extra minutes to help us get our water. And he was always the first man to sit down and get his knees under the dining table too. However, you rarely ran across this type of man in the train crews. Often the train crew would sleep while the wrecking crew worked at night, and then we would sleep on the way home while the train crew was working. But to have a man be so small as that, why I found it awfully hard to take.

The engineer himself spotted us. I gave him signals and he took us over and spotted us up to get our water. Harry disappeared. He never got anywhere near me, because he was afraid what might happen to him, and I was certainly big enough to handle him in those days. But these are the things in life that are very frustrating at times, running up against men like this. I guess it's just part of living.

The next day being July 2nd, some of the Indians turned up for work and some of them didn't, and those who did were a sorry looking lot, I'll tell you. However, we didn't need too much track work done. We were able to get back down there with our equipment put the rest of the cars back on the track, finish up the job, and then get back to Squamish. But we kept being called out, and called out. During those years our track was in just deplorable condition, with 60 pound steel, no ballast, and in the mid-50's it was just pitiful. We would go pick up one wreck, and while we were out another one would happen, and we'd move from one to the next, and sometimes it seemed like we were never going to get home. And we didn't have proper equipment, either. Patience wears a little thin, after you have to work like this for a while.

There is one more incident to tell about on this stretch of line. It turned out rather funny, but it could have been very dangerous. There used to be a small tunnel near Shalalth. The B.C. Electric wanted to put their second power house on the lake front, right on our right-of-way. They purchased the land for it, drilled a much longer tunnel inland from the lakeshore, paid for the track and equipment, and the P.G.E. line was moved into the longer tunnel. This incident happened in the days of the little tunnel one time when I happened to be on holidays, so I wasn't there. But I heard all about it when I got back to work. There was a small derailment just south of the old tunnel, where the bank dropped straight down into the lake, and a boxcar had slid right off into the water, and was floating there right along side of the bank. It was a bit beyond the reach of our crane, and there was no way they could lift a loaded boxcar out. If I'd been there I'd have had the car towed to where we could get at it, but they didn't do that. Somebody came up with the idea of cutting the roof off the boxcar. Then the lumber would float out and the car would sink, and they'd get rid of it that way. We had acquired oxyacetylene cutting torches by then, as part of our wrecking train equipment. Both the oxygen and the acetylene tank were stowed in a cradle with straps and a sling on it, so that the crane could set it where it was needed for work. That saved a lot of heavy manhandling.

So they set an outrigger for the crane and lowered the crane boom, so it would reach as far as it could out towards the boxcar of lumber bobbing there at the edge of the lake. They found a rowboat somewhere, and Bill Gedge and Jim Taylor climbed into the rowboat and went along side the boxcar. The crane operator, Clayton Thorne, (who was one of the best operators we ever had on this railroad, so far as I am concerned), picked up the oxyacetylene rig and swung it out beside the boxcar, holding it there so the two men could reach the cutting torch and start burning off the rivet heads. They started at one end, worked their way along the lake side of the boxcar, around the other end, then back along the inshore side. There was no place to tie on to as they worked that rowboat around the boxcar, so they tied up to the oxyacetylene cradle which was dangling in place at the end of the crane boom. Finally they burned off the last rivet, and things started to happen fast. The roof popped off. The boxcar sank in great foam of bubbles, churning the water under the rowboat. Lumber began exploding out of the boxcar. It was all two by fours, and they were coming up out of the water like arrows from a crossbow, making big arcs in the air. The farther the boxcar sank, the greater the velocity of these two by fours. They came out of the water like rockets.

Clayton Thorne, the crane operator, could see that those men had to be gotten away from there fast, and the only thing that he could do was to lift his boom inland, raising the tank cradle. Of course with the boat tied to the tanks, this tipped the boat up a bit and one of the men fell in the water. Fortunately he had presence of mind enough to hang onto the boat, and men, boat, and tanks were hauled up onto the bank not a moment too soon. It was a regular fireworks display of two by fours leaping out of the lake. The water was covered with wood. Finally they got a power boat, made a boom, corralled all of this floating lumber, and towed it over to Shalalth where most of it was salvaged. Everyone had a good laugh and it must have been comical to watch, although it was a dangerous idea and the boys were lucky that nothing more happened than a good ducking.

And that winds up the stories about the Lake District for now. In the next chapter we'll move up the line past Lillooet into the Fraser Canyon and Cariboo country.

10 FRASER CANYON FROLICS

1950-1951

Just past Lillooet, the Fraser Canyon is very deep, carved out of the rock. A little north of Lillooet is the Moran Canyon, which was at one time examined for a possible hydro-electric dam. However, while it would generate tremendous amounts of electricity, it would practically wipe out the Fraser Canyon fish runs, so it is not a likely prospect. The area is very dry, with low rainfall, and is sparsely settled. After the war, the roadbed in this stretch was in very poor condition with only sixty pound steel. It was very worn and poorly ballasted, which meant that the curves were constantly being pushed out of shape. We had endless small derailment incidents. Our freight equipment was also in poor condition. We had converted to diesel locomotives, however. In 1945 we bought six of the small 660 horsepower units. In 1950 and 1951 we decided to use 1600 horsepower diesel units. This policy was continued until we had acquired a fleet of these units. In 1948 we converted the Lidgerwood from steam to diesel. So by the beginning of the 1950's we had discontinued steam. This meant that we no longer had the problem of running back and forth getting water, as we had done previously. The fuel capacity of diesel engines is also greater than for steam engines so this made diesels more convenient as well.

We had a derailment on April 1, 1952 that produced a few memorable moments. A number of gondola cars loaded with logs had spilled off the track and down the gentle slope of the bank, and there were also quite a few boxcars of lumber off the track. As usual, the back end of the train had pushed into the cars ahead and rode up, so that the trucks separated from their cars. There was quite a pileup of trucks close to the track. Fortunately, there was a nice wide shoulder to work on beside the track. It was a straightforward job. Before we tried to lift the gondolas, we unloaded the logs with the thirty-five ton crane and piled them on that shoulder beside the track where they could be loaded into another gondola car later on. Then, with the outriggers full out, we managed to pick up the empty gondola car and set it back over the track onto one set of trucks, and hold it while the engine pushed the other set of trucks under the car. When the derailed gondola car was close to the track, the crane could lift the loaded car, logs and all, while we climbed underneath and set the trucks in place. We had developed rigging that hooked onto different portions of the cars, usually the centre sill. You had to protect the corners of the steel cars, so that the cables would not cut them during a lift. When we had to lift on an angle instead of straight up, we used these corner protectors to hold the cables out. When the car had been lifted into the air, we had to get in underneath the car with blocking to hold it up. If it was the far end of the car that needed moving over, farthest from the crane, we put blocking in the centre of the car to act as a pivot and see-saw the car over. Then we could lower the near end of the car and lift the far end to swing it over to the rails, or put rails underneath it. Many times we had to lift a loaded car up in the air and hold it there for an hour or more, while the crew built the track underneath that car to the back trucks. Of course, this meant working underneath these huge loads. It may seem a bit dangerous working there when all that is holding between you and sudden death is the strength of the cable. Of course, we made sure our cables were in good condition. I'm proud to say that during all of the thirty-six years that I spent doing this kind of work, we never had a really serious accident to any man of the wrecking crew who was under my supervision, because I was very careful as far as equipment was concerned.

The Fraser Canyon between Pavillion and Moran siding.

The Moran Canyon just below Moran siding. Photograph: E.P. Stathers

Looking south from Moran siding. Note the telephone pole along side the flat that is the P.G.E. Grade about 1000 feet above the Fraser River. Photograph: E.P. Stathers

Derailment Mile 184 just north of Moran siding, April 1, 1952.
Photograph: E.P. Stathers

A nice flat area to work with on the bank side.
Photograph: E.P. Stathers

Note pile of trucks under the loaded cars.
Photograph: E.P. Stathers

Ready to pull the boxcar up to the track. Eric Stathers standing on the crane deck for a clear view and to give signals to the crew. Photographer: Unknown

Note the outriggers full out on the crane with the Fraser Canyon in the background.
Photograph: E.P. Stathers

Up on the crane, getting ready to line it up with the track.
Photograph: E.P. Stathers

After we had all the gondolas back on, we were able to get the rest of the train past the boxcar that was lying down the bank. It was loaded with lumber, and even without the trucks it weighed somewhere in the neighbourhood of 40 tons. There was no way we could lift that loaded boxcar with the 35-ton crane. So, as we often had to do, we unloaded the lumber. The way the car was lying, it was not possible to open the loading door, so it was a matter of cutting a hole in the end of the car.

This is a bit of a chore because of the danger of fire. We used a cutting torch to cut through the steel cladding of the boxcar. Just underneath the steel is a wooden liner, usually full of dried up wheat dust, splinters, and sawdust; dust from all cargoes carried in that car, which is a very flammable mixture. So we carried these forestry backpack waterpumps. As soon as we had cut a small hole, we pumped water in there with the nozzle of our pump. Then we'd start to cut down along the corner of the car, and make a hole big enough for the men to get in and work. By the time we had the hole cut, of course, we had a fire that we could control with these backpack pumps. They are carried on your back with shoulder straps and hold about four gallons of water. There is a hand pump and a flexible nozzle and they will throw a stream of water about fifteen feet.

Then the lumber had to be unloaded by hand and passed into another boxcar alongside. This was a very tedious job. That lumber was freshly cut 2x12's, heavy and slippery. The men inside the car were slipping on them as they pushed them out of the hole. Somebody else grabbed them and slid them into the skidway that we built into the other boxcar on the track, where they were reloaded.

Generally, we used to use section gangs to do this unloading because our wrecking crew usually had lots of work to do on the equipment. Sometimes the cars would be over on one side, and we'd have to repair the trucks and make repairs to the cars before we could put them back onto the tracks, so that they would be able to run again. Often, the cars that had remained on the tracks also needed to be fixed up, and air brakes would have to be hooked up. So our boys were usually quite busy and the section hands did the unloading.

This particular section crew was from Pavilion, the next station about five miles down the track, beside the Indian Reservation. They were all Indians, good working fellows, and the section foreman was an Indian, a big husky fat man. The Roadmaster was there, of course, in charge of the section crews. We also had a section crew from Kelly Lake since we needed the two crews to handle this lumber because, as I said, it was very heavy and slippery. There were only four or five men in a crew at that time. However, there had been a death in the tribe in Pavilion and nothing could stop this Pavilion crew, they had to go and attend the funeral. So at noon they took off, and went back to Pavilion to pay their respects to this man who was part of their tribe. And I guess an Indian funeral is quite a jamboree. However, they were told in no uncertain terms by the Roadmaster that if they didn't show up to help unload this car some time during the afternoon that would be it. He'd go out and find another section crew. So sometime after three o'clock, around three thirty, back comes the whole crew and they were in a sorry state. They had been celebrating. Not only do they meet for the mourning, but I think they also drink his health and wash him down into the grave because they were all pretty polluted. This great big burley section foreman started yelling at his crew. As I was in charge of unloading, I started yelling at him, "You really shouldn't do it this way, or someone is going to get hurt". He would say, "No, this is fine" and keep right on. Finally, he got so obstreperous that he said, "Nooh! We're going to do it this way, this is how it's got to be done, and we know how to do this". And he raised such a ruckus that I had to back off, as he started to tell me off as well. I wasn't running the unloading; he was the boss of the unloading. Well, he was getting so obstreperous that I could see that we might lose the whole gang, and we'd be stuck up there another one or two days waiting to hire a new section gang. Why nobody got hurt, I don't know, because they were stumbling around letting planks slip back onto the men inside the car. After a couple of hours working in that car, even though it was April it was pretty hot up there on the track, they finally got rid of the alcohol in their systems and they managed to get that car unloaded. Then we set out the outriggers on the crane, and lifted the empty car just enough so it would swing, and then slowly swung it around and up to the track. As the boxcar came closer to the track, the crane operator could raise his boom higher and then raise the boxcar higher. We set blocks under it where we set it down, and then maneuvered it back onto its trucks.

As we were working on these cars, people in the area might come to watch the work, and the section crews would watch as the wrecking crew moved in under our equipment. You'd often hear them say, "My God, aren't you scared to go underneath there? You fellows are working underneath, and all that's holding that car up is those tow light cables. What if one of them breaks? You're going to be killed!" And we'd say, "Well, we watch that very closely". They'd say, "You couldn't get me to go underneath one of those cars for all the tea in China". Which takes me back to another wreck we had, which was down in our barge slip in Squamish.

This particular boxcar was being transferred from the barge slip onto our barge, when one of the fastenings that held the barge to the barge slip broke. The barge backed away from the slip and that boxcar, which was loaded with lumber, fell into the water partly under the barge slip. There was no way to use the crane, because if we tried a lift the weight of the crane plus the weight of that car would damage the slip. So we had to get the trucks disconnected from that car and pull it away. It was floating in the water there. Once we got it free of the trucks we could pull it around. So I engaged a small tugboat and got a diver up from Vancouver. We got an empty boxcar down by the track, and they took some equipment down for him and put it all in this boxcar. The Squamish River, icy cold silty murky water, was running in a fast current right past the edge of our barge slip and this boxcar was sitting there anchored with the trucks. He had to go down into this water to disconnect the trucks, then put a line from the boxcar to the tug so that we could pull it away from the slip and tow it around to the bank, where we could get at it to unload it and rerail it.

So the diver went down. He had a set of signals with his helper who stood on the edge of the barge slip.

First he went down with a heavy diving suit on and a helmut, and he had a gasoline pump pumping air down to him. All he had on was a rope which he would pull to give signals to his helper on top to give him whatever assistance he wanted - come up or come down, whatever it was. After a while he came up and said to me, "Mr. Stathers, I don't know whether you know it or not, but there's a great big wad of pilings down there that are broken off and they are just like spikes sticking up". He said, "I thought I'd better let you know". "Well", I said, "How are you making out?" "Oh", he said, "I think I can work on it all right". So he went down again, and he had to get some more tools to get the trucks disconnected from that boxcar. This time, he tore his suit. He got caught on one of those sharp edges of the pilings, and of course he was working in the dark and couldn't see, so he tore his suit and had to come back up. He went into the boxcar, and had a change of underwear, but the suit was no good to him, he had to put on scuba gear. The helper stood by with the line to get signals, and down he went in the scuba gear. He got the trucks disconnected and got the rope over to the tugboat. But when the tug tried to pull away, he had no power. It seemed that the tug, in backing up, had fouled its propeller with the tow rope. So the diver had to go down again into the water and unravel this towline from the propeller of this tug, that I think is a pretty scary job to be doing under the water. If they started the engine up, it would cut him in two. He was taking a chance of getting impaled on these razor sharp pilings, he couldn't see what he was doing anyway, and if anything happened there was no chance of helping him because none of us had any gear or knew how to go down and get him. However, he got the job done. The tug boat got going and finally pulled the boxcar over to the side of the docks. We left it there, and came down the next day with extra rigging to pull it up. The diver came out, went into his boxcar changing room and started to get back into his street clothes. My god, he was cold. I helped him out of his suit, and his body was blue. Luckily I had the forethought to have brought down a Coleman Stove and coffee pot with coffee in it. Although it was contrary to the rules, I had also brought a bottle of 39 Overproof rum. He was standing there shivering when I handed him a cup of hot coffee, liberally laced with rum. "Thank the Lord for small mercies", said he as he downed the restorative, and it didn't take him long to come back to normal temperature. "Let's get something to eat", he said, and I drove him back to the hotel. He'd had nothing to eat that day, no breakfast, no lunch, because he couldn't go down in that cold water with food in his stomach or he was liable to get cramps.

When I was driving him to the hotel he said, "Mr. Stathers, what are those brown marks, those lines going up those mountains there towards the big white mountain, what was its name, Garibaldi?" "Oh, those are logging roads", I said. "What do you mean, logging roads?" "Well you saw those logging trucks coming through town", I said. "They pick up their loads up in the mountain there and drive them down here and dump them in the water". "What", he said. "You don't mean to tell me that men drive those logging trucks down that mountain with those big logs behind them. What happens if they go off the road and hit a stump?" he said. "Those logs would go right through the cab and crush the driver like an eggshell!" "Yes", I said, "I guess they would do that, but they're pretty good drivers and that's their job, and they're used to it, this is what they do every day for a living". "You mean to say", he said,"that those big trucks that come through town here come from away up there in those mountain tops?" "Yes", I said, "that's right". "Jesus", he said, "I wouldn't do that job for any kind of money. No sir, there's no way you'd get me in one of those things. I wouldn't risk my life up there". "Well", I said, "what about what you are doing down on the dock?" "Oh, well, that's nothing. Anybody could do that, that's no problem".

It's what you get used to. If we worked underneath those cars, we thought no more of it than that diver did going down in the water, or that engineer did coming down the mountain with three or four thousand tons of train behind him coming around the curves. Maybe there'll be a boulder on the track as big as the locomotive, and no damned hope of stopping. You know you're going to smash into it, you may have to jump for your life. But whatever your job is, you get used to the conditions of the job and you don't pay much attention to possible dangers, but take them into account and just get on with the job. It was like that when we picked up wrecks. To a bystander, it might have looked disorganized and dangerous, but we all knew exactly what we were doing, and why, and keeping an eye on things.

The general condition of this section of the line was terrible at that time, so we spent a great deal of time picking up small derailments, in seemingly endless procession. I recall one series of three wrecks, because it was the longest time I spent without sleep. The first was in a cut, half a mile north of the Kelly Lake siding. The train was going north and it dumped six or seven cars crossways in this cut, and blocked the line. We worked all day at the shop, and then got the call to take our wrecking train up the line, which meant traveling all that night. I don't sleep traveling in a train. You lie in your bed for awhile, wondering about the wreck and how you're going to tackle it, and then you're up at the stations, arranging for trains coming by, engines, or something. The men got more sleep than I did, I think, but I certainly didn't sleep. So by the time we got up to the scene, I was starting on my second day. As soon as we arrived, we started setting these cars over to one side of the line, and it didn't take very long. We wanted to get the line open as quickly as possible, and then the plan was to run back and forth out of the Kelly Lake siding, between freight trains, and recover those cars. Well, we had just about got the last car moved out of the way when we got a call from the Operating Superintendent, to tell us that there was another wreck down near Moran, nearly at the same place where those log trains had gone off before. So the minute we had that last car out of the way, we picked up our tools and threw everything in to the car, and away we went down to the next wreck. Here again, the line was blocked, so we had to work without stopping. This one was a little more difficult because a bunch of loaded cars in a south-bound train had derailed, and there was a fair amount of damage to the cars that had to be repaired. We had to pick up quite a few of these cars, and worked right into the third night. As soon as we got the line open, we went into the siding at Moran and were getting ready to go back up to Kelly Lake to finish that job. A freight train came by, moving very slowly because the track wasn't in good shape; the section crews were still working on their repairs. As the train moved past, I hollered out to the conductor, a man named Bud Butterworth, "Whatever you do, stay on the track! We've had no sleep going on for four days now; so for God's sake don't go off the track! Get the hell out of the way and don't go off the track". "Don't worry, Eric", he said, "I'll take care of everything", and away they went.

By this time, we were so tired that we were stumbling around like drunks, picking up the last of our gear. We got everything ready for the move back up to Kelly Lake, when the news came that Bud Butterworth's train had gone off the track at Pavilion. Oh, no! So we had to switch the train all around again, back and forth, on and off the main line in order to get the crane onto the south end of our train. The train crew hauled us down to Pavilion, and we grabbed an hours rest, on the way. At Pavilion we hooked onto the rear of the derailed train and pulled it back up the line to a siding. Then we tackled the derailed cars. There were five or six boxcars, loaded ones, scattered all over Pavilion yard. They had to be moved to get the main line clear, and it was easier because there was a siding right there, but while we worked we passed from the fourth into our fifth day straight. When we finally got the line cleared, there was room for our wrecking train to back into the siding at Pavilion. I said to the Operating Superintendent, who was in overall charge, "That's it! We're not going to do another thing until we've had a sleep". I was so beat I could hardly lift my feet up to step over the tracks. I counted it up. From the time we left Squamish, traveling up the line to the first wreck, and with the traveling time we had between wrecks, I had gotten only five hours sleep in five days, and I was bushed. So we tied up right there, and didn't let anybody bother us until we'd had eight hours sleep, and then of course we had to finish sorting out the mess at Pavilion, and go back up to Kelly Lake and put the rest of that equipment together. It didn't take too long, and then we ran back to Lillooet and home to Squamish.

There was a particular problem in this area with derailments. When cars derailed and went off the track, they would often roll over and over down the hill finally coming to rest against a rock or against a bush, but not too far away from the track that we couldn't get them back up to the track again. Generally there was a road of some sort down the railway and we could get a truck in down there. Then we'd build a chute, like the old irrigation flumes, and the section gang would unload the lumber from damaged cars, 2x6's, 2x10's, and slide it down the hill to the road. It would be loaded onto the trucks and hauled back to Lillooet for reloading onto a rail car. This was pretty expensive, of course. By this time we had acquired our own Cat, and we would haul the empty boxcar to some place where we could get at it with cutting torches. After it was cut into sections, if we could reach it with our light line we'd haul it up to the track and load it into a gondola to be sold as scrap. Once in a while we'd just burn it. All of this meant spending quite a bit of time in the area after the line had been opened to traffic again.

I don't want to give you the impression that all of these incidents in our working life were all pain and no pleasure. There was a great deal of challenge to many of these situations, and once you'd overcome them it made you feel good. The crew also felt the same challenge, and there was a great sense of camaraderie between the crew and myself. In those days I wanted strong and agile men on the wrecking crew; that generally meant the younger men. Men in the shops recognized the policy. We did not have the kind of cranes and other equipment that the senior railroads had. There were only six men, plus myself, in the wrecking crew.

Also I preferred men who had some logging experience, because with our Lidgerwood we had to be able to splice cable and run rigging up and down the hills. So while strength was a factor, the ability to move fast was even more important. Under these circumstances, seniority applied in the shop work but was not a factor in placement of men on the wrecking crew, which was agreed to by the Carmen's Union. So we had a great crew of younger men and there was a lot of joking going on, a lot of kidding back and forth.

Even when we got into tough situations, something humorous would happen and the fellows would make a joke out of it. If we hadn't found something to laugh at, we could never have stuck it out. There were different times when men would race one another up to the top of a boxcar to see who could get their rigging fastened first, and the man who came in second would receive quite a ribbing from the crew. Even when it was exhausting and dangerous work, we found some way to have fun with it. The cook at that time was an Italian named Joe Iacovone. Of course, the crew teased him by speaking to him in their version of an Italian accent, imitating the way he spoke. Joe took it all in good humour, and gave back as good as he got. I remember he particularly imitated one man who had a very English accent. Joe really gave it to him. Even when the men were sick or not feeling well, somebody was always making a joke out of it. So in this way, we were able to carry on with the work, even though we knew that it was an uphill struggle and there would be no permanent relief until the roadbed and the grade were improved. But by the early 1950's, we started to see improvement. First in the Cheakamus Canyon, when we went from 60 pound to 85 pound steel. This cut down the derailments over that section. Then we moved up into the Lake District with heavier rail, and improved some more. Also we had been getting a lot of worn out cars from the C.N.R. that caused some derailments. After awhile we refused to accept these cars anymore. We banned them, which caused quite a furor between the C.N.R and us. However, we stuck to our guns. Between not having to handle worn out rolling stock and improving our own stock with new cars, and all of the work that was being done to upgrade the track and the roadbed, things started to look a little brighter. Naturally, as conditions improved at the south end of the line, our crew started to spend more time up at the north end. It was part of the pattern as the railway moved north.

11 STORIES OF THE CARIBOO

1954-1955

The Cariboo section of the Pacific Great Eastern Railway covered a long distance. The line was always intended to reach to Prince George but it took a long time to cross the Cottonwood Canyon. The northern terminus was Quesnel when I joined the railroad. It was only in the 1950's that the service was extended to Prince George as industrial activity in the northern part of British Columbia began to provide heavy traffic and new experiences for our operating crews. So the stories in this chapter come from 1949 and later years, between Kelly Lake and Prince George. You might wonder how I can remember of all these times and dates but actually, in most cases I am just looking them up. I had to keep times and dates on wrecks in order to check the time cards of the men on my crew who were working on these derailments. I also made a rough report on these incidents at the time and these old reports and cards are in my possession now, which is of course a powerful aid to memory. So these accounts really are to the best of my recollection.

You may recall my describing earlier the experience of the first Christmas my wife and I spent in Squamish and how we hoped there would never be another incident of the same kind. Well, on December 24, 1953 a train was coming down from the north and I guess the engineer was looking forward to coming home for Christmas. There was a slight downhill grade coming around Clinton to Kelly Lake, until you hit the canyon. Coming around quite a sharp curve, he saw a rock sitting right in the middle of the track. Just where this rock came from is pretty hard to imagine because there are no rock bluffs for as far as you can see. It was about two feet in diameter and it acted just like a big ball bearing. When the motors on the trucks hit this boulder, the engine was lifted up off the tracks and the wheels came down onto the ties bringing the train to a dead stop. It wasn't too long a train, but right behind the engine were three empty tank cars and the pressure from the momentum of the rest of the train just popped these tank cars onto the side of the line like dominoes.

We were called about 5:30 pm on December 24th and I started to round up my crew. What made it kind of rough for my wife again was that our boys had been away attending university and were coming home for Christmas. One was home, the other was arriving that evening with his new wife, and we had all the trappings and everything ready for a wonderful Christmas holiday at home with our two boys. We didn't see them very often since they were away at university during the year. So I called the crew together and one particular man started to weep bitter tears and said, "I can't go, my wife is sick, and I can't leave her". My wife was standing along side of me and I said, "Mike, my wife is sick and she's getting sicker every minute listening to you over the phone so you better get your clothes on and let's get going". So we managed to round up the men, and away we started.

Now it was quite cold. By the time we got up there, it was early in the morning of the 25th. It wasn't such a bad situation. The engine was sitting off the track, oh, maybe about three feet, just the front truck. The back truck was still on the track. They had already hauled the remainder of the train back to Clinton siding, which was only a short distance away. But this meant that we did not have an engine at the north end to try and pull the derailed engine No. 562, a diesel, back onto the track. In any case, we probably could not have done that because the rock was jammed right under the front truck motor and also driven hard between the ties. It looked as if the best bet would be to try and lift the front end of that engine. I thought back to the time I had made my first lift of an engine at Garibaldi siding (which I described in Chapter 8) and figured, well, three feet is not too far away. I think we can lift it.

Clinton Christmas Day 1953. Empty tank cars.
Photograph: E.P. Stathers

Just taking the lift on Engine 562. 20 degrees below zero.   Photograph: E.P. Stathers

Holding Engine 562 while rock is being removed. Note the angle of the boom. Photograph: E.P. Stathers

However, there was one important difference between Garibaldi and here. It was somewhere around 20 degrees below zero, perhaps a little colder. In this temperature range, steel becomes brittle. The cables are brittle and the safety factor decreases considerably. Still, I thought, we can't sit here all day, we'll give it a try. So we set the crane in position, and put all the outriggers out to make it good and stable. By this time, the engine from Clinton had come back to the wreck. To get maximum lift, we had to have the crane boom as high up as possible and we were sitting on a down grade so we were lifting practically coupler to coupler, crane to engine. The problem was that the couplers were three feet out of line. When we did the lift at Garibaldi, we got that Cat to push the front of the engine back into place. This time there was no Cat and no way of getting one. With that heavy a lift, we didn't dare to try to move the boom for fear it would collapse under anything but a pure lift. And if we lifted, the cables would tend to pull the engine back towards the track and the couplers would bump together and obstruct proper movement. So I had the Clinton engine at the north end hook onto the derailed 562 with the idea that as we lifted, they could pull back slightly allowing the couplers to clear between the crane and the 562.

So we went ahead and hooked the cables up. Of course I had to stand on the deck of the crane, close to the boom, in order to be able to see everything during the lift. That put me right under that boom. So after we had everything set, I had a look around. I had a man on each side of the crane watching to make sure that the back end didn't come up. I made a little prayer that the boom wouldn't collapse and we took a little lift. And nothing happened. We lifted about two inches and let it sit for a couple of minutes. Everything seemed all right. We lifted a little more and the engine came off the rock and started to swing a little bit. We set it down closer to the track, eased off, and boomed the crane over slightly. When we lifted again the engine came over again. This was repeated several times with the cables at a slight angle until the engine was sitting right over the rails in front of the crane. But the rock was still under there.

The safety factor was nil in these cold temperatures and every lift we took I half expected something to give. We were hoisting somewhere between 65 and 70 tons of front end of Engine 562 and the breaking strain of our cables was only 90 tons. I thought even the boom might break. It was a very ticklish situation. There was no way to get the ties out and dig a hole to pull out that rock because everything was frozen solid. But that gave me another idea. Our crane was being supported by the outriggers, which were big steel beams straddling both sides of the railroad sitting on feet, and securely wedged with hardwood wedges. In fact, the strain of the lift was supported on those feet. But with the ties and the ground under the track being frozen so hard, we could lift just from the rails alone with our crane. So we took another chance and took the wedges out of the outriggers, and moved the blocking up a foot or so, and left the outriggers out but with no wedges so they were not actually carrying any weight on a lift. This way the crane could move along the track but not tip over if anything hung up or broke.

The rock was not too far under the 562. It was jammed near the motor. If we could get it clear then we could roll it between the cowcatcher and the wheels. So the plan was to lift the engine, then the Clinton engine would back away to pull the 562 off the rock, the crane would follow up with the engine clear, and we'd roll that rock out of there. It was kind of a dangerous thing to do but what other choice did we have? There was no other equipment to work with. So we made the lift and everything went according to plan. In a little while we had the rock out and Engine 562 was back on the track. There was very little damage to it. The cowcatcher was bent so we cut it free with a cutting torch and hoisted it onto a flatcar. The tank cars were empty and with the ground frozen hard we were able to drag them up to the line with our crane and didn't need the Lidgerwood. The crane set them back on the track, we hooked up, and by nightfall we were rolling back on the line to Squamish. So although we missed Christmas, we were home early on Boxing Day and I had my Christmas dinner, or at least what was left of the turkey that the family hadn't consumed. So that was another time when Christmas Day was spent on the road with a wreck instead of being home with my family. It was just one of the things that you had to put up with being in such an occupation as I was.

Late in 1953 and into 1954, the West Coast Transmission Pipeline was being built and our railway up to Prince George was hauling most of the pipe. There was a loading landing this side of Prince George from which the pipe was trucked to various sites. This pipe was loaded in gondola cars, level with the sides of the car, and then in a pyramidal form nesting one pipe into another. There were no wires or anything holding it because you couldn't let the pipe be chafed or have the ends damaged in any way. It was just riding there held in place by its own weight. We had an incident early in the summer of 1954 involving one of these trains of pipe at a place called Enterprise, just north of Lac La Hache. It is located beside a shallow valley where the low points are sloughs and the higher points are meadows. The San Jose Creek runs through this area from side to side. The area is more than two miles long and is a great feeding place for waterfowl. In fact it was a good place for hunting ducks and geese in the early days. The railway passed through this valley, crossing over some of these sloughs including the biggest one, an L-shaped marsh with a long arm reaching to the West. The original railroad builders instead of building around the slough decided to push straight through, which would have added a lot more mileage and would have been all this side hill work. They did this by providing a wider roadbed by dumping a lot of gravel and laying marsh ties. Marsh ties are three feet longer than standard railroad ties and tend to give great stability in soft ground. This is standard practice in Canadian railroading.

However, during the Depression and the War and the years between, but especially since the War when ties were extremely hard to get, the track gangs had been replacing rotten ties with standard length ties instead of marsh ties. By summer of 1954 more than 60 percent of the ties were just standard issue and of course they could not supply the same stability that the builders had counted on. This big slough required about a quarter mile of marsh ties and they weren't there. So if you stood on one side of the swamp and watched a train come across, you could see the roadbed sinking under the weight of the engine, which was making the rails rise in front of it so the train was going uphill all the way across the swamp. There was no problem in the wintertime, of course, but this happened in the summertime when it was very warm. These gondola cars loaded with pipe were pretty heavy and we had three different incidents at this point on the line. They were all similar; I will describe only the worst one.

When we got there, there were three carloads of pipe over on their side with the cars partially in the water. Most of the pipes that had been riding on top of the load had gone into the slough, some of them partially, some entirely submerged. We had a count and knew how many pipes there were on each car, so we knew how many we were looking for, but even then we had to fish around with poles to find some of them. These pipes were specially machined for a welding fit and great care had to be taken not to damage the ends. They would be inspected very carefully when we got them to their destination to see if any damage had been done and the railroad would have to pay for the damage. So I had special rigging made up to handle this pipe, special slings with special hooks on the end so we could pick up a pipe without damaging the ends. We cleared the pipe away from the derailed gondola cars first, and then went to work to rerail the empty gondolas. They weren't in too bad shape because they'd just run into soft mud and ooze. Then we brought up some empty gondola cars that we had brought with us behind the crane and it was a matter of salvaging the pipes out of this slough. We sat there on the wobbly roadbed and the men had to scamper on these pipes and attach the sling hooks to each end. Of course, as time went by the pipes were sinking deeper and deeper into the mire. As we lifted a pipe, one end would have dropped a little lower into the ooze that would pour out in a geyser of back mud, slop, and plants. And the smell!

The smell was atrocious. I mean, we knew about ripe, but this was rotten! And, of course, the more we worked and the water and muck splashed around the more everything got covered and contaminated by ooze, and the more often the men slipped falling on their bums onto the pipe with both feet in the mire. We started loading that pipe early in the morning and by the time we had all the cars out and the entire pipe picked up all of the men, including myself, were saturated with the stinking ooze from these pipes. So after we got everything picked up and ready to move, the crew said, "Well boss, can we go for a swim?" And of course I said, "Sure, away you go", and they headed for a hay meadow not far from the slough. Well nobody bothered to take off their clothes; they jumped straight into the creek, hats and all. It was quite warm and I tell you they had a ball! They washed and splashed back and forth and they actually washed all their clothes and themselves in San Jose Creek. They were cavorting around like a bunch of seals in there, and when they came out and got back into the sun, it was so hot and dry up there that everything dried right off while we got ready to leave. It was the right way to finish up a dirty smelly job.

We had two other small derailments in that area, one where only one car and a few pipes went in, but that one piece of track was a queer setup. I understand why they had the same problems running north of Winnipeg into Churchill, Manitoba. The ground was frozen hard in the winter and there was permafrost in this section but it would thaw a bit in the summer. So the engineer made a grade about twice as wide as the standard grade and put in extra long ties and there is less pressure under load, the ground never thaws out and even if it does, the roadbed will support traffic. Just the same, it is very unusual to see track moving up and down as it did at Enterprise. But we had no more trouble there after the marsh ties were renewed.

Just a little farther up the line is the town of Hixon, which was the scene of a wintertime wreck on January 7, 1960. It took place some time after the refinery went into operation at Taylor and we were handling difficult cargos. By this time I had become the General Car Foreman for the railway and I wasn't the wrecking crew foreman any longer. They called me out on this one because it was our first experience with having to handle liquid gas cargos. There had been a derailment of quite a number of cars including two tank cars of propane. The ground was frozen solid, there was a side hill on one side of the line and a flat spot on the other side, and the cars had run over the frozen ground quite a distance from the track right close to a bank that sloped down into a little creek. Water from the creek flowed right through the town of Hixon. We were in a dangerous position here because it was quite cold, no wind, and propane being heavier than air it would roll down the embankment into the water and be carried through the gullies and by water into the town of Hixon and there could have been a disaster. We were in somewhat of a predicament.

As I had never handled propane before, I was at a loss to know just what to do. However, we had telephoned the Taylor Plant and also the Explosives Inspector, who was situated in Chilliwack. These two men are experts in their field in handling explosive gases and this is where I got my first experience. These gases are transported in liquid form, but will gas off when exposed to normal air pressure. Propane stops gassing off at 18 degrees above zero. These two derailed tank cars were filled with propane and as it happened it was quite cold, somewhere between ten and fifteen degrees below, and very little wind. We had a conference between the Assistant Superintendent from the operating department of the railway, the two explosives experts, and myself with a lot of discussion. It was decided that we would send to Squamish for some three inch pipe together with fittings, valves and so forth, and this gear was sent up in a hurry on the next through train. It was dangerous to handle the cars so far from the track and it was decided that we would let them "gas off" by burning off the contents of both cars.

The cars were not damaged at all just sitting there full of propane and very heavy. We rigged the three inch pipes up to the domes of these tank cars and ran the pipes out down a little runway supported on little wooden A-frames so they projected just a little way over the bank. That part was okay, but I was a little apprehensive when I asked the explosives man from Taylor, "Who is the guy who is going to have to hold the flame when the gas starts to flow?" "Oh", he said, "that's no problem. I'll light them". So we cut some long poles out of the bush (there were lots of slim poles around there) wired a bunch of waste onto a pole, and saturated it with coal oil. "Now", he said, "I'm going to light this torch and hold it on to the end of this pipe and then you just open the valve on the tank car, and the gas will roll out down the pipe and I'll light it". Well it was quite a bit above 29 degrees below zero, so it would certainly gas off. "Open the quick

118

valve now", he said, "don't open it slow. I want full pipe". So I opened up the valve fast and he held his flaming torch in front of the pipe and there was a tremendous boom, an explosion, and flame shot out from this pipe like a gigantic blow torch. It was a huge flame shooting out there twelve or fifteen feet. Then we went to the next tank, got it opened and flowing and burning and there was nothing else we could do but sit there and make sure they kept burning.

Somebody had to be there all night because if the flame went out we had to be ready to light it again, otherwise that gas would roll down the hill right into Hixon. The wind started to get up, so we built a shelter out of ties, right on the edge of the bank between two tank cars. We had two men and two sticks on duty all the time to watch the pipes. We took shifts during the night sitting in this little windbreak with all of our heavy clothes on. On my shift, the wind got quite strong and every once in a while we would lose the flame, especially on the second night, because the pressure was going down in the tank because it was getting colder. When the flame went out, there was a mad dash to shut off the valve at the tank car. Then one man would hold the flaming torch up to the pipe, and the other man would spin the valve open again, the gas would flow, there would be an explosion, and away it went again.

It was quite a sight watching these tongues of flame shooting out in the middle of the gully. We were sitting there in the middle of the night and all at once we heard a crashing noise in the bush down below. Crash and creek. Crash and creek. We couldn't figure out what was going on because everything was quiet and still except the wind blowing through the trees. Finally I got up from our little shelter and walked over, down the bank a little way, and peered out into the bush that was lighted by the two flaming pipes. It was an old cow moose wandering through the bushes below in the creek bed looking up to see what was going on, and attracted by our light, I suppose. As soon as she saw me, she took off. We had a laugh about this, and kept the gas burning.

There have been a lot of catastrophes with propane gas. Down in the United States, there was one wreck where a propane tank car was derailed on a bridge and sprung a leak. The gas which flowed out was carried downstream by the river, and about two hundred yards downstream was a summer resort. There were a whole bunch of trailers, campers, tents, what have you, and the people all came out to watch the crew working on this derailment. Nobody realized that the propane was rolling down towards them. Somebody struck a match for a cigarette, and there was a terrific explosion. Quite a number of people were killed or burned. It was disaster stories like this that made us apprehensive about possible damage at Hixon, only a mile away.

It took us two nights and a day and a half to burn those tanks out to the point where we could handle them with a crane. Partly this was because it was so cold, the tanks gassed off slowly. Then we got the tank cars back onto the track and hauled them down to Squamish where it was much warmer. Being old hands by that time, we rigged up the pipes again, gassed them off, burned off all the gas, and then we could repair the damage to the trucks and the running gear. We were able to put those cars into running order again and send them home. So that was our first experience with propane gas. Another cargo that gave us trouble was sulphur, as I will tell you later on.

Farther up the line is Abhu. There is a small creek at Abhu that has dug a tremendous canyon through that countryside for miles and miles. The railroad has a huge bridge there. On the north side of the bridge the country was quite flat on both sides of the line. There was an up train with a lot of empty cars that derailed on February 16, 1955. The ground was frozen hard and derailed cars will slide a long way on frozen ground and snow. They don't dig in the way they would in the summer time. We left Squamish about noon and as we got to Alta Lake I could see the snow blowing off the top of Black Tusk, just a spume of snow. The north wind was really howling up there. It wasn't so cold down on the flat at Alta Lake but the mountain tops were streamers of snow. I told the boys that it was going to be a cold trip.

Before we left Squamish, we had enough forethought to start the engines on the 35 ton crane and the Lidgerwood. The farther up the line we went, the windier it got, and the colder it got. When we got to Lillooet, the Lidgerwood engine had stopped. We carried battery cables long enough to reach from the diesel locomotives to the starting batteries of the Lidgerwood and the crane. Fortunately, the Lidgerwood had not been shut down too long and we were able to get it running again. Then we got some plywood and some canvas from the roundhouse and boxed the Lidgerwood in as best as we could to protect it from the cold. It was already about twenty-five below zero in Lillooet and with that north wind blowing we knew we'd have problems keeping the engine going. The crane was housed in with doors on the front that kept the wind from blowing through so it wasn't exposed like the Lidgerwood, which was open front and back. So we blocked up the front as best we could. After we pulled out of Lillooet heading up the line, there was a different train crew, of course. I said to the brakeman, "You know we're a little worried about these engines with this cold, we want to keep them going. We're going to try and get some sleep now so will you keep an eye on these crane and Lidgerwood engines and if they stop, come and wake me".

Well about two o'clock in the morning somebody shaking me by the shoulder awakened me. It was the brakeman. "Eric", he said, "the Lidgerwood engine has stopped. It's not running". So I got hold of the Lidgerwood and crane operator and we both just pulled a pair of pants over our pajamas, pulled on a sweater, and a parka; neither of us got properly dressed. We climbed out of the bunk car and over the top of the tool car and got down into the Lidgerwood to start it again. Well the operator tried to turn it over and turn it over and turn it over, but nothing would happen. I said to him, "Bill, do you feel cold? Because by God I'm freezing to death". I could feel the cold right through my pants and my pajamas. My legs and my whole body felt like I was being pricked with needles. And Bill said, "Yes, I'm freezing. I'm so damned cold I can hardly feel the buttons". He had taken his mitt off to handle the starter buttons. "I'm so damned cold, I can't stand it much longer". "Neither can I", I said, "We're going to freeze. To hell with it", I said, "let's get back in the car before we get badly frostbitten". So we took off back to the bunk car and it took us an hour or so to get warmed up enough to get back to sleep. When we stopped at Williams Lake to get a fresh train crew, we found that the crane engine had also stopped. By gum it was cold. We got the locomotive up along side of the crane and managed to get the crane engine turning over again. Then we tried the Lidgerwood but it wouldn't go at all. I said, "Never mind boys. Forget it. We'll worry about it when we get there".

So we left Williams Lake heading north and I said to the train crew, "How cold was it last night?" "Well", he said, "they registered between 63 and 65 below when you fellows were coming through Lone Butte". That was just when the two of us had been outside on this open Lidgerwood travelling at twenty-five miles per hour through the air at sixty-five degrees below zero. No wonder the engine stopped. That provided a wind chill factor of between 85 and 90 degrees below zero. No human being could stand that unless they had the finest of equipment on, and we didn't. Inside of five minutes, we'd had it. After leaving Williams Lake it was so cold in the car that you either laid on your bed or sat on the dining room table because the floor of the car was so cold. I was sitting on the dining room table to keep my feet off the floor when something hit me a sharp blow on the side of my face and it hurt like the dickens. I hollered to the men in the car, "Who's horsing around and throwing things?" Everyone in the car denied doing anything so when we looked we discovered that one of the water pipes on the side of the car had burst and thrown ice at me like a bullet. We had the three stoves in the car going full blast at the time too.

P.G.E. Bridge over Abhu Creek north of Quesnel. The crew that built the bridge panned gold out of the gravels from the excavations for the footings. Photograph: E.P. Stathers

Finally we got to Abhu siding. That was just south of the Abhu Bridge, and not very far from Quesnel. The crane engine had stopped again in the cold. The first thing was to try and get both of our engines running again. We got our train all switched around at the Abhu siding and got the cables from the locomotive over to the Lidgerwood. We even got our blowtorch to heat up that engine and revved up the locomotive engine trying to make that Lidgerwood engine turn over. The batteries were dead and nothing would turn. It was thirty below zero. So we turned to the crane engine. The crane operator got out our supply of ether capsules that we used to start diesel engines. They consisted of little gelatin capsules about two inches long filled with ether. Either is much more explosive than diesel fuel, that's why it is used. The system was to put a capsule into a little chamber on the engine manifold. You pushed the container button to puncture the capsule at the same time as you pressed the starter button to turn the engine over and it was supposed to start. It didn't. We used up all of our ether capsules. No result. So I suggested that maybe we could put the crane into gear and push it along the track with the locomotive. The crane operator managed to get it into gear but when we pushed it, the wheels just skidded along the track.

So we phoned Vancouver to ask the Superintendent what he could suggest. It was a Cummins diesel, so he contacted the Cummins plant. The answer came back: Take off the breather, get hold of a cutting torch, get warm air going into the engine, and turn it over. The breathing tube supplies air to the engine. But who was going to climb up into this cab that was stinking of ether fumes? The cab was full of ether, you could smell it everywhere. I put it to the men, and the crane operator said, "You get a fire extinguisher and I'll get the cutting torch" So we had both doors of the crane open, the operator took the breather off, we hooked up the cables from the locomotive to provide starting power, and he pressed the starter button. I lit the torch. There was no explosion. I held it over the breather cap heating the intake air as the engine ground over and over and over and eventually it fired. I kept that torch going, heating intake air as the engine kept firing, working, going faster, and faster until it had finally caught. We had to run it for quite a long time until the engine oil got warm enough in the base of the engine. The running gear was frozen up with the cold as well, stiff, so we ran the crane along the track and pushed it with the locomotive at the same time, until everything was warmed up and loosened up before we started work.

While we were having this trouble starting our wrecking crane, the Operating Department got the notion that we really needed help. So they contacted the Prince George wrecking crane from the C.N.R. to see if they might borrow it and down came a C.N.R. crew from Prince George with their crane. It was a steam-powered 50 tonner that could pick up one end of a car, loaded or empty, with no trouble. Our 35-ton diesel was faster and more versatile. So when we finally go to work there were two crews, the C.N.R. with a 50-ton steam crane at the north end and the P.G.E. with a 35-ton diesel crane at the south end. Our Superintendent, Mr. Stewart, had come up from Vancouver with another man and they were watching the two crews at work. It took two days to clean everything up, plenty of time to see our different operating styles.

I prided myself on our crew. They were just like the finest baseball or hockey team. Every man knew his job, where he was supposed to be, and everyone was so well versed in the operations that most men took their places without me even asking them to do it. The Prince George crane was a different design and awkward to handle, and we were actually putting two cars back on the track to one of theirs. There again, they had a bunch of older men and they worked by seniority. Any man could take the job by seniority but I wouldn't allow that with my crew. All my men were young men, agile, fast, who would run up the side of a car to hook a line up; while their crew were slower and they didn't make a move without an outrigger on. They were a very slow moving crew. I was highly complemented on the wrecking crew we had and the way they did their job and I was proud to be part of a bunch of men like that.

Well, there isn't much more to tell. We pulled all the cars back to Quesnel where we had to do some work on them before we could haul them back to Squamish. We ran really short of water by the time we got to Quesnel. Traffic on the line was building fast and keeping ahead of construction and replacement, so our wrecking crew was kept pretty busy. Routine picking up doesn't make much of a story, but we were always running into new problems and also moving farther up the line as service was extended.

12 PUSHING NORTH

1956

About a mile south of the Ahbau Canyon is a siding called Greening where we were called to a derailment on January 7, 1956.

This particular wreck took place at Mile 408 just north of Greening and very near Ahbau Canyon. It was caused by a mudslide that took place after a heavy snowfall before there was much frost in the ground, and a number of boxcars were derailed in a cut. Before going into details of how we picked up this wreck, I want to say something about the kind of country we have in the Cariboo and the north of British Columbia, and what happens when old Mother Nature is disturbed. There was a considerable hooraw a few years ago over the various decisions made by different governments to press on with construction of the Dease Lake extension of the railroad and then to cancel it. These public announcements seem to come from people who have not lived in the north. Very little is ever said in the newspapers or in public about the engineering aspects of railroad work or the soil conditions there. I'm not a geologist or civil engineer, but I've talked to men with those kinds of training and experience and had more than enough personal experience right in the mud during various incidents over the years. Soil and drainage are the governing factors. When you alter the natural lay of the land in the north, it tries to slide back to the way it was. That's the simple fact. Nature has lots of time and you may not notice anything right away, but if you go back and look that land is sneaking back into its old shape.

For more than 15 years after I joined the P.G.E. in 1929, we had trouble with our line into Quesnel. There's an area there known as "Mud Hill" where the railway went through a huge cut through the clay bank. Water seeped down this clay bank from Six Mile Lake, seeping between the clay, glacial till, and hardpan layers, and that clay was in constant motion; creeping, creeping down the hill and carrying the roadbed with it. I can recall going over the track there and seeing five sections of wooden railway bridge between the one we were traveling over and the Fraser River. We had many instances of the same kind when we extended the line from Quesnel to Prince George in 1952. And they had the same trouble when they went from Prince George to Fort St. John and Dawson Creek. It wasn't only the railway. The hill climbing out of Peace River and Taylor and up to Fort St. John presented the same problems. You may recall the highway bridge that the American Engineers had put in, a suspension bridge. The soil became saturated with water and the tension of the cables pulled the anchor bastions right out. They were even able to say, based on the rainfall and water flow, just when it would collapse, and a cameraman filmed it falling. Then there are people who make derisive remarks about laying rails on plywood. Hell's Bell's, I've seen ties laid on puncheon and logs in order to get the machinery in there where it was needed to do the work. Lots of times they put down wooden mats for track to sit on in order to get into these cuts because it is so slippery.

In this particular spot at Greening, we were facing the same problem. There is a layer of hardpan, impervious rock, and seepage water that ran over it. The soil above it is high in clay content. When it is dry, it is hard. When it gets wet it works, it oozes, it shifts, and it creeps. When you are trying to push a railroad bed through this country there are places where you must cut away the hillside and lay a grade and interrupt the flow of water over the hardpan. That's when trouble begins. There are ways around this problem but they involve very expensive construction and that kind of money is not available for a pioneering railway or highway. People are very quick to criticize the P.G.E. and the B.C. Rail without understanding the situation. To complicate matters in the north there is the effect of soil freezing and thawing with the passage of years. Everybody in the north knows about "break up" when highways cannot support regular traffic. But some critics may not understand the challenges of freeze thaw conditions and the related drainage and runoff problems.

Just north of the cut where this Greening wreck occurred was a small bridge that crossed a gully. In the original construction the footings were not set down into the bedrock and they had been having trouble with the bridge moving, with the foundations shifting after heavy rains. Looking up the hillside from the cut you could see five hundred feet up where the whole hillside had broken away from the crest of the hill and was sliding down into the cut. It was a continual battle digging out along side of the rails between the high side of the bank and the track to keep the ditch clear and keep the bank from sliding and covering the track. In fact, many times that bank did slide over the tracks and trains were delayed. It was a continual fight just to keep the line open, never mind rebuild it.

It was 408 miles from Squamish going on for two days travel so by the time we got there it was after lunch, early afternoon. We had the Lidgerwood and the 35 ton crane with us. The cut was full of boxcars loaded with lumber. The boxcars were on their sides and a lot of them were quite a distance from the track, too far for us to use the crane. I could see that we'd have to drag these cars up close to the track before the crane would help us. So we ran the crane ahead, out of the way, and got ready to pull the Lidgerwood. The temperature had dropped since the derailment and it was pretty cold, under thirty below zero by that time.

We were on a pretty straight pull for the first boxcar so we didn't have to put any deadman in, just hold the Lidgerwood back with our Lidgerwood stops. There were four inch square steel stakes with a Y-shaped bottom that fit around the track being secured with a wedge driven tight under the track. Then we piled ties up against them, backed the whole train up about ten feet from the stops, put all brakes into emergency, and rigged up for the pull. If whatever you're pulling doesn't come, then you pull the whole train down against the stops and generally the load you're pulling will come then. If it's a big pull, you rig up for extra mechanical advantages. There are plenty of combinations, and you choose one that will take the load that you've got to shift.

We had to dig down through the snow to get hold of the coupler on the first boxcar and get our heavy cables around it. I gave the signal to pull and watched the boxcar. It didn't move, but the Lidgerwood took up cable and hauled itself and the whole train, with all brakes set full on, down the track and up against the Lidgerwood stops and hesitated there. You couldn't see anything under the snow, but I thought by golly this must be a heavy car. I signaled for another pull. That inch and a quarter cable was just singing, tight as a fiddle string. The Lidgerwood was starting to climb right over the stops. So we slacked off and chained the Lidgerwood down to the rails so that it couldn't come up over those stops. Then I told the operator to take a pull and haul that boxcar out of there. He gave a pull and a two inch shackle (that's two inches of steelm, like a big clevis) snapped as if it were glass, flying through the air, and all of the rigging collapsed. So we rigged it up again and put another block down on the boxcar to give us double purchase. Another pull and this time the end of the block broke and it came flying back up to the Lidgerwood. I was beginning to be suspicious by this time. I got things organized for one more pull with a heavy block that we seldom used. We had two of them in the tool car that were used for heavy pulls on locomotives. It took about four men to handle it. We hauled it down to the boxcar and coupled it on, and set up our cables once more and started to pull again. The engine roared as we pulled and pulled and all at once there was a sound like two cannons going off and both of these Lidgerwood stops, four inch steel, exploded and flew through the air like cannonballs. That's what can happen to steel under stress when you are working in temperatures like thirty below zero. So we stopped everything, of course, and got out the snow shovels and started digging around that boxcar.

Finally with the snow all cleared away, we could see what had happened. The ground had not been frozen to any extent before the derailment and when this boxcar left the track fully loaded with lumber it had so much momentum that it actually punched through the snow and through this soft ground, dug itself a trench, and pushed a little wall of mud ahead of itself. As the temperature dropped the mud had frozen solid, and we had been pulling against that wall of frozen countryside in front of that fully loaded boxcar, one frozen mass. Well, what to do now? The Lidgerwood couldn't shift it and it was too far away from the track for the crane to lift it. What about pulling it back the other way? And maybe we could free it up by pulling it back onto its feet again. So we went back into the Greening siding and changed everything around, putting the Lidgerwood and the engine ahead of the crane. Since this boxcar had broken away from the others, there was room to move back north of it.

We wanted to exert a pull on an angle with a rolling hitch from our crane, and at the same time try to break the car away from that mud bulkhead by pulling with a line from the locomotive. It would take all the power we had. So we set the crane with all four outriggers fully extended, tipped it back to lean away from the pull which would raise the boom angle and give us more effective lift. Then we dug down under the boxcar, down the far side, and passed the crane cable over top of the car down the far side and back underneath, hooking onto the bottom of the car. That gave us a rolling hitch, so when we took up on the crane cable the car would tend to roll back onto its feet in an upright position. With the crane boom at right angles to the tracks, we didn't have too much effective lift. Then we hooked another cable from the north coupler of the boxcar to the south coupler of the locomotive and everything was set.

I gave the signal to the train crew to move the locomotive and they started pulling and smoke started pouring out from the motors. The crane operator took tension and worked his line, lifting and pulling, and that boxcar broke away an inch, another inch, and then slowly it rolled back into an upright position, about six inches from the mud bank. They held it there while the crew put wooden cribbing underneath to prop it up and it was actually standing upright. Then we slacked off and it was just a matter of unloading the lumber with the crane. Then we used the Lidgerwood and the crane to haul the empty boxcar back to the track and rerail it. The rest of the cars were easier to handle because they had not been embedded in frozen ground. We pulled them closer to the line with the Lidgerwood, used the crane to unload them, then rerailed them and pushed them out of the way. When we had everything picked up, we moved back to the siding at Greening to repair these cars so they could travel back to Squamish. Of course they were all covered with snow underneath, the brake rigging was broken, some of them had no air brakes, and they were a mess. So we had to repair them before they could be moved.

There were quite a lot of these cars to repair so we worked for an entire day at the siding. There was about three feet of snow on the level at the side of the track that made it kind of difficult to move around. Somehow or other, the whole crew developed dysentery. There was a continual parade and of course we couldn't relieve ourselves near the track where everyone was working. We had to dig a trench into the snowbank on the edge of the Greening siding and then dig out a clear spot. Every once in a while, somebody would break off and make a mad dash into this trench and there would be words later on. We can laugh about it now, but it wasn't very funny sitting there with your pants down at twenty-five or thirty below zero. You didn't stay there any longer than you had to. I remember one man had it particularly bad. That led to an incident that seemed very funny later on, although he didn't think so at the time. We'd had our supper and were preparing to go out again to work on these cars that night, and we needed some more tools. So I asked two of the men to come with me to the tool car to get these tools and take them with us. As one fellow bent over to pick up these tools, the other fellow goosed him. The first man let out a yell saying, "Don't do it! Don't do it!" and of course the second man said, laughing, "What's the matter? What's the matter?" and the first fellow jumped out of the car and ran down the track with the second fellow chasing him trying to goose him. He only ran a few car lengths down the track when the first guy said, "You've done it! You've done it! You've made me poop my pants, you dirty dog", and oh my golly the row that went on there, and the language! The poor fellow had to come back in the car and they were both laughing so much there was nothing anybody could do but laugh. Well, with the conditions these men had to work under, you had to have a sense of humour or they'd have all gone on strike or gone berserk. Afterwards, they went back to work crawling under these cars with a cutting torch to heat and straighten rods and cutting off the parts that were broken, and bending and straightening so that we could get the cars to roll again. And all that snow melted, and the water dripped down on you, and as soon as you got out and away from the torch your clothes would freeze. You were wet one minute and freezing the next, your clothes would freeze solid and it was so damned cold that we couldn't get enough heat in the bunk cars to dry our clothes. So that was quite an episode. These men worked under what today would be called appalling conditions and managed to find something to laugh about.

But that is the kind of country it is in the north. Things were rough. When people ridicule the engineers and the men who worked so hard building this railroad up through the north country, they don't realize the hardships and conditions that men work under to run a railroad or a highway. I travelled over the Cariboo Highway when it just wound like a rattlesnake up and down and around the different bluffs. It was a gravel highway and in the springtime when the frost came out of the ground, you got mired to the axles with your car and quite often you got stuck and the farmers made a lucrative thing of pulling cars out of these mudholes. When they built the highway where it is today, they had to do the same thing as they did with the railway. North of Cache Creek, and especially between Clinton and Williams Lake, there are huge fills and cuts. I travelled that highway in automobiles and the first two or three years after it was built, whole sections would give away and slide down. There would be huge cracks in the paving and only half of the highway would be left. The hillside would slide down and cover the highway, the same as it was doing on the railroad tracks. That country is tough to build in. It's not like the prairies where you can run a long line, put in some gravel, and dig two ditches and that is it. That Northern B.C. is tough country. Some of it is actually worse than building in the mountains where you're blasting rock. At least when you get the road blasted through rock, you know it's going to stay there. But that northern upland plateau country shifts and slides. So I wish the critics would get out from behind their office desks and go up there and see for themselves the conditions that men have to face to keep the roads and railroads open.

* * *

This next episode was fairly routine, but we have a nice set of photographs to illustrate how we went about picking up a wreck. This derailment took place at MacAlister (Mile 387) in April 1956, when a southbound train of logs and lumber derailed on a slight downhill grade. The engine left the tracks and stopped dead the minute it hit the dirt and of course all the following cars in the train (which was quite long) continued to exert their forward momentum on the cars ahead. The conductor who was riding the train told me didn't feel any shock but all at once he began to see boxcars popping out into the bushes. He said they were going like a herd of sheep, one after another, until finally the whole train had come to a stop. Some of these boxcars had run down the hill through scrub and trees and had been pretty badly damaged and they were too far away to recover with our crane or Lidgerwood.

South end Mile 387, April 1956.
Photograph: E.P. Stathers

Building track on top of piles of trucks before trying to pull the loaded car off. Photograph: E.P. Stathers

Loaded boxcars down the bank near the old Cariboo Highway.
Photograph: E.P. Stathers

Damaged cars opened up to facilitate the lumber transfer.
Photograph: E.P. Stathers

Piece by piece the lumber had to be taken out.
Photograph: E.P. Stathers

Sling load coming up to be put in to another car.
Photograph: E.P. Stathers

First we dealt with the cars that were lying around the track and tying up the line. Some of the boxcars were lying over on their side, and some were partially standing. These had to be unloaded to be made light enough for our crane to handle them. As frequently happens in a derailment, some cars had separated from their trucks and there was a cluster of trucks three high still over the track. We went to work to empty a car, then jacked it up, and built a false section of railroad right over the top of those trucks, so we could hook onto the car with our crane and slide it over those rails back down to the permanent line where we could rerail it. There were some cars with cottonwood logs which were very heavy and the crane had to unload these and set them aside. The empty cars could be slid out with the crane, again on temporary rails. It was a matter of systematically pulling cars and trucks out of the tangle, pulling them back to where they could be put back onto their trucks, and rerailing them. Un-piling the lumber from the cars down the bank was a long tedious process. The men broke into the cars as best they might and piled a load of lumber onto a sling. Then the crane boomed out as far as it could, picked up that slingload and swung it to the high side of the track for reloading into another boxcar.

There is a story to go with these boxcars down in the trees. The old Number One Highway ran just below those trees, more or less parallel to the track at that point. Below the road is a nice big flat area and there are several ranchers around there. They used to have good potato farms there, and raised hay and alfalfa. Of course, these ranchers gathered around to watch us at work picking up the wreck. It was something new for them to look at. Three of them got interested in these damaged boxcars. They wanted them for granaries and hay bale storage. So we made a deal with them, that they could have the boxcars for a dollar a piece if they took them away, but they had to take them out of sight. So they got hold of a Cat and hauled them away out of the road somewhere. The agreement was that they would put these boxcars into their fields where they could not be seen from the track or from the road. But one man put one of these boxcars right alongside of his barn which was close to the highway. Every time you went by there you would see this boxcar with CP or CN numbers on it. We kept asking him to paint out the numbers. It wasn't very good advertising for the railroad having that car stuck out there as part of his outbuildings. So while we got rid of the boxcars, we had a bit of trouble with the people who took them away.

The unloading of the lumber from all those cars was a long and tedious job. But the weather was fairly good, as it was in the spring, and we didn't have too much trouble picking up the cars. We were working quite close to the siding so we were able to set cars off as we recovered them and we had the line opened quickly enough. Being close to the siding, we didn't have to move very far when trains wanted to come through. It was a pretty routine operation.

* * *

Just at this time we were pushing the railroad north from Prince George to Fort St. John and Dawson Creek. This called for a major railroad bridge across the Fraser River just north of Prince George, which was being constructed by the Dominion Bridge Company. They had a special 99 ton railway crane with a long boom designed for this work, and their crane had been tied into one of our trains and shipped up from Vancouver. We got a call in Squamish about two o'clock in the afternoon of May 17, 1956. There had been a derailment at Mile 381, about three and a half miles south of Quesnel, and that big crane was off the track. So we pulled the crew together and hooked on to our 35 ton crane and our faithful Lidgerwood and got up there the next day.

There was the Dominion Bridge crane, down the bank sixty feet below the track, and piled up against it and above it were several of our gondola cars and logs spilled all over the crane. By the time we got there they had brought in a Cat from Quesnel to push a couple of cars to one side so the line was open. This was a pretty unusual derailment and it took awhile to figure out what probably happened. The boom had been removed from the crane; that is standard procedure. Then the crane was coupled into our train, boom-end forward and with no boom on. The leading trucks were riding with very little weight on them. Most of the weight was at the cab and engine that was the back end. There is always a little movement and some bounce on the springs. Travelling over rough track, the front trucks must have hit a low spot and, being light, bounced up so that the front wheels could climb the track and over the bank it went. Anyway, that was what we put down as the cause of the derailment.

Now this crane was very important to the Dominion Bridge people because they were working to a pretty tight contract schedule to get that bridge finished. The railroad had to get across the Fraser River before we could push the track north, and Premier Bennett had already announced that the line would be open to Fort St. John and Dawson Creek by the fall of 1958. The bridge company did not have another crane of this type with the long boom. They sent one of their superintendents up to work with us to inspect and recover the crane without damaging it, if possible. Otherwise it might have to be sent back down to Vancouver for repairs, which would set back the whole construction timetable. We looked the situation over as best we could. With the gondola cars and logs there it was not possible to see how much damage had been done to the crane. But it was obvious that our little 35 ton crane was not going to lift a 99 ton crane back onto the track. We would have to construct a steep grade spur line from our main line down beside that Dominion Bridge crane, put temporary track in, rerail the crane, and haul it back up to the mainline with our Lidgerwood.

South end Mile 381, May 17, 1956. Photograph: E.P. Stathers

North end Mile 381, May 17, 1956. Photograph: E.P. Stathers

Middle part. Photograph: E.P. Stathers
Underside of the crane. Note the mud covering the tracks and under the crane that had to be removed to put in the solid bed of ties. Photograph: E.P. Stathers

Still digging to get at the gondola trucks. Photograph: E.P. Stathers

All ready to put up the rigging and haul up to the main line.

So our Operating Superintendent hired a big D8 Cat in Quesnel and had it brought down on a flatcar. We marked out a line for the Cat operator and he started in on the side of the railroad line to cut the gravel out on the downhill side of a cut, and to make a grade down beside the crane. It was about a 35 percent grade, which is very steep, but it was about all the room we had. It took him a couple of days to complete this grade and the section gang were right behind him dropping ties and getting rail ready. While that was going on, our crew was picking up logs with the crane and recovering the gondola cars. Now I guess it must have been wet before the derailment because the trucks, the underside of those gondola cars and that derailed crane had dug deep into the mud. And then it turned hot and that mud dried out. The men were working in their shirtsleeves and the ground was like cement. It was so hard that you couldn't shovel it. You could put your whole weight on the shovel, but there was no way it would go into the ground. So the men were driving into that hard mud with lining bars, sharp-pointed crowbars with a straight end, and using picks to break up the ground in order to move it with a shovel. Before we could pass a cable underneath a piece of equipment in that mud, you had to tunnel inch by inch underneath in awkward positions on your hands and knees, lying on your belly, to make a hole through the ground to push a cable through. It was tremendously hard work. Finally, we had picked up all the logs and pulled back all of our gondola cars and we were able to get a better look at the crane.

Cranes are designed so that they can be swung around in any direction to pick up and transfer loads. In order to move them safely from place to place, they are provided with big tiedowns, turnbuckles that fasten the rotating portion of the crane into a fixed position. Screwdown stops also hold the cab and engine section down in line with the crane bed. During the derailment, these turnbuckles and stops had broken loose and after rolling down the side of the bank the crane had come to rest with the back end of the rotating cab resting against the bank. Before the crane could be safely recovered, the rotating part had to be swung back into line with the crane bed and tied down again. This was a tricky job because it involved easing the machinery around the cogged gears. The Dominion Bridge Superintendent managed to get into the cab and he juggled with the controls while the D8 Cat operator used his big blade to take the strain and they cheated that rotating cab around, step by step, until it was parallel to the crane bed. Then we tied it down with cables. The superintendent was quite relieved to find that, although the cab had been battered up, the operating machinery seemed to be in good shape.

Meanwhile the wrecking crew was struggling to pry that baked mud out from underneath the crane. The Cat could not reach under with his blade, so it was a matter of chopping the mud out with picks and prying it out with bars. It was especially difficult clearing the trucks of the crane that were pretty well in line with the crane body. On most railroad rolling stock (practically all of the freight cars) the trucks are not attached to the cars. They stay in place because the weight of the cars rests on the centre casting of the truck, with a long pin in the centre that permits movement and pivoting. During derailments these trucks often separate from the railcars. However, cranes are assembled differently. In order to take advantage of the weight of the trucks as a counterbalance during heavy lifts, the trucks are pinned through the centre castings of the crane with a heavy pin and keyed so that the trucks cannot come away from the crane. The wheels and the entire undercarriage of the crane were encrusted with mud, which all had to be removed. The crane was leaning over into the bank, with the bankside wheels dug right into the mud and the offside wheels hanging in the air. The D8 Cat had made a flat landing area beside the crane so that when he got it back onto its feet it would sit there and not roll away. But all that mud had to be removed and replaced with a solid bed of wooden ties. This meant chipping out the mud under the crane to make room for a tie that had to be wrestled into place. Then start again and make room for the tie next to it. And again, and again. So men were crawling under that crane on their hands and knees and lying on their backs and on their bellies prying with bars and banging and scraping off that hard-baked mud with crowbars and picks and shovels, and then sliding ties in, one at a time, to make a bed of timbers. This was exhausting work. After awhile, we were working in shifts, twenty minutes at a time, then sitting down and getting our strength back. Two days it took, two of hard, hard work by hand to get that mud out and those ties in, and to get all the wheels of the trucks free and clear. We were able to set rails down on the tie bed, and took a pull with the winch of the D8 Cat, and the crane was sitting upright. When it was securely on the rails, we blocked the wheels with wedges.

Before we could pull the crane up, it was necessary to lie out the rigging for the job. This involved a number of factors. First of all when you pull with a cable you pull in a straight line. When you are pulling railroad equipment that is on the rails and you want it to stay on the rails, you have to pull more or less parallel with the track, or you pull everything off the rails. Since we had that crane to haul up on a spur line and the Lidgerwood on the main line that ran in a different direction, we would have to use the pulley blocks. Secondly, in order to haul a 99 ton crane up a 35 degree slope, we would need some mechanical advantage that we could get by putting a pulley down on the crane coupler. This meant rigging a line from the Lidgerwood through the pulley block by the main line, down to the crane and through the lower pulley on the crane coupler, back up to a pulley on the main line and back to the Lidgerwood. Since there were no suitable trees or rocks we would have to dig in a deadman to hold the slings, which would position the two pulleys at the main line. Thirdly, the crane was now sitting more or less on a flat spot, but once we started our pull we would have to do the whole thing in one try because there was no way in the world to block off such a load on a hill, or hold it half-way up a grade while we changed our rigging around. It was really a problem in geometry. We had to set the top pulley blocks in such a way that they would stay more or less in line with both the main line and the spur line. By setting a block down at the crane, we could gain a smoother pull from the Lidgerwood, since two feet of cable would be wound onto the Lidgerwood for every foot the crane travelled up the hill. However, at the end of the pull the lower pulley block would be right up against the upper two pulley blocks.

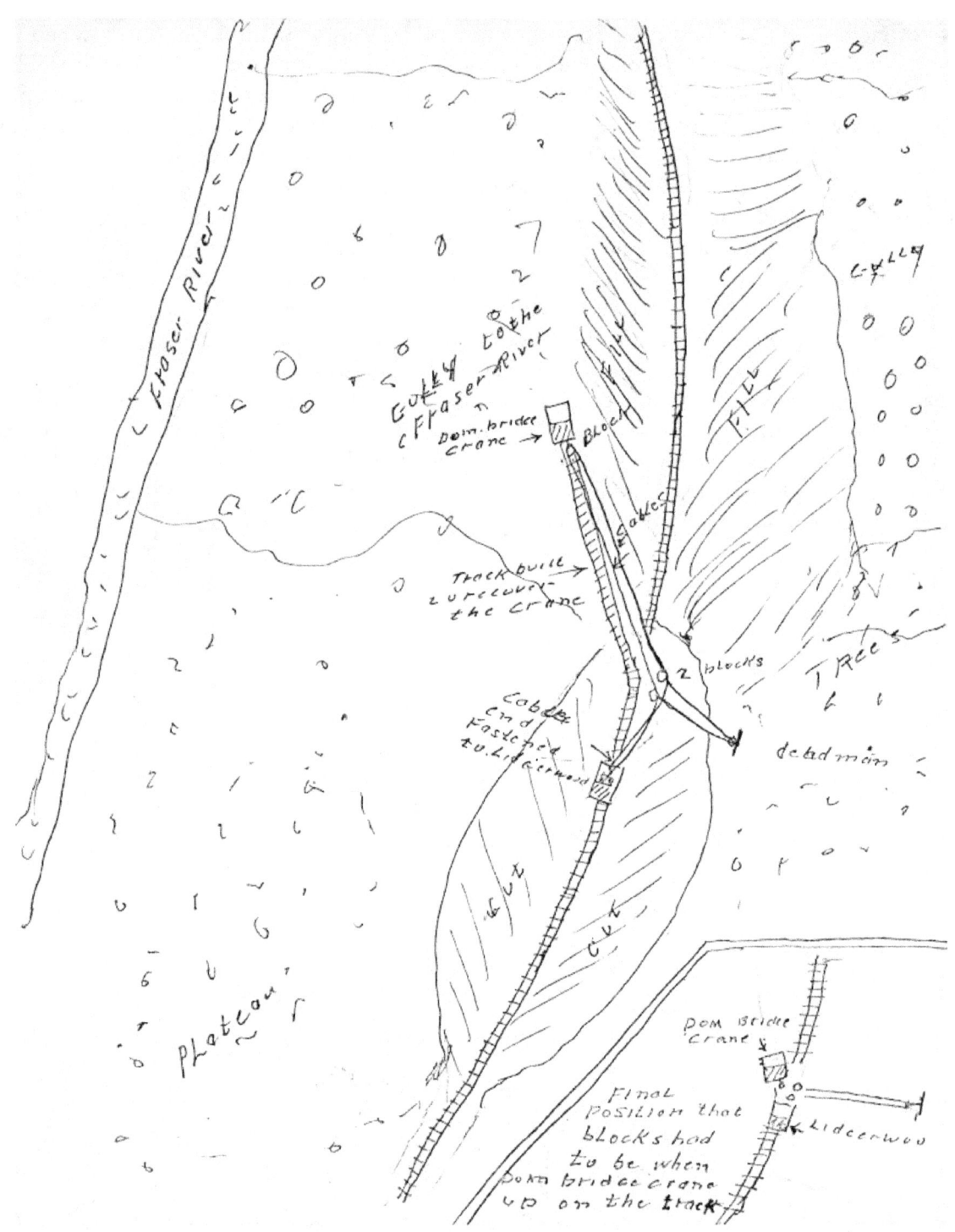

Map Diagram of crane derailment at Dominion Bridge. Photograph: E.P. Stathers

So the question was, where would these three blocks meet? This would determine where we set the deadman, and how long the slings which held the upper blocks would be. As the pull went on, the angles between cables and tracks would steadily alter. If the slings on the upper blocks were too long, we would not be able to pull the crane high enough on the hill. If the angles were too extreme, we'd be pulling sideways on the crane. There was quite a discussion about this. I had always talked things over with the crew before any difficult pull, and they often came up with good ideas. Sometimes I'd let them go ahead on their own, do the whole thing, and they did a very good job too. But there was no room for error on this pull. We wanted to end up with the three pulley blocks together and the crane sitting on the top of the grade where it flattened out again, up against the Lidgerwood. So I calculated where the Lidgerwood stops should be set, where the deadman should go in, and where we wanted those three pulley blocks to meet. When I told the boys how I had it figured, there was some heated discussion. The Lidgerwood operator especially spoke up saying, "You'll never make it! If you hook up there, you'll pull the crane off the track". Well I had to overrule him and say, "No, that's the way we're going to do it and here's where we'll hang the blocks", and I kicked holes in the dirt as markers. "No way", he said, "I'll bet you five dollars it doesn't work. You're going to pull that crane off the track from there and we'll lose it, it'll roll over". As if I didn't have trouble enough. "Okay", I said, "You're on!" and we had a five dollar bet. The Dominion Bridge Superintendent was listening to all of this and eyeing the situation, and he was pretty worried. It was altogether new to him, doing work like this. Mind you, I was just as anxious as he was. Anyhow, he was pretty much of my opinion that we'd finish up in the right spot with our pull and we wouldn't lose the crane.

So we went to work to rig up for the pull. We got the deadman dug in and set with slings to hang the top blocks onto. The section gang broke the track on the main line and connected it up to our temporary spur down to the crane. We set the Lidgerwood stops on the mainline track, put the Lidgerwood against the stops, and chained it down to the rails. The locomotive and work train were set right behind, with all brakes on emergency. Using the Lidgerwood line, we cinched up the slings around the deadman. Then we ran the Lidgerwood cable through the three pulley blocks and took up the slack and tightened up the rigging. There could not be any chance of a slipup. We eased that crane a little bit up the spur line off the flat so there was room for the Cat to follow. I gave the Cat operator instructions to follow close behind the crane as we pulled it up the hill. If anything happened, he was to jump out of the way. If he had time to put the brakes on, fine, but never mind the machinery, never mind the crane, just jump and get out of the way. On each side of the crane I had two men, one man with wedges and a hammer to follow up placing wedges under the wheels, and another man with an armful of wedges ready to hand to the first man. Those were about all the precautions or safety measures we had available to use if anything broke.

The wedges might slow things down a bit and the D8 Cat would slow it down for sure. The crane might not stop but it would move slowly so it would not be able to run right off the hillside, just wind up in the mud again. One more thing to be done, we greased the inside of the rails. Then I took a deep breath and lit my pipe. It was one of the favourite sayings of the Lidgerwood engineer, "Here we go, fellows. There's smoke signals coming up from the boss" because it was a habit of mine that whenever we got in a dangerous position ready to do something, I would fill my pipe and light it before I started giving signals.

So the smoke signals started to come up and I gave them the go ahead to pull easy. The crane inched up the hill, bit by bit, and the wedges were driven in and the whole works moved slowly, very slowly and steadily up the hill. We didn't dare stop. We had to keep moving slowly. I must give the bulldozer operator great credit for the way he followed that crane, with his big blade barely touching the coupler of the crane all the way up the steep grade. When we started there was quite an angle between the cable and the spur line but the track was greased and we were moving slowly. As the lower block moved up, the angle on the upper blocks changed. It lessened as the blocks swung on their slings, moving slightly towards the Lidgerwood and slightly away from the anchor holds which were fixed to the deadman. We stopped the pull when the three pulley blocks were almost touching and they were exactly in line. The crane was safely up onto the flat beside the mainline. Then the bulldozer operator dropped his blade down behind the crane as a brake and we ran a cable for safety. We slacked off the main line and took down the rigging and hooked the Lidgerwood onto the crane with another cable. Then our train slowly backed up and took the weight while we knocked out the Lidgerwood stops and pulled the crane right onto the main line. The section gang moved right in to cast off that spur and joined up the main track again, and there we were, all in one piece again.

That Dominion Bridge Superintendent was a very relieved man. He came up to me and shook me by the hand and said, "Well, sir, that's one of the finest pieces of engineering I've seen. I was sure scared that we were going to lose that machine back in the hole again, and God knows what we would have done then, because there's nothing to replace it with. I want to congratulate you and your crew on the way they handled it, bringing that crane out of the hole". Well, of course, it was all part of a day's work but we felt quite good about it, everybody was happy about the way we handled it. I forgave the Lidgerwood man his five bucks because he did such a wonderful job of running that Lidgerwood. Part of our success was that it ran so smoothly, not once was there a jerk on that line, at any time. So we took the whole train into Quesnel, crane and all. The Dominion Bridge Superintendent had a good look at it and he figured that it did not need to go back to Vancouver. They could get the work done in Prince George to fix it up. So we left it on a siding and headed back down to Squamish with our wrecked cars and logs and what have you. Another train picked up the crane from Quesnel and took it into Prince George and inside of a week it was put back into shape and went to work building the bridge across the Fraser River, so that we could get to work on the run to Fort St. John and Dawson Creek.

In those years, the early fifties when the track was in pretty bad shape, we were getting many derailments in the Cariboo and spending many busy days and nights there. One time we had three wrecks, one after another. We were on our way home from picking up the first one, but only got as far as Pemberton before getting word that there was another wreck up the line, and after that another one. We were away from home about two weeks on that series, just chasing back and forth. For some time I had been calling for better equipment to handle wrecks and the Dominion Bridge crane incident was one of the last where we had to cope using only the 35 ton crane and the Lidgerwood and the methods which I have described in these chapters. Help was on the way. How we got it, and what we did with it, makes a new set of stories.

13 DAWN OF A NEW ERA

1956

In the previous chapters I have shared with the reader some of the highlights of my education, from the time I joined the Pacific Great Eastern Railway in 1929 up to the 1950's, and about how we went about picking up train wrecks using whatever equipment and crew that circumstances provided. There were always better days coming, we were told. One day we would run right into Prince George. One day we would get proper shop equipment. One day the roadbed would be permanent instead of construction standard. We worked through the Great Depression of the 1930's and through the Second World War of the 1940's, and now we were into the 1950's. And darned if the railroad didn't get to Prince George. And that was hardly done before they announced that the line would be punched through to North Vancouver. With the expansion of the railroad activities, there were some changes in management. In 1955 I was appointed General Car Foreman, so I was in a position to ask for better equipment for the shop and to speak about the needs for improved gear on our wrecking train. Construction of the 40 mile portion of line between Squamish and North Vancouver more or less followed the coastline of Howe Sound, which is very scenic but extremely rugged. Through West Vancouver and into North Vancouver, it passed through built up residential areas, following the right-of-way which had been part of the original service between 1914 and 1928. There was an obvious likelihood of derailments in this new section, which may have had some effect on the Board's decision to finally allow me to budget for a big wrecking crane.

So early in 1956 an order was placed with the Industrial Brownhoist people (who are manufacturers in the Southwest US) for a brand new 150 ton diesel-powered wrecking crane. This machine had six-wheeled trucks, instead of the regular four-wheeled trucks. It had outriggers front and back on each side, which were operated by gear cranks. It also had a telescopic type of outrigger, to operate additionally from the centre of the crane, which would run out twenty-five feet from the track. This meant that if the ground was at all stable, we would have a platform with this machine that was practically impossible to turn over. There were a number of additional specifications which were made because of experience over the years picking up wrecks. There were extra heavy lights on the front and back of the crane to illuminate the area where we were working or moving at night, and a light under the boom which shone directly onto the area where we were hooking on to pick up equipment. There was also a gasoline engine to be used to start the main diesel engine of the crane. This gasoline engine was quite easy to start and could be hand-cranked if necessary. When you got it warmed up and going at its proper rate of speed, you could turn over the big diesel and the crane engine would start. The crane company was surprised by this request and told me that they had built many many cranes and no one had ever wanted such a thing, and it would cost a bit more because it was an extra. But I was adamant that we have this starting mechanism because of all the problems we had in the past with battery starting and cold weather.

Shown sitting on the deck of the "Big Hook," capable of handling most derailments, are (left to right): Terry Aldridge, Sonny Rennie, who is the crane operator at the controls, Dick Riemer, Bill Bachuk, who is the other crane operator, Shelby Lipsey, and Armdan Constantin. Tom Fowler, the Foreman in charge of operations is sitting over the coupler of the "Big Hook." Two other very important men who are missing in the photo are Joe Iacovone, the cook, and his helper, Val Iacovone. For story, submitted by Terry Aldridge, Carman, Squamish Shops, see below.

The original wrecking crew that manned the big hook on its first run.
Photograph: The Coupler, P.G.E. Rail's employee newspaper

Well it took a while to get delivery on this new crane. It had to come up by slow train and we didn't get it until late in the fall of 1956. Along with it travelled the man who was going to show us how to operate it and break it in and make sure everything was working according to the specifications. Oh, it was a most beautiful piece of machinery. We put it on the repair track behind the shop, where our operators could get their training from this crane man, and we put it through its paces. It had a huge boom on it and the big hook was double, rather like an anchor, with two hooks back to back in one so you could put a sling around each end of a car and hang a sling along each side of the hook; the slings would not foul each other and you could lift the whole works at once. It would lift 150 tons right at the coupler, on the level. This meant that we could pick up one end of an engine quite easily. Of course, the lift limit would decrease the farther we were from the centre of gravity, but with these huge outriggers and with this great heavy boom we felt no fear of lifting locomotives or rolling them over so long, as we had a stable piece of ground to work on. There was also a smaller hook with a separate cable drum and drive. The new crane was built so that the boom would lock into a travelling position and did not require a cradle on the idler car, which made it a lot quicker to get ready for travelling. Because it had six-wheeled trucks, it could handle rougher trackage and move more smoothly. This meant we could travel faster going up the line and could get to wrecks quicker than we had before.

In order to make full use of this new crane we had to build a new wrecking train, which meant extra cars, new cars, different types of cars. We made up new slings. We had to build new blocking. We had to build an idler car for the crane, with fuel carrying capacity. We had the caboose fitted up with an electric generator and backup lights, so that when we picked up a car or a locomotive and were backing up to the nearest siding we could see what was going on and weren't running blind, as we had been doing with the old equipment. We had already acquired a better crew car, a big old Milwaukee sleeper which we had fixed up and were already using. It was fairly comfortable living accommodation, especially when compared with our old tin can of a crew car. We still felt real cold weather but things were changing very much for the better. Having this new crane meant that we could send our 35 ton crane up to the Prince George area along with the Lidgerwood. We had to build another work car for them and they took our old cars. This provided the company with a complete wrecking outfit at Prince George, which was a great step forward. Now, in case of bad derailments, we could bring a crane in from each end of the mishap and be able to work from both ends at once. Altogether, the new crane and its gear gave us a wonderful advantage and it was a beautiful piece of equipment. It did not take long before we had a chance to try it out. The first scheduled passenger service from North Vancouver to Squamish began operating on September 1, 1956. The new highway was under construction just above and more or less parallel to the railroad. For several years after that it gave us quite a bit of trouble because of rocks coming down into our track. There were many minor incidents. However, in this chapter I'll mention some of the major opportunities where we tested our new crane.

About three or four miles south of the town of 100 Mile House there was a level crossing where the highway came down a hill and made a right-hand turn across the railway track. This crossing was practically hidden from the railroad tracks by the rock bluffs until you got quite close. On February 7, 1960 a trailer truck hauling a tank of gasoline came down that hill to cross the track at the instant that the Budd Car passenger train rounded the corner, and the two collided. The front of the train struck the tank and ruptured it, and the gasoline exploded. Flames engulfed the front end of the train and the truck and trailer as well. The first reaction of the engineer and train crew was to evacuate all passengers from the lead car of the two car train, getting them onto the ground. Fire had taken hold of the lead car. The men then turned their attention to saving the rear Budd Car. This meant unhooking the control and brake connections and uncoupling the two cars. The engineer had been quite badly burned in the cab of the lead Budd Car during the collision, although he did not realize it. In uncoupling the hoses and disconnecting the two Budd Cars, he actually ripped the skin off his hands. His face was badly burned and it required almost three years of medical attention before he was finally able to come back to work.

When the fire died out, the Budd Car had been burned to a shell. In the heat, the steel beams of the car had sagged under the weight of the two diesel engines underneath so that the engines and all the undergear were resting on the track. The car could not be pulled anywhere without damaging the truck or derailing the train which was pulling it. The yard crew from Williams Lake managed to coax it along by putting ties under it and skidding it to a mill siding a short distance south of the crossing, to get it clear of the main line so it didn't hamper the passage of train traffic. Meanwhile the wrecking train was called to go up and bring this burnt out Budd Car home. So we arrived, bringing the insurance man with us. The Budd Car was insured for its full value, of course, and before we did anything at all he looked the whole situation over. The car was absolutely gutted by the fire, a charred mess, and hopeless as far as rebuilding was concerned. But some of the parts underneath, below the source of the heat, weren't so bad. However, the engines were actually sitting on the track holding up the car. The problem was how were we going to transport this car back to the shop.

Well, we now had the big crane to work with. If we could pull the engines up off the track, we might straighten out the two centre main beams, at least enough for the Budd Carr to be safely moved. So I came up with a plan. We were able to get along side of the Budd Car with our crane. We cut a hole through the roof of the car, in the centre, and passed a heavy strong cable down around the two main beams. It was quite cold and the ground was frozen and of course the ties were frozen into the ground. So we chained the couplers on each end of the Budd Car down to the rails so they could not move. The section gang brought us some steel rails which we were able to slide through the end of the car and pile up like a little pyramid sitting on the body bolsters over the front and back trucks. You could see the sag in the steel backbone of the car dipping below these steel rails. Then we took a lift with the crane, easing it up until the centre of the Budd Car was actually supported by the crane. We passed heavy chains around the car beams and our steel rail backbone, then set jacks under the car beams and forced them higher in the air, bending them back into a straight line and pushing the sag out. More pull from the crane, more pressure from the jacks, and we re-wrapped the chains tighter. Then we drove wedges in to make the chains bind very tight. Little by little we straightened out that Budd Car, reversing the sag until the engines had about three inches clearance above the track. Then we eased off with the crane and undid the couplers, and that car was sitting there on the siding with three inches clearance. Of course, if we moved it the sag might come back.

The front Budd Car on fire at the crossing just south of 100 Mile House, February 1960.
Photograph: E.P. Stathers

Here we were able to take advantage of the long boom on our new crane. Even when the crane was on the same track as the Budd Car, we were able to reach the centre of the car and make a lift. So we coupled the Budd Car next to the crane for the journey home, thinking that possibly those engines would sag as we travelled down the track. Surely enough that is what happened. As we went along we would stop at every siding to inspect the centre section of the Budd Car and drive in wedges that were loosened in travelling. Twice before we got to Lillooet we had to pull into a siding and take another lift with the crane, then retighten all the chains and drive in the wedges again. By the time we arrived at Lillooet, it had pretty well stabilized so we were able to hook into a standard train and were taken home. When we got to the shops, the Budd Car was demolished and any salvageable parts were used for repairing other cars. Without the use of that new crane, we couldn't have moved that Budd Car at all. We'd have had to cut it up into pieces and load them with the old 35 tonner. We had already tried out that long boom in a small incident, and found out how it could make life so much easier. For instance, we could move into a heap of boxcars all piled up on each other, get a sling around the nearest one, back the crane away and tighten up the big hook, and that crane would drag the car over to the centre of the track and pull it right out of the mess. Then we could take the light line and string it around behind the cars to pick up the trucks and set them on the track. If the boxcar was loaded, we'd have to lift the front end up and seesaw it on blocks, but we could still set it on its trucks and rerail it from the rear end, because with more power and a longer boom the light line could reach right across the length of the car, which you could never do with the small crane even if the boxcar was empty.

While I'm talking about Budd Cars, there were a couple of other interesting incidents with the Budd passenger cars. They were also a part of our era, as was the microwave communications system which allowed our dispatcher to talk directly to engineers and conductors, even when their equipment was on the move. It was these improvements in communication which made it practical to send patrol speeders ahead of the passenger trains in troublesome sections of the line, such as the Lake District and Cheakamus Canyon. We had 85 pound steel in the Cheakamus Canyon by this time and a lot of the curves had been eased there and better ballast put down for the track. Anyway, a Budd Car was heading south through the canyon, running late and it was dark by this time. The patrol speeder had gone ahead and everything appeared normal. As the train rounded the corner of a bluff the engineer caught sight of a huge rock on the right of way. He immediately applied the brakes in emergency but there wasn't enough distance to bring the train to a stop in time. The Budd Car struck the rock, which was not on the track but right beside the track, and was deflected off the rails into the gravel. I guess the Good Lord was looking after the passengers and crew of this train because they skidded down the ballast along the side of an abutment just beside the end of a bridge. The engineer still at the controls was staring out into space hanging over the edge; he could look down the side of the bridge which passed over the Cheakamus River, 150 feet below.

We were called out immediately. By the time our wrecking train arrived the passengers had been taken off and had continued on to North Vancouver, and there was no one there but the train crew. It was an extremely difficult place to work. The second car in the train was jammed up against the boulder and could not back up. There was no place for the crane to work from except off the bridge itself, which was both difficult and dangerous. The outriggers of the crane could only be set out the width of the bridge itself, which is about half the width of the crane platform when outriggers are fully extended. What was more awkward was that, the men, including me, had to sidle their way along the edge of the bridge past the crane to reach the wreck. We got out the lanterns to carry with us. Ordinarily we would have strung up work lights, but there was no place to string them. There was a steep wall on one side, the river was on the other side, the second Budd Car was sitting just off the track, and jammed between that car and the rock wall was a damned great boulder which was as round as a baseball. It must have weighed a good ten tons, I'd say. We couldn't blast it because that would also blow up the Budd Car. We couldn't get a regular cable on it or around it because it was sitting right on the gravel, jammed against the canyon wall and jammed against the Budd Car and it was almost completely round.

When we tried to put a cable on it, the cable slipped off. But there was another way. We might try to pull it out with a bunch of light cable. There were a number of smooth protuberances on this boulder. So we got a number of light cable chokers and made a kind of wire basket hooking them up through a light shackle which acted like a slip knot. We took a pull and the rock shifted a bit and all the cables immediately slipped. So we tried it again and moved it some more. We were working practically in the dark by that rock as the crane lights illuminated the end of the bridge but didn't reach behind that car. Well, I guess it took five or six tries before we managed to get that rock out to the front of the Budd Car. We set a final hitch on it and eased it onto the edge of the bridge where it balanced. Then the whole crew got set on the bridge side, to push when we gave the signal to slack off and loosen the shackle. Maybe you've seen kids throw rocks into rivers or lakes. Well say, you should have heard the splash that rock made a few seconds after we let it go when it hit the Cheakamus River! That was the biggest rock I ever threw in a river, believe me!

Then it was time to tackle the Budd Car, and I was very nervous about trying to lift it in these circumstances. A Budd Car weighs 60 tons, so picking up one end meant a good 30 tons. We were going to have to do it off to one side of the line from the bridge, with practically no help from the outriggers, so our lifting capacity was way down. Of course I was conscious of that river 150 feet below. It was dark and hard to see. We had to take some care in setting the slings around the Budd Car. Because we had so little purchase from the outriggers, I put a man at each corner of the crane and instructed the operator not to lift more than an inch at a time. We set the boom over so that the slings would drag and lift at the same time. The trick was to cheat the end of the car up the bank and more in line with the track. So we took the strain and everything held. Then we worked the car up away from the concrete abutment up through the gravel, inch by inch, until we had it more or less close to the track so we didn't have to lift from the side of the bridge. Then we took a straight lift and set it back down on the track, cleaned up, and took everything back to Squamish. We were lucky no one fell off the bridge working back and forth around the crane.

Those were the days when we had a lot of trouble in the canyon with overheating brake shoes, which caused numerous fires along the line. There was a lot of logging going on at Alta Lake and various points along the line, and we had a logging train running every day picking up all the logs. They used to load these logs onto specially designed log cars and there was a lot of cedar and the bark would hang down. Coming down the canyon on a two percent grade, the brakes were kept half on by setting what is called retaining valves which meant that the brakes were applied continuously. The trains would come down about twenty-five miles an hour, in fact some logging trains were held to fifteen miles per hour in some sections in those days and those cast iron brake shoes grinding away on cast iron wheels threw a lot of sparks and got very hot. If the brake shoes were badly worn, a chunk of red hot metal could fly off and lay on the grade and ignite trailing bark. In the very hot weather, those rock walls in the Cheakamus Canyon would soak up heat all day and stay hot all night and everything became tinder dry. We had numerous fires start because of these logging trains; some of them quite serious, when the bridges would catch on fire and the whole crew would have to get out and fight them. We actually designed water tank cars which were tied in at the end of the logging trains, just ahead of the caboose. Operated by the train's air system, they pumped water from the tanks through a specially designed spray bar which wetted down the track after the train had gone through. These cars more or less replaced the forestry speeder patrol which used to follow each freight train to put out any fires.

Well this particular time I had been up to Lillooet, and on the Budd Car coming back with me were my wife and two of my grandsons. A logging train had gone through ahead of us, and there was a forest fire raging in the canyon. We stopped at Garibaldi and waited for a call from the dispatcher to tell us it was safe, because it was burning fiercely on both sides of the track. The patrol speeder went through ahead of us and I guess he reported that it was all right, safe for the train to come through. So we started off. I guess a wind must have come up between the time he went through and we went through. As soon as we crossed nineteen mile bridge I could see flames leaping along both sides of the track, ties were burning and all you could see was smoke. By this time we were committed. I ran up to the Engineer, Alan McDonald, and said, "Alan, what the hell you gonna do? Are you going through?", and he said, "I can't very well back up now, we're right in the middle of it. We'll keep on going". I got hold of the brakeman and we took all the fire extinguishers up in the engine compartment of the Budd Cars. What I was afraid of was fire in the train engines. Those diesel engines underneath the Budd Cars were quite oily and of course if they caught fire the whole train would be set alight. The passengers, of course, had no notion of that there was any danger. They were enjoying the fire immensely, looking through the sealed windows and pointing excitedly to the blazing trees. I was sweating blood. I had the doors open at the back of the first car and was standing on the steps with the fire extinguishers. The engineer was alerted to come to a stop immediately on my signal so that the brakeman and I could dash out with an extinguisher and put out any fires on the engines. I guess the engineer decided he wasn't going to hang around there, so the train was really moving and there was quite a draft so we were choking with smoke and burnt by sparks. I guess we ran through about five miles of this fire before we got into the clear and believe me I was a very, very pleased man when were through there without anything happening to us. There must have been 160 or 170 passengers in those Budd Cars, including my wife, and two grandsons as well. There we were travelling along in the most modern equipment through a fire caused by tired old logging train equipment. It was the dawn of a new era, when we started operating with new equipment, but it took awhile before we had replaced all the old stuff and completed the renewal of our right-of-way and roadbed.

The new crane proved of great advantage every time we were called out, but the next tricky and interesting occasion was September 11, 1961. A train proceeding south towards North Vancouver ran into a rock slide at Mile 28 and Engine 590 was carried off the line and down the bank. It landed upside down with the front coupler jammed against an outcropping of rock, which was all that held it from sliding straight into the deep waters of Howe Sound. The rest of the train stayed on the track. It was only a matter of rerailing a few cars and the line was open again. Although there was actually no special reason to get there immediately, I arrived on the scene as did a number of other company officials. I could see right away that our big crane would not have room to work because the track ran right along side of a rock face past a very narrow band. There was no place to put the outriggers on the sea side of the track and not enough room to swing the crane on the land side because the back of the crane would hit rock wall. If we tried to make a lift from the track, with no place to put out our outriggers, we would just pull our crane on top of that engine. So it was an unusual situation, and it called for an unusual solution. Instead of a land-based crane, we would have to use a sea-based crane. Since a derrick would not be able to hoist Engine 590 back up onto our grade, we could load it onto a barge instead and tow it back up to our railroad barge dock in Squamish to handle the lift.

Well sir, it was quite a scene. The dredging company provided two derricks, one a 40 tonner and the other a 50 ton dredge. There were some tug boats and a barge standing by. We had our wrecking crew and the big crane on the track, immediately above our stranded engine. Now that entire locomotive weighed about 120 tons and those two derricks would only hoist about 90 tons between them. However, the engine trucks weighed about 25 tons apiece, so the first thing was to disconnect those trucks and pick them up separately. The trucks and the engine were partially covered in the rock slide, so the derrick operators went to work with their clam-shell buckets to pick off this rock and debris. Now, although we could not swing the boom on our crane, we could still exert quite a powerful pull with the main cable. The feed pulley on the crane was swiveled so that it would pivot and turn when we pulled from the side and the cable would not jam or hang up in the sheaves. We could change the angle of our pull by moving back and forth along the railroad line. So when the rock was cleared, our crew got a line on one of those trucks and we managed to disconnect it from the engine. Then by working with the crane and the two derricks together we were able to ease the truck away clear of the engine. It was hoisted up and set down onto the barge which was sitting just behind the derricks. Using the same technique, the second truck was removed from the engine and also transferred to the barge.

These derricks are floating, of course, so that when they try to lift a heavy load on one side, the other side tends to tip up. So where our crane was equipped with outriggers to provide a stable platform, these derricks had what they call shear legs. They were wooden pilings, like telephone poles, with steel point on them which are driven down onto the rock or whatever bottom they find, like big stilts and they sit down there and stabilize the front of the derrick as it lifts. I just don't know how they were transferred or set out. So these shear legs carry a lot of the load during a lift.

This whole operation was supervised by a superintendent of this dredging company. One of the requirements for such work was a loud voice. I believe my men must have figured me as rough man to work with, because I had a good loud voice and I didn't hesitate in using good strong language to get things done in a hurry. Sometimes I think I've actually saved men's lives by yelling at them when they couldn't see what was happening, when a boom or hook was swinging and they didn't see it coming. On more than one occasion, I think, I saved a man's life by yelling with such a forceful voice that they jumped when they heard me yell. But compared to me, this dredging company superintendent was a tyrant. He stood up on the ledge of that rock where he could see the whole operation and directed the whole crew, including me. I took orders from him because he had the gravest responsibility of handling the derricks. I didn't have any experience or know-how with floating machinery, and I wasn't looking for any either. I didn't want that responsibility. So when he hollered at anybody to do something, they did it, and they did it on the dead run; they didn't stop to wait or hesitate. He had a big loud voice and he could make himself heard over the whole distance. We were all members of this crew and it was instant command, instant response. He handled those men like a coach handling a football team. It was a treat to see. Each man knew that he was watching everyone, and every man was dependent on the other fellow doing his job. That's the kind of teamwork that is necessary on the big salvage jobs. I imagine that it's the same on the big oil drilling rigs and big lifting jobs, where there are always salvage operations. One man has to have absolute control over every person on that job and his orders have to be obeyed immediately.

Now came the ticklish part. We had to combine the lifting capacity of the two derricks, one a 40 tonner and the other a 50 tonner, to pick that engine up. But we wanted to pull it over into an upright position, and as soon as we moved it all and the front coupler shifted off the rock, the engine would start sliding into the water over a very steep dropoff. So the slings had to be set up so that when the lift was made, the engine would lift and roll and the crane line would keep it from sliding towards the sea. The shear legs on both derricks had been set, and the superintendent checked to see that everyone was in place. He signaled for the lift and the engine lifted up off the rocks and rolled into a more upright position. Just at this critical moment, the shear legs of the far-side derrick slipped and it started to drift out from the shore. The front of the deck dipped down until there was about a foot of water over the front of the derrick deck. However, there was a tug standing by and they might have been expecting something like this, because as soon as the superintendent saw what was happening he had that tug in there in just a few seconds, pushing the derrick in and holding it in place against the shoreline until they could reset those shear legs. When this had been done, the two derricks had to rebalance the load so that the locomotive was upright and being carried proportionally by the two different machines. We kept the strain on with our crane line while they readjusted the slings, and then when they were ready to back off from the shore the crane line was cast off. The derricks backed away and almost immediately the barge was brought in underneath the load by tugboat and the engine was set down onto the deck of the barge. Our section crew built trackage right down the centre of the barge while our machinists and the wrecking crew inspected the trucks and got them ready for service. The derricks then lifted the trucks onto the track where they were chained to the rails so they wouldn't slip. Then the two derricks picked up the engine again and set it back onto the tracks and the engine was back together again on rails in the centre of the barge, safe except from a heavy storm. It was the end of the summer and luckily the weather was good, no high winds or problem with rough water. There is quite a difference in levels through the tide in this part of the Pacific Coast, but that had been taken into account in the calculations of the dredging company.

The derricks removing the gravel so the trucks could be taken off.   Photograph: E.P. Stathers

The barge being slipped underneath the engine.
Photograph: E.P. Stathers

Tying it down to the rails on the barge. Photograph: E.P. Stathers

So the barge was towed up to Squamish to be offloaded at our barge slip. And this also provided some anxious moments. The barge slip of course is hinged so that it will move up and down with the tides. It is supported in the front by cables and a long beam. You raise or lower it to match the height of the barge deck and then the barge is locked onto the barge slip with huge irons and turnbuckles. The barge was fairly small and everybody realized that when the load of that locomotive was transferred from the centre to the front end of the barge, the back end would tip up. The yard crew had the job of rolling Engine 590 onto the dock and they were apprehensive. So when everything was locked in they started their move and sure enough as the engine moved to the barge slip, the barge began to tip and the crew hesitated and slowed down. I yelled in my biggest voice, "Get goin', get goin'!".

They still weren't on the barge slip, they had another six or seven feet to go but the barge was tipping and we had to take the chance. So I gave them the highball sign, and they slipped that engine right off the barge. Actually, when the last truck came off, the back end of the barge was right out of the water, because there was nothing on the back end to counterbalance the weight of the engine on the front. However, we made it without even going off the track and the engine was hauled up to the shop. It was back in service in a short period of time. This was quite an expensive business, making a salvage contract with the dredging company and bringing in those derricks and tugs and barge and our crew and crane, and it was dangerous work as well. But we were looking at a quarter million dollars worth of locomotive at that time. It would be much more now. So it was a bargain provided that we got our engine back. I can tell you we were very glad and very relieved when 590 was back in the shop.

That was the second major incident where the extra capacity and features of our new crane proved to have great value in saving expensive equipment. Of course we used it on many occasions for routine work; and because it was so versatile and had such capacity we could sort out incidents very quickly and restore service before much time had been lost. This was a great contrast to the old hand-working methods of earlier years. There was a particular problem between Squamish and North Vancouver between 1956 and

1958 because they were punching the highway through above the railroad tracks, working from both ends and in the middle. It was arranged that they would blast every Thursday morning after the Budd Car went through and there was no rail traffic until the night freight train. This would give the road-building crews a chance to blast and to clean up the rock and debris. Many times they would not have the line clear before Friday. Even after the highway was completed, it took time for the banks and cuts to settle down so there was a period of several years when there was a great amount of loose rock on the line. These derailments generally didn't amount to much, and with the big crane we were able to handle them quickly and easily. So our wrecking train equipment looked after the south end of the line while our old wrecking train with the 35 ton crane and the Lidgerwood worked out of Prince George on the north end of the Pacific Great Eastern Railway.

We knew it would happen that some day we would be calling on the two wrecking outfits, one from the south and the other from the north, to work together on a particular derailment. This small piece of P.G.E. history was made on January 23, 1962. Just as you entered Williams Lake yard from the north end there was a small siding which had put in to serve as a loading platform for the sawmill there. Lumber was loaded onto boxcars at this siding. Now there had been some snowfall, and the yards were being cleared. The section crew was working to clear snow out of the switches at the north end of the yard and got past this siding just about the time that the Budd Car service was due from the north. So the foreman ran his speeder back into this siding out of the way and left one of his men to throw the switch. Then they all sat down in the speeder and waited for the Budd train to go by so they could resume their work. In a few minutes the Budd Car came roaring down into the north yard right off the main line into the siding, tilted over slowly with the snowbank, slid into the speeder which was demolished struck the boxcar and bumped it down the spur, smashed into the loading platform, and came to a stop lying over on its side in the snow. Somebody had forgotten to throw that switch. Luckily for us, there were only a few passengers on board that morning. They were all rushed to Williams Lake Hospital. There were no injuries of any consequence but they were shaken up.

So the call came in for the wrecking crew and I was told what had happened. I asked for the Prince George auxiliary to be sent down from Prince George at the same time. Now I knew that lifting this Budd Car was quite a different problem from handling freight cars. If we took a straight lift with cables around the passenger car, we might bite right into the shell of the car with our cables, or crush it. I recalled that we had been storing a lot of mattresses for the outfit cars under cover in our big storage shed. So I had the crew load these into the wrecking car along with the usual slings and timbers and other gear, and we headed up the line.

Actually, it was not a difficult wreck to deal with. When they cleared off the yard trackage the snow had been pushed to the side forming a snowbank, and this snowbank had acted as a cushion for the Budd Car when it tipped over coming down the siding. The car came to rest leaning over against the wrecked loading platform and the snow, off the track. We had to dig quite a bit of snow away in order to feed out cables around the car. These Budd Cars are self-propelled equipment, with an engine on each truck making a dual drive. Made of stainless steel, it was handsome equipment worth about $225,000 at that time. We couldn't see how much damage had been done until we got it away from the platform, but we had to take every precaution not to make any further scratches or damage if possible when we handled the car. Each of the wrecking crews was a smooth working team and in this case they would have to work together during the lift. I took charge of overall operations. All the men worked well together, which pleased me very much. They got the cables fed around the Budd Car and brought the two cranes into position for the lift. Then they laid those mattresses against the skin of the car and set timbers across the mattresses to spread out the pressure of the cables. Of course while the train operators took up the slack, the men had to stay in there and keep the mattresses and timbers in place, so there were people all over the place and plenty of things to keep an eye on. When we had taken the strain, the men moved out of the way. They set up blocking which would hold the car high enough off the ground so that we would be able to inspect the running gear. Then we made a slow and careful lift and the car was upright sitting on the blocks. We looked it over and fortunately little damage had been done, largely because of the effect of that snowbank. Then it was a simple matter to rerail the car.

That was a very special day for me. For all these years we had worked with inadequate equipment always being told that it was coming, that there would be better days ahead. By this time, thanks to the interest of the Premier (Mr. W.A.C. Bennett) and the government, we were actually getting these improvements. We had heavier rail, diesel engines, better equipment, better tools, and the company was finally promoting their men up through the ranks. The south end wrecking foreman that day was Tom Fowler and the north end wrecking foreman was Barry Hunt. These two men had come into the shops when they were only 16 years old, as apprentices. They were the two lads who climbed up the rock with pickaxes to secure the tailhold for our rigging the time Engine 53 went into Seton Lake. I looked upon them as if they were my adopted sons all the time we worked together, and I still look upon them the same way. So it was the culmination of some 33 years of hard work and back-breaking labour, and many anxious moments rerailing cars and locomotives with inadequate equipment, to be able to command two crews, with two cranes, and retrieve a valuable piece of rolling stock in a combined operation. In the old days with the small crane, we would have been at it for days and done a terrific amount of work, but with our new equipment it was much easier and safer. Gordon Thornton, the loading supervisor from Prince George, managed to get a photograph of me with my foremen and the cranes. There I was, Superintendent of Car Equipment, with a fine team of men and the right machinery. It was a historic day in my service life with the P.G.E. Railway.

14 THE BIG HOOK

1963

The second time that the two hooks (one from Prince George and one from Squamish) worked together was on a derailment at Mile 310.5, right on the shore of the lake just south of Williams Lake. It was not particularly difficult to pick up because once again we had all our equipment on the spot. The train had been southbound out of Williams Lake and derailed in a cut, losing some sixteen cars altogether; fourteen boxcars loaded with lumber and with grain and two empty oil tank cars. Lumber and grain had spilled out and some of the boxcars had burst under the compression force of the moving train behind them. The Prince George crew got there first from the north end and recovered the first tank car, which was partially on the track. Then, using their Lidgerwood and their crane and also a Cat, they hauled the other tank car up the bank back to the tracks and rerailed it as well. The Cat operator worked alongside and nudged some of the boxcars a bit further out of the way. The section crew were able to run a shoefly track around the wreck so the line was open again; traffic was able to flow around this wreck. By the time that we got there from the south end, the work gang were transferring lumber from the broken and derailed cars into other boxcars. Some of the lumber had been smashed up and also some of the boxcars. All we could do with some of them was to cut them up and load the pieces into gondola cars or on flat cars. A few were still in good enough shape that they could be hauled back to the shop on their own wheels. One car loaded with wheat had dumped part of its load onto the track. In order to transfer the wheat from this damaged car we used a grain augur, the same as farmers used quite often to handle their grain.

Mile 310.5, first view of the scene from the north end, April 1 1963.

The Prince George crew continued working from the north end while the Squamish crew worked from the south end, and we both made good use of the Cat. The 150 ton crane could pull cars back up to the track with the aid of the Cat, pick them up, and rerail them. We set a rolling hitch onto one boxcar in the water and put another line onto the coupler from the Cat so that we could roll it over with the crane line and pull it back to the grade with the Cat in a combined move. Then, with the big hook still holding it beside the track, the 35 ton crane was able to move up on the shoefly and pick up the other end of the boxcar; it was rerailed by lifting from both ends. The bigger Cats were becoming more common by this time, and they are a wonderful piece of machinery. They can cut down gravel and move snow around. A Cat will clear in a few passes as much as a complete day of shoveling by our crew in the old days. They can get into awkward places and push cars out of the way, or pull them, tow them where you want to. Where we would have had to rig for a pull with our Lidgerwood cable in the old days, these Cats can push or pull.

The Cat with its line hooked on to the rear end pulling it back on to the track.

This wreck took place very close to town and a lot of people were watching us work. They must have had a tremendous number of chickens in those parts, because overnight a great deal of the spilled grain disappeared and the same thing happened the next night. There was one special boxcar that we called a heated boxcar with a very good decking in it, maple wood 2x2's compressed together and glued, which made very good flooring and also very good table tops. The car was damaged so badly that it had to be broken up. The flooring came out in large pieces, which we were saving to take back to the shop. But each night part of this flooring disappeared along with the grain. We did manage to save some. All of the pieces of the boxcars were put into gondolas or onto flatcars, and that was the end of the derailment.

Before I can tell the story of the next derailment, I'll have to make a detour via the Norfolk & Southern

Railway. By this time, as the line was being extended and the traffic was expanding, we were purchasing a variety of new rolling stock; and among other things we needed another Business Car. These Business Cars are used by company officials and by important guests of the railroad in their trips up and down the line. The company heard that a car was available for purchase from the Norfolk & Southern Railway. So, in my capacity as Superintendent of Car Equipment, I was sent down to look this car over with the authority to make the decision whether or not to purchase it if I thought it was suitable for our purposes. This railroad ran from Norfolk, Virginia down into Florida. It was purely a freight outfit and did not run any passenger service. The General Purchasing Agent, who I had been dealing with, told me that the head of the Board of Directors, who had delusions of grandeur, wanted a special car for himself. This Colonel (I have forgotten his name) purchased the car from Pullman Company and had it converted at great expense into his private Business Car. I think it was somewhere between 130-140 thousand dollars, which was a great deal of money in those days.

It was a very luxurious car. It had a full-sized bedroom and a tiled shower, then two more compartments, a dining room, a stainless steel kitchen, the crew's quarters, and a sitting room; all done in the finest of furnishings. The linens were something to see, the finest obtainable. There was a whole complement of wine glasses, for all different kinds of wines, and specially built cupboards to hold and protect these glasses from any shocks during travel. It was all crystal; when you tinged it with your finger the glasses would tinkle just like bells. There was a complete service of plates and crockery, all china, and beautifully trimmed with gold around the edge and golden initials "N.S" (for the Norfolk and Southern) in the centre of each piece.

The old Colonel used to enjoy going to the horse races in Florida. He would fill this car with his friends and female company (you might call them entertainers) and off they'd go to the horse races in Florida. In fact, I was told by officials of the Norfolk & Southern Railway that the Colonel's parties were costing more money than the railroad was making on freight service and they had to put the Colonel into forced retirement, which is partly how this railcar came up for sale. Now it happened that the Colonel was a great friend of Barnum & Bailey (the circus people) and he used to take Mr. Barnum along on these trips to Florida. So when Mr. Barnum found out that the Colonel was building this new car, he gave him the old silver from his original Barnum & Bailey Circus Car: knives, forks, spoons, the silver tea set, cream jug - the whole works! Barnum had purchased more modern silver to use in his second car, so the original set was all given as a memento to the Colonel. It was all curlicues, a real Victorian design of silver cutlery, and it had quite a history behind it.

Well I decided that the car was suitable to purchase and telephoned our Vancouver office long distance to give them my opinion, and they gave me authority to sign the papers and bring it home. How I brought the car back to British Columbia is another story in itself. I had to ride the car, of course, and travel over a lot of different railroads before I got to Vancouver. When I got to the border between the United States and Canada, they were going to lock me out of the car. There was no way that I could look after that car if I was locked out of it, so I was put into bond. I was handed a bonded seal by Canada Customs, with instructions that as soon as I got off the car I had to put this seal on. It is a crime to break a bonded seal. Anyhow, we finally got back with the new Business Car. It was a beautiful car. With everything marked "N.S"., we had to find a name for the car which matched the monograms on the tableware and the silverware, so it was called the *Northern Summit*. All of the sleeping cars and special business cars have their own name. The *Northern Summit* also had the Royal Insignia on it, commemorating the trip made in it over our line in that car, from Prince George to Williams Lake. As you might imagine, after acquiring that car and living in it all across the United States and into Canada and being bonded with it, I developed quite an interest in the *Northern Summit*.

The *Northern Summit* at the shop. This is the car the men were sleeping in when the wreck happened.

The weather was really dirty, windy, rainy, an awful night, on October 21, 1963. When the night freight train pulled out, immediately behind the diesel engines was the *Northern Summit*, and right behind that was our other Business Car, *Cariboo*. Only a few miles up the line, just south of Brunswick Beach, on a curve there was a cracked rail. Whether it was hit by a rock that came down from the highway above is not known. But when the weight of the lead diesel engine came onto that rail it snapped, and the lead diesel derailed. All three diesels came off the track and spilled over in the ditch, coming to a full stop. In the caboose at the rear of the train was Conductor Joseph Pakulak. It not certain where Pakulak was at the time of the derailment, whether he was sitting or standing, but the sudden shock travelling down the train when the engines stopped abruptly threw him down to the floor of the caboose. His skull was fractured and he died of his injuries, just a young man, leaving a widow and two children. It was an unfortunate and unusual accident which was fully investigated in a coroner's inquest.

In the crew quarters of the *Northern Summit*, asleep in their beds, were the cook and the steward. The momentum of a moving train is greater than the force which can be applied by the air brakes, so the cars at the back press forward and either telescope the cars in front or push them off the track. There were about seventy freight cars behind the business cars in this train, and their momentum drove the *Cariboo* halfway up into the *Northern Summit*. Although it was a wooden car, the *Cariboo* had a steel frame underneath and the cars and frames actually penetrated one another, locked together in one huge mass of grinding metal. The front end of the *Cariboo* was thrust right through to the dining room of the *Northern Summit*, and stopped not more than a foot away from the bunks of the sleeping men. Neither man was injured, but they were trapped in their compartment. The man in the upper bunk managed to squeeze down to the lower bunk to where both of them could see out of the window. They could see out, but there was nothing to break the window with. Fortunately, the other men in the train crew (the engineer, fireman, and the two trainmen) were not injured. By this time we had radio telephones in the engines, so that even though his locomotive was partially over on its side the engineer was able to contact the Chief Dispatcher and tell him the train was in the ditch. Assistance was immediately sent out from North Vancouver, and we were also notified in Squamish. The front end crew then made their way back down the train where they saw the two trapped men banging on the window. They waved for them to move aside and threw a big boulder through the window to smash it. Then the cook and the steward threw a mattress over the broken glass and they were assisted out of the car to safety and taken immediately to Vancouver. Conductor Pakulak was rushed to the hospital.

The *Cariboo*, with its wooden body and metal frame, was written off after the wreck.

In Squamish we could hear on the company radio some of the arrangements which were made to take care of the men and crew of the train; there was nothing for us to do in that regard. But the first thing I thought of was all that valuable china, cutlery, and glassware on the *Northern Summit*. So instead of waiting for the wrecking crew, I jumped in my car along with the Chief Electrician, Jack Mahood, and we drove down the highway to Brunswick and got down onto the line beside the wreck. All of the crew had been taken away and the train was deserted. We could smell propane gas from the tanks underneath our business cars. The feed lines had been damaged and were leaking, so we disconnected the tanks and cut them off, and got them of the way. Then I said to Jack, "Now the first thing we've got to do is to get that beautiful cutlery and china out of here, before any vandals get in her and steal it". So by pulling and prying on it, I was able to clear away some of the loose metal and managed to get into the kitchen and into part of the dining room of the *Northern Summit*.

In order to pick up this wreck, we had to start with the big crane on the north end to recover the engines. The line was closed, so it was a case of keeping at it until everything was picked up. They brought an engine and the shop crew from North Vancouver with rerailers and various other equipment to begin straightening out at the south end. Using the big hook, we eased the first engine back onto the track and then went back for the second and then the third. By this time we were into the second night and it was terrible weather, blowing a gale and the wind howling and the rain coming down really hard. I remember that second night very well. Stan Goad, the Superintendent of Motive Power, who was in charge of engines was there with me. We had both just purchased new nylon rainproof suits with pants and a coat, with a parka on top so that we could wear a cap and pull the parka over top and we were dry. That wind was so strong that you could lean against it. Really! And when gusts of wind came along, you had to hang onto something or it would blow you along the track. And the rain! It was pelting down so thick it was obscuring the lights. By this time we had a string of electric lights and a light plant going and sometimes the wind would blow the lights over. It was a terrible, terrible night to work. However, we stayed with it all night, and eventually we had all three engines back on the track.

Then came the time to pull the business cars apart. We couldn't actually see how much damage had been done, but there was no use trying to take them apart delicately because we couldn't save anything anyway. So we put a locomotive on one end with the big hook, and the other two engines on the other end. When we tied on, we gave a little nudge and another little nudge, pushing the cars a bit further together to loosen things up. Then I gave the engineers the highball to back up. There was this most almighty tearing sound a teeth-chattering noise, with wood splintering, glass breaking, tortured steel being ripped apart as the two cars separated. Finally, they were apart. It didn't take too long to clean up the rest of the train and we hauled back to Squamish and set the two business cars in the coach yard. The *Cariboo* had a wooden body on a steel frame, and it was too old a car to do anything with so after the accident we just wrote it off as a dead loss. Joseph Broadbent, General Manager of the railway, wanted to know what we were going to do with the *Northern Summit*.

So I got together with my Car Shop Foreman and four or five of the best mechanics we had in the shop and asked their opinion. After the Chief Electrician had made his survey, we figured that we could rebuild the car and put it back in shape. So that's what we did; cut off the damaged section and rebuilt the whole end of the car. That work was done in our little wooden shop in Squamish. This was long before the construction of the big shops they have there today. The *Northern Summit* was completely restored, so that if you examined it today you'd have trouble believing it had ever been smashed. Of course we had to replace that beautiful crockery and the only place it could be acquired was England. We sent some broken pieces back to England and they produced crockery of very much the same pattern with "N.S". on it. The *Northern Summit* is still operating as one of the business cars for the B.C. Rail.

On November 4th I was called into Vancouver to attend the inquest on the death of Conductor Pakulak, which was held at the police court on Main Street under the Chief Coroner of Vancouver. Early in the inquest proceedings, the lawyer for the trainmen's organization made the claim that facilities provided in the caboose were not adequate for the protection of the crew and that therefore the company must be held responsible for the death of Mr. Pakulak. Now it happened that the railway had built that caboose. As railway activity had expanded and many more trains were being operated, more cabooses had been required for these trains. After examining various possibilities, it had been decided that we would construct our own cabooses. I made the general design and we consulted for some time with a committee from the trainmen's organization who offered many suggestions. Among us we arrived at an approved design and our crew at Squamish built 48 of these cabooses. So then the trainmen's lawyer pointed out that there were a number of conflicting statements in the evidence given as to where Mr. Pakulak had been at the time of the accident. If he had been seated at the table doing his billing, or up in the cupola of the caboose, it did not appear possible that he could have fallen as he did. Moreover, these cabooses had been built exactly as the trainmen wanted them. Therefore, the company could not be held liable in the manner that the crewmen's lawyer suggested. Both lawyers were busily pressing their case, hammer and tongs, accusing and defending. And the coroner was the most exasperated man I think I've ever come in contact with.

I don't believe that the coroner had ever before held an inquest involving railroad operations. He had some difficulty knowing who to question from not understanding how the railroad worked, I suppose. It's like the army with very diversified duties. Each person had an area to look after and responsibility for that area, but was not responsible for any other area. All of the company officials who might be required for any questions were present. There was the Chief of Operations, the Chief Dispatcher, the Chief Engineer (who was in charge of track and bridges) the Operating Superintendent (who was in charge of operating the trains), the Roadmaster (who was in charge of keeping the track in shape), the Superintendent of Motor Power (who was in charge of looking after the engines), and myself, the Superintendent of Car Equipment (responsible for cars and equipment, and in this case especially, cabooses). When some statement was made concerning the condition or circumstances at the time of the accident, the coroner would direct a question at one of the officials in order to establish the facts. He would ask the Operating Superintendent, "What was the condition of the track?", and the Operating Superintendent would get up on the stand and say, "Well sir, that is not my field of work, you'll have to ask the Chief Engineer". So the Chief Engineer would get up and say, "Well, as far as I know it was in good condition. The Roadmaster never reported it wasn't. It could have been a broken rail, it could have been a rock. We don't know yet for sure". Then the coroner would ask the Chief Engineer, "What about the speed of the train?", and of course the Chief Engineer would say, "Well I'm sorry but doesn't come under my department. You'll have to ask the Operating Superintendent".

Then he'd ask the Operating Superintendent something about the locomotives and he said, "Oh, that's not my department, sir, that up to Stan Goad, the Superintendent of Motor Power". So the coroner would have Stan Goad to the stand and turn around and ask him a question about matters in the Car Department and whether he thought the caboose was in a safe and proper condition, and he'd turn around and say, "Well, I'm sorry sir but that's not my department, it's up to the Superintendent of Car Equipment to answer that question". Finally the coroner became so exasperated that he stood up from his chair and said, "Who the hell's running this railroad, anyhow?" While each of us was correct in our field, we didn't want to stick our neck out in anyone else's field. When it came my turn, I had to get up and say that all these cars had been built and produced with the cooperation of the trainmen's committee, that we had built them according to their approval, and the agreed specifications were strictly adhered to. The inquest went on all one afternoon and the morning of the second day before we were dismissed, and it was quite an experience for everyone there. While many might have had a good idea what happened, we were not able to speak on matters outside our own department. Just how it ended up, I don't know, but with a man losing his life it was a very sad affair and an experience I wouldn't want to go through again.

By this time our railroad had become a big time transportation system, handling new cargos and having to figure out answers to lots of new problems. The P.G.E. now had an interchange with the C.N.R. at Dawson Creek, at Prince George, and at North Vancouver, as well as with the Milwaukee Railroad by barge between Tacoma and Squamish. With so much traffic, the company could not afford to have the line tied up any longer than absolutely necessary. There was an occasion when we had a small derailment at the Brunswick Tunnel, and of course our crane could only operate from the north end, so the Operating Department made arrangements to borrow a crane from the C.P.R.. It came up and cleared the wreck from the south end while our Squamish hook cleared the north end. Having moved up from the Car Shop Foreman and Wrecking Foreman to Superintendent of Car Equipment, I was having to make decisions in a lot of unexpected situations, but by this time, I had gotten used to it, I guess, and took things pretty much as I found them. There was more pressure, though, and more people looking to see what we were doing, and relying on us to come up with the right answers.

Another memorable derailment took place at Mile 35.6, just south of Shannon Bay (which is about four miles south of Squamish), on December 2, 1963. This was a very mixed train of loaded cars, and some 17 or 18 cars were off the track in a big mess with the back end of the train piled up in a heap. There was no room to get a shoefly around the wreck, so the line was tied up. We were called in Squamish, and the Operating Department shortly afterwards called upon the C.P.R. crane for assistance from the south end. As soon as the Squamish wrecking crew was called out, I got into my car with Stan Goad (Superintendent of Motor Power) and Jack Mahood (the Chief Electrician) and we drove as close as we could and scrambled down to the track. My God, what a mess! And what a stink! It was another pitch black night, raining hard, the wind howling along the Sound right beside the track, and the smell of blood and guts all over the scene. Amongst all this mess were two cars of Cariboo cattle and a carload of pigs. The pigs were running all over the place, squealing and howling. They couldn't get up the bank very well because the cut bank was too high and there was ocean on the other side. But the worst of it all were the cattle which had gone crazy with the smell of blood. Quite a few animals had been killed or injured and were crumpled up in their cars in a tangle of guts. The cattle were bawling their heads off, eyes glaring, completely spooked, and charging back and forth across the line. Lorne MacNamee (the Assistant Superintendent) had come up from North Vancouver with two or three other men, and they and the train crew were trying to rescue the livestock. It was quite dangerous, actually, down there along side of these derailed cars with cattle charging at you out of the darkness. If they ever caught you with their horns, you'd be ripped to pieces.

There was a place down the track from the stock cars where some overturned boxcars formed a little vee with the wall of the cut. We found some timbers and broken slats to construct a makeshift fence, and managed to herd these cattle away from the smashed up stock cars and down into a corral. They quieted down some, away from the smell of blood. They could have smashed through the "fence" at any time, of course, but they treated the barrier as if it were substantial. The damned pigs were another matter. It was almost impossible to handle them. They came roaring out at you in the darkness and hit you in the legs and knocked you ass over kettle, and there was a constant screaming and grunting and groaning until you didn't know whether you were coming or going.

There was an access spot, a flat area, a little way up the track and somebody managed to get hold of a one ton truck with a body and a tow truck to help winch it. They backed this truck down off the highway until it was close to the track. Then we put together a platform ramp running up to the truck and a fence so we could herd these pigs into the truck. The cattle were still making noises and these damned pigs were still tearing around, and suddenly a brilliant flash of light right behind us scared the pants off me. I turned around and here is a man with a flash camera taking pictures. So I stepped right up and said, "Hold it, Mac, what do you think you're doing?" He said, "Well, I'm taking pictures of the wreck". And I said, "You're certainly not, you're not going to use that flash camera around here, we've got too much damned trouble here now without you scaring these animals, they're scared bad enough now". I said, "If you're not careful, you're liable to get knocked over by one of the pigs and you're liable to get hurt. Will you cut it out now and get off the property, this is private property here, you've got no business here".

He said, "I'll have you know, sir, that I'm a reporter from The Vancouver Sun and I'm perfectly privileged to take whatever pictures I like and report on the scene as I see it". "Oh no, you're not", I said, "No, you're not, you are on private property and you're trespassing". "Now", I said, "Will you please remove yourself from the property and do not take any more pictures". I said, "Mister if you don't go, you'll be forcibly ejected". And he said, "You can't do that to me". Well I didn't argue with him any more. By this time, the sergeant of our company police from North Vancouver was there, so I turned to him and said, "Sergeant, will you escort this man off the property. Take that camera away from him until he is off the property and when he is off the property and on the road away from the wreck, you can give him back his camera". The sergeant took his camera and he said, "On whose authority are you doing this to me?" I said, "On my authority". And he said, "What authority have you got?" So I said, "I'm the Superintendent of Car Equipment here, I'm in charge of picking up this wreck, and I am helping to quiet these animals, and I have the authority to put you off this property". So he turned back and said, "This is not the last you'll hear of this. I'm going right to Mr. Bennett about this". I said, "Well you do that. You go to Mr. Bennett, go up to him right away and give him my name, Mr. Stathers, I'm Superintendent of Car Equipment, and tell him that I ordered you off the property on account of taking flash pictures and endangering our lives here with all these animals running around. However, you're not entitled to take pictures of wrecks on private property". So he went away, boiling mad, and the police sergeant escorted him scrambling back up the hill, got him onto the highway, and set him loose.

By this time our wrecking crew had arrived on the scene and we had enough fellows helping that we managed to round up all these pigs and chase them into our corral beside the truck. They couldn't get past the truck up the hill, and they didn't want to go into the water. So we chased them up the ramp, where a couple of husky fellows could pick them up and throw them into the truck. Or so we thought. Months later there were reports from people who lived along there of funny wild animals running in the bushes making squealing noises. However, we had a very hard winter that year so I don't think any of them survived. The next thing was to bring the cattle in. By this time daylight was coming along and the cattle were a bit calmed down. We were able to use the same ramp and got hold of two trucks and we were able to herd the cattle down the track, get them to the ramp, up the ramp, and into the trucks and they were taken to Vancouver. Then we faced the messy business of burying all the dead animals and getting to work to pick up all of this spilled equipment.

It was a stinky, dirty job. By this time, of course, I didn't have to do the actual work. The wrecking crew had the messy jobs of taking out those dead cattle and pigs. Luckily there was quite a shoulder of land there where the bulldozers were able to dig a deep trench and the remains of the dead cattle and pigs were buried there. Then it was a matter of picking up the derailed equipment. By this time the railroad was into piggyback service and there were three piggyback cars involved in the wreck. This service was designed to combine the best features of door-to-door highway trailer delivery with long haul rail service, which could be done without the individual truck and driver. The semi-trailers were backed onto special flatcars and tied down with cables. At the destination point another driver would hook onto the trailers and deliver them to the customer's plant. These semi-trailers are in effect big boxes with thin aluminum shells. We had to take great care when lifting them so that our crane cables did not cut into the sides of those thin aluminum skins. So the crew had to do a bit of finagling with the big hook and our derailment equipment to recover these three piggyback cars and the trailers. Once they were out of the way, we continued working on boxcars from the north end, while the C.P.R. crew worked on the boxcars from the south end.

Now two top C.P.R. officials came out to this wreck to watch the work. They had heard what we could do with our big hook, and they had requested their company to put one on order for Vancouver. My wrecking foreman was in charge of the crew, and I did not interfere with him too much. The C.P.R. crane capacity was 150 ton lift but it was an older design and steam powered. Our new crane was also 150 ton, but was diesel powered and had traction under its own power with drive wheels on both ends, which gave it almost the same traction as a locomotive and a terrific pulling capacity. By this time our operators had put in some time and gotten some practice, so they were able to do a great deal of work with it. They could move up the line to a car that was off the track, pass the cable out and put a hitch around the car, lift it up in the air and then back up, swinging the boom a bit from side to side at the same time to loosen the car from the pile, and easing or pulling or tearing it out of the heap (as required) right onto the track. They didn't even need to put out any outriggers unless the car was too far away from the track. Even when the car was loaded, that crane could lift it and swing it clear of the wreckage, pull it up the line, and then either set it back on its own trucks or set it over to one side of the line where we could get at it later. Then the crane would move right back into the pile for the next car. The C.P.R. steam crane crew were not able to swing over very far unless they put their outriggers out, and of course their crane would not move very far on its own traction. This older crane was not nearly so flexible to operate as ours was, and the crew had to be cautious about overextending the capacity of their lifts or they might tip over. The two visiting officials were amazed at what we could do with our new crane, and the top man of the C.P.R. said to me, "We must have one of those new cranes. We've got to have it. I'm certainly glad I'm out here to see this tonight". And they stayed with us all night long watching the work. We were pulling two cars to their one, or even better, because we had the newest crane in Western Canada. I don't know about Eastern Canada, but we had the finest piece of wrecking equipment of any railroad west of Winnipeg. So they were very impressed. We kept on working until we had the whole mess cleaned up. Altogether it was about a three day job, but it didn't take long to clear the right of way because we were able to get Cats from Squamish, and the Cats assisted the cranes to get things clear. Once the cars were pushed out of the way and the line was open, we could let the traffic flow and then went back in between trains to clear up the mess.

The end of this story came about a month later when I was called into the General Manager's office. Joseph Broadbent didn't give me any reason why he wanted me to come down specially, just that he wanted to see me in his office at such and such a time. There was a staff meeting every Friday at that time, where all the executives from different departments used to meet and work with one another but this meeting was just for me alone. So I was wondering what the hell I'd done wrong, or whether I was going to be fired. However, he said, "Eric, I hear you had some trouble with a reporter. I have a message here from Mr. Bennett saying that you used force on a reporter from The Sun to remove him from railway property. Is that right?" "Yes, sir, that's right I did. Mind you there was no physical force. You were out there, you saw the mess we were in. You weren't there the night the cattle and pigs were chasing us all over the ruddy track", I said, "but the reporter was and we were darned scared we were going to get horned by one of those cattle steers, whatever they were". I said, "The pigs were knocking us off our feet every once in a while and this man came up and started flashing his camera taking pictures of the wreck. We were very much afraid he was going to stampede those cattle again. On top of that", I said, "you gave us strict instructions about six months ago that we were not to allow anybody to take pictures of wrecks on company property. You couldn't stop them if they were taking pictures off the property, but no one was allowed on company property", I said. "He was right on the track behind me and he refused to go. So the police sergeant was there and I asked him to take his camera, take him up to the road, return the camera to him, and tell him to go". I said, "The next morning as soon as it was daylight he was back overhead with a helicopter taking pictures. But of course, I couldn't do anything about that", I said. "Anyway, by that time we pretty well had the cattle and the pigs out of the way so it didn't matter. That's the whole story, Mr. Broadbent", I said, "and as far as I'm concerned there was no physical force used. He went back because the sergeant took him by the arm, he got his camera back as soon as he was off company property, and as far as I'm concerned I was carrying out instructions". So he said, "Very good Eric, thank you very much. I'm quite sure that Mr. Bennett won't take any objection to what you did". And that's the last I heard of it.

There was a minor derailment in Brunswick Tunnel, where the cast iron wheel on a loaded car broke in half and the train piled up behind it. Our crane had to go into the tunnel from the north end and yard out the derailed cars. It is hard to get much of a lift in a tunnel, because of course you can't lift the boom on the crane very high. However, the operator was able to lift those loaded cars clear of the track, and back up under his own power clear of the tunnel. He did say that on account of the unevenness of the track, which had been torn up a bit, he hit the boom two or three times on the roof of the tunnel and smashed the lights on the boom. But he succeeded in getting all of the cars out. Meanwhile, I was working down at the south end with a crew and a locomotive trying to remove that car with the broken wheel. You couldn't do anything with it. So we built up a series of timbers and ties, and we tried to skid it out. Well, hell's bells, every time you moved it ten feet the cribbing would collapse. We finally had to jack it up and change the wheels, and it took us a good half day just to get that one damned car out of the tunnel.

In another minor derailment, one of the piggyback cars wound up teetering on the edge of the bank, just balancing on the edge of the track, overhanging a straight drop down into Howe Sound. With the new crane they could get the boom out in order to make a lift, but the problem there was how to hook on. One of those boys had to go out onto that car, feeling whether it bounced or not depending upon what extra weight they put on it, with the risk that it might tip right over and go down. I wouldn't have wanted to go out there myself, particularly. However, I wasn't in charge of the actual work by that time. It took some guts but the wrecking foreman and his crew managed to get a cable onto the overhanging end of the car and the crane was able to take the weight and swing it, easing it back onto the line. As you can see, the new crane was making it possible for us to recover cars and cargoes which we could never have retrieved with the equipment and methods of the old days. And that completes the account of serious derailments between North Vancouver and Squamish in my time up to 1965.

15 RUNAWAY AT MILE 110

1964

When it comes down to it, picking up train wrecks is largely a matter of experience. You can learn a lot from other people's experience in school and in books, but what you learn for yourself on the job is probably the most important. From experience in the Car Shop the men know how cars are put together. This helps them in a wreck to imagine how the cars come apart, or sometimes how to take them apart, or get them apart. We have to know where the couplings are, where the hose lines are, where the brake rods are. We have to know where to hook onto the structure of a car to pick it up or turn it over or pull it away. And we keep an eye out for the probable cause of the derailment as well. I used to watch each car and look at each portion of the track as we uncovered it, and I got so I could tell from the marks and scars on the railcars which car was first to derail. Sometimes it was a problem with the cars themselves. Sometimes it was the track. You could see by the way the track was torn, if it had been twisted or fractured or split, just what the circumstances were.

Generally the people who were around at the time of the derailment are gone long before the wrecking train arrives. Our first duty, of course, after the people are clear and the animals are clear, is to get the line opened to traffic again. So we try to reconstruct the situation in our heads as part of planning how to recover all of the rolling stock. When the wreck had been completely picked up, I would file my report with remarks and comments as to the condition of the equipment. More than once, it was only when we picked up the last car of a derailment that we discovered the probable cause of the incident.

Driving up the highway north from Pemberton to Darcy, the tracks are on the right hand side. As you get near Mile 110, the highway crosses over the tracks over a small railroad crossing, and you come to a little stream with an old wooden building on the left hand side, and a hay meadow on the right hand side. At this point you are traveling over the 1858 Gold Rush route to Lillooet. That wooden building was the watering house for oxen and horses and cattle. Inside was a trough arrangement where the owners kept their cream and milk from going sour, by diverting part of the stream to surround their milk cans. This was long before refrigeration, of course. There used to be a two-story log house with accommodation for travelers, and a big barn for animals. They were still there in the 1930's, but they became vandalized and were finally burned. In 1964 the watering house was still there (with a shake roof) and you could get the most delicious drink of pure, clear, ice cold water there. Across the road on the right hand side was a big hay meadow and on the far end of that meadow was a little ranch with beautiful little buildings all painted green and white, and the stream meandered through that meadow. As you passed the ranch, the road became steeper. There was an old logging road running up to the left, through quite thick bush, in more or less a flat area. This section had been logged off many years before, perhaps to build the ranch buildings. At any rate, you could walk through this area and get to the railroad track from the highway.

This beautiful little historic spot was the location of the most costly wreck that ever happened during my time with the P.G.E. When everything was totaled up, including the damage and loss of rolling stock, cargo, and everything else that happened, the bill was over half a million dollars. This wreck took more out of me than any other wreck I ever was at in my whole 36 years of experience with the P.G.E. Exactly how it happened, I do not know. I wasn't at the inquiry. I do know what we found when we arrived on the scene, and from the position of the cars I created a scene with my imagination. It was just a short train, only 51 cars, with two diesel engines. They left Lillooet on the evening of January 18, 1964 on a straight run into North Vancouver. They were not expecting to set out any cars along the way, so the engineer and fireman were up in the cab of the engine and the two brakeman and the conductor were in the caboose at the rear of the train. All the way from Darcy to Cheakamus the line is either going up a hill or down a hill. There are some flatter grades and some steeper grades. Between Birken and Mile 110, the grade is shown on the elevation map as 2 percent, but at this particular spot (where the line is also very curvy) I'm sure the grade was 2.2 percent, and this is what might have happened.

It seems likely that the train was running pretty fast when they came over the hill at Birken and started on the down grade. Maybe the crew in the caboose thought they were going too fast into the curvy section. There is an emergency valve in the caboose, which a conductor can pull, which will stop the train by putting on the brakes. However, you have to do this gradually by just cracking the valve open a little bit or you will have brakes on at the back end of the train while the engines are still pulling at the front end, and the train might break in two.

Maybe they tried to crack that valve. I don't know. I did hear, just hearsay, that the fireman went over to the engineer's side and told him they were going too fast, and he'd better brake it a bit to slow down, but the engineer disregarded the suggestion. Anyway, the train entered into the series of curves at excessive speed. In this train were a number of loaded tank cars, and with the momentum of their load shifting as the car swings through a curve, then the opposite curve, then back, it might have worked up a bit of whiplash effect. Many of the boxcars were loaded right to the ceiling with lumber, which would give them a high centre of gravity, also susceptible to a whiplash reaction. However, it happened that the train came apart with the back end on the first curve, the middle on the next curve, and the front end on the third curve. Of course as the cars went off the track, some went one side and some went the other because of the way they piled into one another, and the track was blocked. At the back was a group of fifteen or sixteen cars including a refrigerator car, an empty tank car, eight loaded boxcars, and five loaded tank cars. Further down the track sitting on the straight stretch by themselves on the rails, were four cars loaded with grain, which I suppose had less load higher up and were less subject to tipping in the curves. On the next curve down there were twenty-six assorted boxcars and flatcars (all loaded with lumber) and two tank cars of molten sulphur, and on the next curve again (opposite curvature) there were four more cars all loaded with lumber and the two locomotives, all off the track. It was very fortunate that the two engines left the track at that point because on the next left hand curve, if they had kept on at the same speed or the engines had broken away from the train, those locomotives would certainly have left the rails and plunged down over the bank to drop more than a hundred feet to the highway below. Both men would most likely have been killed.

The crew in the caboose, which remained on the track, phoned right to the dispatcher in Vancouver and reported the accident. Officials came up from Vancouver immediately to pick up the train crew, and took them to Vancouver. A fire had started in the centre group of cars, from molten sulphur leaking out of one of the ruptured tank cars onto the broken lumber during the wreck. At the rear of the train a tank car containing liquid butane had derailed and punctured, and there was a strong smell of butane all around. When we were told of these cargoes, I telephoned for special help. I called Mr. Coughlan, the explosives inspector for all of Western Canada, who had assisted me on other wrecks where we had to handle propane, butane, and explosives. I also asked Mr. Dunn to come from Taylor. He was the safety man for Taylor

Refinery and worked with these gases all the time. He knew his business very well and was a good man to work with. I'd worked with him before. The Prince George auxiliary and the Squamish auxiliary were called out at six o'clock Sunday morning, January 19, 1964.

First on the scene was an engine from Lillooet, whose crew managed to pull the empty tank car back onto the line at the north end and removed that tank car and caboose out of the way for the Prince George crew. When the Squamish auxiliary arrived at the south end, the section gang had already swung the track so we could get around the derailed engines, but we couldn't get our crane past the first car so we started working on the south end of the wreck. I left the wrecking foreman in charge, and Mr. Coughlan came with me up the line to take stock of the damage. One sulphur car, the one on fire, had stayed up by the tracks. The second sulphur car had been carried down the hill and was very badly mauled, but not leaking. The burning sulphur created a toxic gas, so when you got within twenty or thirty yards of the car you'd cough and your eyes would run. It was a severe irritant to eyes, nose, and throat and you couldn't breathe that stuff too long, although there was no danger of anybody being gassed. However, the burning sulphur was not the biggest problem. During the wreck, lumber had been flung off the flatcars in all directions and some of the boxcars had broken as well. The sulphur had oozed over a lot of this wood, which caught fire immediately. The fire had spread down the hill and burned away the wooden decks of some of the cars. A number of cars came to rest against trees, and the trees were also burning. From time to time, a tree would burn through and let go and the boxcars would roll farther down the hill, right over the highway below. Some of the lumber cars had not yet been attacked by the fire, but many of them were already beyond saving.

A distance farther up the line, the four grain cars were sitting together on the track with the brakes locked on, waiting to be hauled out of there. Up at the first bend at the north end of the wreck, Tank Car 88774 lay across the track on a slope with her steel sills driven into the side of the boxcar ahead so that the steel frames of the two cars were enmeshed, practically welded together. A hole had been torn in the tank and more than two-thirds of the butane had spilled out onto the ground, saturating the whole area below that car, including the ground beneath several other butane cars, which fortunately were still intact.

Well, we had a pretty good idea by then what we were up against. Two engines in the ditch at the south end and the way blocked. A sulphur car on fire, blocking the line, and a number of cars so damaged or burned in the middle cluster that many of them would have to be written off. The beginnings of a young forest fire, which also threatened the highway below. Four grain cars to be pulled away and, at the north end, the line blocked by the makings of an explosion. If anything set off the gas from the butane tank and spilled butane, the explosion would ignite the other butane cars and take out the entire area right down to the ranch buildings on the far side of the highway. To make matters worse, I was pretty well on my own to handle this wreck. Usually, as the reader will have noted in previous stories, there is an Operating Superintendent in attendance and sometimes the Chief Engineer or an engineering assistant who takes care of the track. The Operating Superintendent takes care of the movement of the trains and the train crews and anything to do with the public, and generally assists the wrecking crews to help handle the wreck. But in this incident, the train crew was taken out of service immediately and taken right down to Vancouver. An investigation was held the next day (Monday morning) and the operating people were all at the investigation. So I was left with all of these problems: arranging with the police for the evacuation of the people living at the ranch house; the protection of highway traffic from explosion and fire; arranging to fight this forest fire; finding some way to handle the butane; looking after the gangs of men working on the track; and picking up the wreck at different places spread about a third of a mile apart. I had to make all the decisions myself, because there was no help there from anyone else from the P.G.E.

The first thing to do was try and get that fire under control. We had no means of fighting a fire of that magnitude. All we had was fire extinguishers and the small backpack units. However, we got in touch with

Chief Dispatcher, Norman MacPherson, and he managed to contact the forestry department at Pemberton. They came out with two pumps and all the hose they had, hooked their intakes into that little wooden watering house with the stream running through it, and set up to spray the fire as best they could. There was no way for them to actually put the fire out, so I gave instructions to try and concentrate on the cars which were loaded with lumber and not yet on fire, and let the other cars burn. We would handle sulphur cars ourselves. We had gas masks in the crane so we did all we could, which was to put gas masks on, take shovels up with us to the burning sulphur, and cover the sulphur with gravel from the hillside. This sulphur had been liquefied, but by this time it was turning solid. It was very hot, but, by shoveling gravel on top of the flames we were able to control it. After a while it would flare up again and we'd go back and shovel on some more gravel. Mr. MacPherson also contacted the R.C.M.P., who set up a patrol of that section of the highway and stayed in touch with the situation.

In order to get the line open, we would have to get past the burning sulphur car and the mess there and get past the butane car and the danger there. So the Squamish crew went to work and threw the cars on the south end out of the way and worked their way up into the mess at the centre. By the time we'd come this far, darkness had arrived and there was not much use trying to do anything during the night because we knew it was going to be a long session. I left my Squamish wrecking foreman to work on the south end while I concentrated on the explosion danger up at the north end. Now there was no way we could get by that butane car. It was laying across the track and there was quite a steep gully there on the bank side. In order to put a shoefly around the butane car, we'd have had to fill in the gully with gravel and there was no way to get gravel cars or any part of a train in there. What it came down to was, we would have to move that car. I told Mr. Coughlan this.

Early Tuesday morning Mr. Coughlan and I went back to Pemberton by truck, and he called by long distance telephone to the head office of the explosives bureau for North America in New York City. He explained the situation, how we had eighteen inches of snow on the ground and a temperature between ten and fifteen degrees above zero, how the butane tank had been holed and the liquid butane had run out all over the ground under this snow, how you could smell it all over, and reported the various readings he had taken with the explosion meter around the tank car and surrounding area. Then he asked about how we should move that tank car. They would not give him an answer. It was the first time they had recorded any experience of this type and they would not say how to move the car or whether to move it, or how to handle it. Naturally I thought of pumping out the remaining butane, so I sent down to Squamish for an air pump. Actually, we had some pumps off the old steam engines, which we found we could run off the compressed air line feed from the diesel engines. This rig arrived on Tuesday and we hooked it up and put the hoses in place. But the pumps wouldn't handle the butane. They would handle water, but they wouldn't handle butane.

On Wednesday Mr. Coughlan again telephoned New York, and all they could tell him was that they had not found anything. They had no record of a person who had this particular experience. No one could tell them what should be done, so he'd have to use his own judgment as to whether it was safe to move the car or not. Well, he did not wish to take that responsibility. But he suggested perhaps we could pump out the butane with a different kind of pump. So we sent to Vancouver and got a gas pump, which was rushed to the wreck, and we tried again to pump out that car. By Wednesday afternoon the Prince George auxiliary, using their 35 ton crane, had set over all the boxcars and other cars from the north end and worked the line clear right down to this broken Tank Car 88774. They were ready to assist us in moving it. In the meantime the south end crew with the big hook was blocked by the group of cars in the centre of the wreck, jammed up against the bank and down the side and still burning.

We got a Cat from Squamish, which came up on a flatcar and unloaded at the small crossing. There was some excitement when the Cat was unloaded. We piled up a bunch of railroad ties to make a ramp, and when the treads of that big D8 Cat rode onto those ties they started to turn and spill like roller bearings and the Cat just went skidding sideways right off the car and onto the track. For a moment I thought we were going to lose the Cat and the driver as well. However, he did not tip over and was able to run his machine up to the wreck and start moving those burning cars out of the way. The crane could not get in close enough and the cars were jammed too tight. But the Cat was able to nudge them apart and push them out of the way. The Cat operator was Mr. Goss from Squamish, and he had a difficult and dangerous job to do. There was smoke and flame all over the place and very little room to work among the burning cars, particularly right between the bank and the track where the heap piled up. With the Cat pushing and the crane lifting we managed to work through this group of cars until we had only one more knot to shift. Mr. Goss had to nudge three other cars farther down the hill to make room for the final car, and we'd be past the fire. So we got the crane line onto this car while the Cat operator swung his machine up the bank and edged north to come down on the uphill side of that last car and push it down the bank off the track. Well, he made his turn and then the Cat slipped right down against the side of this burning boxcar. He couldn't turn, his tracks were just spinning, and he was trapped in there in the smoke with flames shooting up along side of his Cat. What he didn't know was that there was a boxcar door lying there under the snow, and the treads were just sliding over this steel door. I was afraid we were going to lose him. But the wrecking foreman gave a little extra swing on the crane and was able to move the car, which allowed the Cat to back up and get off the door. Then using his blade, he was able to scoop this slippery steel door up in the air and get it up against the side of the boxcar, between his blade and the boxcar floor, and then by maneuvering back and forth and pushing and swinging by the crane and more pushing, we finally managed to get the line clear. To get past the sulphur car tank that was on fire, they shoved it far enough so that there was room to swing the track over. The crane was finally able to travel up the line to the grain cars. These were hauled down to the nearest siding, and we were finally able to run the Squamish crane up to where this Butane Car 88774 was still fouling the grade.

It was getting late in the evening and I said to Mr. Coughlan, "Ed, this car has got to be moved. We've got to get this road open". But he would not give permission. So I said to Mr. Dunn, "What do you think?" "Well," he said, "he's the man with the authority, and if he won't give you the authority to move it, why then you've got to take it on your own shoulders. I know you've got to get the road open but his hands are tied too. New York won't give him the authority to touch that car and I certainly can't give you the authority. It's out of my field. So," he said, "it's up to you". "We can't wait any longer", I said, "we've just got to move this car". So I went back and we got all the fire extinguishers from the locomotives, one from the north end and two on the south end, and we had four (I think) in the auxiliary, these big fire extinguishers, all CO_2. Then I told the crew what we were going to do. "This is going to be very dangerous", I said, "and I don't want anybody to do this unless they feel sure of what they are doing. You can't have a man who is unsure of himself in a spot they have to be in order to carry out the job safely. "I'm sure we can take it out safely without any explosion", I said, "providing we use those fire extinguishers". What I planned to do was to spray the steel with CO_2 which would smother any sparks which might be made when we pulled those two cars apart. The tank car was still more than a quarter full of liquid butane, but the temperature was only about plus ten degrees Fahrenheit and butane stops gassing off at eighteen degrees above, so there was no gas coming off from the tank car. Of course, the whole area was saturated with liquid butane.

I had the Prince George crane crew hook their crane onto the north end of the butane car. The Lidgerwood was set behind the Prince George crane anchored to the track behind the Lidgerwood stops, and their cable was run out to the end of the butane car. The idea was to make the pull north with the Lidgerwood, pull the butane car right away from the boxcar, and then swing the tank away from the track with the crane. On the south end the big hook couldn't help us, because it would be pulling wreckage back onto the track and we wanted it pulled off the track. So I sent the Squamish crane away from the area and in the clear before we started to lift that butane car. The R.C.M.P. had been warned, and they stopped all traffic for a mile on either side. Meanwhile the forestry crew were still in the area fighting the fire, and I left it up to them to handle it for themselves. These extra details had become my job as the wreck itself. So everybody was moved out of the area except five people, one of whom was Mr. Coughlan. Give that man credit, he was not authorized to approve what I was doing but he did not shirk the danger, he assisted as much as he could. Terry Aldridge, the assistant wrecking foreman, was with Mr. Coughlan on the fire extinguishers. Barry Hunt was in the crane, and the Lidgerwood operator (I forget his name) was at his post. And me.

When we were all set, Aldridge and Coughlan climbed down into the hole beside that car. Each man had a big foam extinguisher ready to fire, and another right beside him to keep it going. The machine operators sat watching me and waiting for the signal. And as I stood on the track, I thought to myself, "well, Stathers, this might be the last thing you do on this earth. The minute you raise your hand for the signal to start the pull, there could be the biggest damn explosion that ever took place in this country, and they'll most likely find all of us spattered around the rocks up the hillside somewhere. Well, it's been a good life so far, although I'm not feeling too good, but here goes". So I told them, "Start spraying, fellows. Open up those fire extinguishers". Well as soon as that CO_2 foam hits anything, it will freeze. If you put your hand in front of the CO_2 nozzle, it will freeze your hand immediately. So the second that foam hit the steel frames of those cars it froze, and they covered the whole area with frost. After about twelve seconds, I gave the signal to pull. There was a screeching and a groaning, the grinding squeal of the steel being torn apart, scraping, and those men stood right there in that hole and kept spraying with their extinguishers and finally that tank car had pulled free from the boxcar. I signaled the Lidgerwood operator to stop pulling, and the Prince George crane was able to swing that car over clear of the track. And by Wednesday night around nine o'clock we had the track open. Believe me, I heaved a sigh of relief when that operation was done, because we were now free to let trains through and the most dangerous task had been completed. We still had to get rid of that butane but at least we were in the clear and the temperature was staying down so it was not as dangerous as when we first got there. I don't want to bore the reader with my own personal problems, but at that time I knew I had angina and it was slowly getting worse. That wreck was scattered over a good quarter of a mile of track and it snowed practically every night. I was tramping back and forth, back and forth between the two auxiliaries and the fire crew and I was swallowing nitroglycerine pills to keep me going, and I was not in good shape. I'll tell you that I was suffering quite a bit of pain and the angina was certainly not improved by these worrisome times.

Well that night we ran short of water and we had to go back to Pemberton to get water. We ran right into Pemberton station. Mr. Coughlan called his boss in Montreal and told him what I'd done, how we'd handled it, and how successful it had been and that the line was clear. But we still had to get rid of that butane that was left in that ruptured tank car. I gave the Chief Dispatcher the okay to let trains through but they were to shut off their engines and try to coast through the area where the butane was spilled because even diesel engines will throw sparks. Then we tied up and tried to get a few hours sleep.

A way freight came up the line from North Vancouver or from Squamish to bring supplies, and while we were sleeping they came into Pemberton and tried to spot a boxcar at Pemberton station on an old siding, which hadn't been too well looked after. The frost was starting to come out of the ground, it was getting a little milder, and the engine had hit the ground. So we were called out at four o'clock in the morning. We didn't dare go in on this rotten track with our crane, so we had to put the outrigger out and reach a long way across from the main line. The Pemberton yard was built on a swamp, so the track was not too stable. We had quite a tussle with this problem. When we tried to lift the engine from the siding on the opposite track our outriggers were pushing the blocks down into the ground, and there was some danger of tipping over. To make matters worse, we were working on a reverse curve and the elevation was against us. So it wasn't until practically eight o'clock in the morning that we managed finally to get this damned engine back on the track and get the way freight on its way. Of course we had to follow it back up to the wreck and start to work, so we got very little sleep that night too.

The two cranes set to work to recover the first engine while I went back up to the butane car with another pump that had just come up from Vancouver. Unfortunately, not all of the fittings arrived with it. We spent much of the day trying different hoses, different methods, different schemes, but could not pump the butane out of that tank car. Then we tried to siphon it out. We'd fill the hose right up with water and stick it in the butane and flop the outfeed end down quickly below the butane level. But the water wouldn't pull the butane out. There would have been no trouble siphoning water. But butane is heavier than water and the gas is heavier than air, and for some reason or other it just would not flow. We wasted a lot of time messing with the pump and the siphons.

Well, we finally managed to get that first locomotive back on the track with the two cranes, and we hauled it down to the nearest siding with the wrecking train and got rid of it. The Prince George crew, in their enthusiasm, brought their 35 ton crane down beside the second engine, set the outriggers as far as they could and blocked it up. By the time I got there they were trying to get that second engine back on the track. I could see from the strain in the pull they were taking that they might get into trouble, and I hollered out, "For God's sake, what are you fellows doing?" "Why", they said, "we were trying to get this engine back on the track before you got here". "Well", I said, "you're crazy". Then I took a closer look. "My God", I said, "you've broken the outriggers". And sure enough, I got down and took a close look and they had taken so much lift that they'd cracked the front outrigger on the 35 ton crane, which made it useless so far as we were concerned. We couldn't put any strain on that outrigger, and we couldn't reverse it. It was made to fit only on the one side. So we gave up on the second engine for the time being. The next day we tidied up by clearing things away a little further from the line, easing the shoefly sections, and getting the track in better shape for trains to go through without danger of going off the track. Friday night we took both cranes back to Squamish. Some of the wrecking crew changed over, we got supplies all replenished, and the shop crew worked on the 35 ton crane to put it back into working condition.

While the crew were resting up in Squamish and getting prepared to go back up again Monday morning, I had to go down to Vancouver Saturday morning. I took with me all the data that I had acquired, and gave an account of what we had found, what we had done, and what I thought had caused it, to the officials. This took up all day Saturday and all of Sunday morning. Then I got home for a few hours rest Sunday afternoon and Sunday night, and of course we were away again Monday morning.

The first thing to be done Monday was to recover the second engine, and with the two cranes we managed that. Then we spent the rest of the week actually cutting up cars and loading them; it was largely a matter of hard work. Those cars which we could not reach with our cranes from the track had to be pulled up. We were not able to afford the expense of the big D8 Cat too long so we had loaded him up and taken home to Squamish. By this time our own Cat and the Cat operator had been brought down from the north. Boy, he was a wild man, was that guy. By the time the forestry crew had managed to put out the fire, a lot of those cars had worked their way right down close to the road. So our Cat operator built a road down from the south end through these broken trees and debris. With his help and the big hook from Squamish, we were able to pull some of the loaded cars up near the track where their loads could be transferred because the cars were so badly smashed up. First we tried to get the cars that weren't burned. Then we went after the empty cars. When we got the big D8 Cat hooked onto one of those cars and wound it up, he'd gun it and head right for the track, come hell or high water. You stood well clear because there were trees coming down, parts of cars flying around, dirt flying up in all directions, and once he got going he didn't stop until he got that car near the track where we could handle it with the big hook. We worked this way for the rest of the week until Saturday.

We also went back to work with the gas pump on Monday, trying different types of lines, and the temperature dropped some more. It was quite cold but we finally got that pump going somehow or other. Then the lines kept plugging up, frozen solid, and we spent practically all day trying to pump, freezing the line, thawing out, breaking the ice in the pipe. Oh, what a time we had trying to get the job finished. Finally Mr. Dunn came up with an idea. He said, "Why don't we flush it out? Flush it out with water and let it go. The ground is saturated now, it can't hurt to spill some more. Let's fill the whole damned tank with water and flush it out and then we can pull it up ahead and turn it over and pump out the water". So I asked Mr. Coughlan what he thought, and he said, "Well, you're going to put more butane on the ground. However, I don't see any way out of it. So you go ahead. Do whatever you think". By this time the forestry crew had pretty well got the fire under control. They brought their pump up to a little creek up in the north end which flowed down along side of the tracks, and hooked up their lines to this creek. By nightfall Tuesday they were about ready to start pumping water into this tank. Early Wednesday morning we started the water going into the tank, and with two pump lines it didn't take long to fill it and it flushed all the butane out. That butane spread all over the place, but the temperature continued to stay low. So we finished up the second week on Saturday and came down to Squamish. The road was open so there was no need to stay there.

During the second week, my south end wrecking crew foreman, Tommy Fowler, was down with the flu and the second in command, Terry Aldridge, had to take over. He was just a young lad at the time, and he did a commendable job, but he did scare the hell out of me a couple of times lifting cars without putting outriggers out. So I stayed on and worked through the third week. However, all went well and he didn't turn it over, so everything went nicely. By the end of the third week we had most of the boxcars up and I had finished up all the damage assessments. The sulphur had solidified by this time, and the sulphur cars were in terrible condition and very heavy. The crew spent another two weeks recovering the sulphur cars, and the other tank cars of butane, which were tipped over on their sides. They used the same technique operations with the big hook and the D8 Cat. To finish up this wreck, Mr. Coughlan and I went back to the site in May and dug holes in the ground to test the whole area which had been saturated with butane. He took readings with an explosion meter and no trace of gas was found, so he gave clearance for the area to be used again.

I was actually up there as superintendent of the whole area for three weeks and they were three tough weeks. Of course, I never get as much sleep as the men do when we're out on these jobs, and what with my own bit of trouble. I believe that three week period had quite an effect on my health. Later in that year, October of 1964, I suffered a severe heart attack and had to be sent to the hospital. After that, I did go back and try it again for a couple of weeks when I suffered another heart attack and that was the end of my career with the Pacific Great Eastern. We had other derailments before I retired, but nothing of any importance worth noting, as far as this story is concerned. This was the biggest and most trying time that I ever had on a derailment, because I was in full charge and because of the danger that was involved. We had handled derailed propane cars before, but we had never had this situation where no one could tell us what to do. In the other derailments with butane and propane cars, we were able to rerail them loaded and get them out; or if we couldn't do that, because they were too far away from the line, we burned them off as I described in an earlier incident. But this time we were absolutely stuck there and I had to take it upon my own shoulders to make the correct decision. If anybody had been killed or burned or hurt in any way, I would have been responsible. But I was right in the middle of it, so I don't think I'd have been around to answer for it if anything had gone wrong.

When I started this series of stories, the idea I had in mind was to leave a record of the hardships that men underwent before the days of modern equipment. People today have a hard time imagining what railroad work was like in the days when everything was done by hand. But even the big railroads started small, and the men just worked with the equipment they had. I came from the C.N.R., where they had heavy steam equipment, to the P.G.E., where the wrecking train was the seven ton crane and the

Lidgerwood and some auxiliary cars, and the crew was made up from the small group working in the small shop. Up at Lillooet they had another Lidgerwood on a small flatcar with a few cables and small blocks, and foreman Stan Malm and his crew, who also put a lot of equipment back on the rails by jacking and blocking. We had the steampot and the bigger crew. And from there, I have tried to tell the story of the work the men had to do during those 36 years, and how they had to do it.

Left to right: Tom Fowler, Eric Stathers, Barry Hunt; in the background Sonnie Rennie, crane operator.

It is a different world today. Since 1964 the company has acquired another 150 ton crane, a newer model. The first 150 tonner went up to Prince George with its full complement of equipment. They've gotten rid of the Lidgerwoods, figuring they don't need them when they can set down the outriggers on the two big hooks and between them they can make a 300 ton pull. They can do tremendous things with these two machines. I haven't been back and have no experience with the two of them but the men like them very much. The first 150 tonner had six wheeled trucks, which I always thought was an advantage in rough track. The new one also has six wheeled trucks. Also they have men in the crew now who can use dynamite. This would have been a very useful thing for us. We had to fight for hours sometimes to get cars untangled, hours of hard labour. You can understand that when cars are jammed into a derailment in a cut, the couplers are sometimes locked together just like steel bars, and it takes a long time to drive the mechanism up and get the ears of the couplers apart. We sometimes had to cut those couplers off with a cutting torch. Today they just put a stick or two of dynamite in the right place and blow those couplers and cars apart. It's another skill, another tool.   Then today they have these big D8 Cats, and plenty of them, available along the line, and other mobile equipment as well. With the volume of rail traffic along the line, they don't try to save the cars as we had to do, they just can't afford to tie up the line. The big Cats come in and push everything clear so the track can be restored and the line opened again. Then the big hooks can come in between trains and rescue the derailed equipment, while traffic continues up and down the line. The men also have proper equipment to work with, good lighting plants, a place to sleep, and much better accommodation. Their cars are well looked after, and they are treated much better.

So the last thing in the world that I want to do is give the impression that the B.C. Railway of today is anything like the old P.G.E. of my day. The long trains and the tonnage they pull can compete with any railway on the North American Continent under similar geographical conditions.

The repair shops and facilities have been improved to such an extent that they can do work that was impossible in the early years. The road bed, along with the heavier rail and crushed rock ballast, has cut down the number of derailments dramatically.

Some day in the future the railroad will have to be built in Alaska, so there can be a north-south rail link to bring down the heavy mineral products that now lie dormant in the north. When that portion of the line is being built, men will have to undergo similar hardships in order to overcome the problems of muskeg, sliding banks, and glacial fill that make up the land mass north to the Arctic. It is true that they will have better equipment to work with and better living conditions, but the hard and sometimes dangerous work will still have to be done. These future men should be give the credit due.

I don't expect that I will live long enough to see this happen, but I hope that many of the readers of this book will.

I hope that you have enjoyed reading it and you now have a better understanding of the hardships that men endured in keeping the P.G.E. operating in the early days.

ABOUT THE AUTHOR

Eric Prince Stathers (E.P.) was born in Hull, England in 1907 and emigrated to Manitoba, Canada with his family in May 1914. He lived in Oak Lake, Clearwater, and Pilot Mound before moving to Winnipeg. He completed Grade 9 secondary school in Winnipeg in 1921 and in 1923 began an apprenticeship as a carman in the C.N.R. Shops in Transcona from 1923 to 1928.

Eric was married to Mary Uhrich in September 1928. In 1929 Eric and Mary moved to Squamish, British Columbia where Eric began his career with the Pacific Great Eastern Railway (P.G.E.) as a Car Foreman in the Squamish Shops where he managed the apprenticeship program. Over the years Eric served as Wrecking Foreman, General Car Foreman, and Superintendent of Car Equipment for the P.G.E. and the British Columbia Railway from 1929 to 1965 when he retired from the railway for health reasons.

Eric Stathers, third from left, with his first group of apprentices outside the Squamish shops (Eric Stathers).

This story chronicles his 36 years of work as a wrecking foreman between 1929 and 1965. It is primarily an account of how the men went about picking up train wrecks with detailed accounts, methods, original pictures, and hand-drawn maps connected together with anecdotes about the operations and hardships of working on the railroad during those years

ACKNOWLEDGMENTS

The manuscript for this book was originally written by Eric Prince Stathers for family and friends in May 1981. In the words of E.P. Stathers, "This book would never have been written without the encouragement and very capable help of my good friend Dr. A.L. (Dick) Lazenby B.A., M.A., PhD. who set the narrative into proper phasing and spent many hours searching through archives to obtain better copies of the pictures that I had gathered over the years".

Photo Credits:

Mr. Artie Phair, Lillooet, B.C.
Mr. Stan Malm, Lillooet, B.C.
Mrs. Mildred McDonald, Squamish, B.C.
Mr. Colin Nicholson, Squamish, B.C.
Mr. Gordon Thornton, Retired Loading Inspector, B.C.R.

Typing Credits:

Mrs. Nancy Chalmers, Squamish, B.C.
Mrs. Irene Stewart, Squamish, B.C.

Eric Prince Stathers
Squamish, B.C.
May 1981

E.P. Stathers' manuscript of In the Ditch was transcribed and digitized for publication by the Stathers family:

- Kim Stathers, great granddaughter of E.P.S. and archivist at the University of Northern British Columbia, served as Project Manager, developed the web approach, transcribed and edited the manuscript, and digitized the original photographs.
- Nicola Stathers, great granddaughter of E.P.S., copy-edited the transcription and helped with photographs
- Jacob Eric Stathers, grandson of E.P.S., transcribed, edited, and managed publishing of the manuscript
- David Pettitt, great grandson-in-law of E.P.S., edited the final proof of the manuscript
- Harold Eric Stathers, son of E.P. S., provided guidance
- Mary Lou Stathers, daughter-in-law of E.P.S., provided copies of "My Story"
- Catherine Stathers, granddaughter of E.P.S., provided the original manuscript of In the Ditch

Throughout the editing and transcription of In the Ditch, our intent was to preserve Eric P. Stathers' voice and storytelling style.

GLOSSARY

Boxcar	A railroad car designed to carry most loads. Boxcars are enclosed and have side doors of varying sizes; some include end doors and adjustable bulkheads to load very large items.
Brakeman	On early trains, iron wheels, located atop cars were connected to a manual braking system underneath the car by a long metal rod. The two brakemen would ride on top of the cars and would begin turning the iron wheels to engage the brakes. When one car was completed, the brakeman would jump the thirty inches or so to the next car and repeat the operation. The brakemen would work towards each other until all cars had their brakes applied.
Budd Car	A Budd Rail Diesel Car (or Buddliner) was a self-propelled diesel railcar built by the Budd Company of Philadelphia used mainly between 1949-62. They could be used singly or coupled together in sets and controlled from the cab of the front unit. The cars were adopted for passenger service in rural areas with low traffic density or in short-haul commuter service.
Business Car	A railroad passenger car that was either originally intended or later converted for service as a business car for private individuals. They were used by railroad officials, dignitaries, and wealthy individuals for travel and entertainment.
Carman	A Railcar Repair Carman is responsible for inspecting, rebuilding, and repairing freight cars.
CCF	Co-operative Commonwealth Federation (CCF) Party was a social-democratic political party founded in Calgary, Canada in 1932. In 1944, the CCF formed the first social-democratic government in North America when it was elected to form the provincial government in Saskatchewan. In 1961, the CCF was succeeded by the New Democratic Party (NDP).
Conductor	A railroad conductor works aboard the train and coordinates the daily activities of train crews. A freight train conductor oversees the loading and unloading of cargo whereas a passenger conductor is the captain or overseer of passenger operations.
Coupler	A locking mechanism to join or hold railway cars together.
Deadheading	Riding off duty on a train.
Deadman	A long trench, about six to eight feet deep, dug into the hillside filled with timbers in a T-shape used to attach a cable to pull wrecks out of a ditch.
Fireman	The fireman's job was to shovel coal into the firebox of the steam engine. Another job of the Fireman was to keep the cylinders on the drive wheels oiled while the train was underway.
Flanger	A flanger is a track-clearing car that has a snow plow under its centre. It is generally pulled by freight trains to remove snow between the tracks and at switch points.
Flatcar	Railway rolling stock with an open, flat deck mounted on a pair of trucks, one at each end containing four or six wheels. The deck of the car can be wood or steel, and the sides of the deck can include pockets for stakes or tie-down points to secure loads.

Gondola	A gondola is an open-top type of railway rolling stock that is used for carrying loose bulk materials. Because of its low side walls, gondolas are used to carry either very dense material, such as steel plates or coils, or bulky items such as prefabricated pieces of rail track.
Jordan Spreader	A removable front plow about two feet high that can be lowered down to the track to clean out snow or gravel for about two inches below the top of the rail or spread gravel as track ballast.
Lidgerwood	A steam-powered winch mounted on a wooden railcar that was manufactured by The Lidgerwood Company. It was similar to a donkey engine used in logging operations.
Master Mechanic	A Railway Master Mechanic performed highly skilled and complex mechanical repairs on both light and heavy equipment
Observation Cars	A type of railroad passenger car, generally operated in a passenger train as the last carriage, with windows on the rear of the car for passengers' viewing pleasure.
Piggyback Cars	Piggyback cars refers to a flatcar that is used to carry trailers, semi-trailers, or containers.
Replacer	Replacers are specially-shaped pieces of metal with grooves and ridges in them, designed to guide the wheels of a derailed car up beside the track, and above the track so that the car wheel flanges lift back into their normal running position.
Rerailers	A metal casting secured to the track to guide the wheels of a derailed train back on to the track.
Roadmaster	A road foreman or roadmaster is assigned a territory of track on the railroad to maintain and see that it is kept up to railroad standards. They are also responsible for overall maintenance personnel and for coordinating with surrounding roadmasters and territories.
Roundhouse	A roundhouse is a building used by railroads for servicing locomotives. Roundhouses are large, circular or semicircular structures traditionally located around or adjacent to a turntable.
Section Crew	Also known as Section Gangs, they were responsible for a section of track. They typically rode handcars to look for and replace rotted ties, tamp loose spikes, and tighten bolts.
Shoefly	A short bypass rail line often around a wreck built as needed for temporary use.
Snow Plow	The wedge plow was first developed by railroad companies to clear snow. The mountain wedge plow forces snow to the sides of the tracks and requires a large amount of force to be able to handle buried rocks and trees.
Tailblock	A pulley block with a loose tail of cable or rope attached to it for pulling.
Tender	Every steam engine requires both water and coal to operate. This is supplied from an auxiliary vehicle called the tender, which is usually coupled immediately behind the engine.
Trucks	Railway trucks are the chassis or framework-like structure underneath a train to which wheel axles and wheels are attached through bearings.

INDEX OF NAMES

A list of P.G.E. Employees that managed or braved the hardships and risked their lives to keep the rail line open and operating between 1929 to 1956 is provided below.

First Name	Surname	Role	Location
Harold	Bailey	Master Mechanic	Squamish
Minor	Bazley	Engineer	Squamish
Paddy	Bowman	General Manager	North Vancouver
Mr.	Bristol	Apprentice Shop, CN Railway	Transcona
Joseph	Broadbent	General Manager, Pacific Great Eastern Railway	North Vancouver
Bud	Butterworth	Conductor	Squamish
C.M.	Conley	Brakeman	Lillooet
Frank	Conway	Conductor	Lillooet
Jack	Cooper	Engineer	Squamish
H.P.	Cummings	Fireman	Squamish
Terry	Dedridge	Assistant Wrecking Foreman	Squamish
George	Devine	Wrecking Crew	Squamish
John	Duncan	Fireman	Squamish
Fred	Eadie	Engineer	Squamish
Tom	Fowler	South Wrecking Foreman	Squamish
Jack	Frost	Master Mechanic	Prince George
Bill	Gedge	Wrecking Crew	Squamish
Mr.	Giles	Fireman	Squamish
Stan	Goad	Superintendent of Motor Power	Squamish
Barry	Hunt	North Wrecking Foreman	Prince George
Andy	Hutton	Work Train Engineer	Squamish
Joe	Iacovone	Cook	Squamish
Mr.	Johnson	Engineer	Squamish
Don	Kirkwood	Blacksmith	Squamish
Andrew	Kyle	Master Mechanic	Squamish
Jack	Mahood	Chief Electrician	Squamish
Stan	Malm	Foreman	Lillooet
Angus	McCrae	Senior Locomotive Engineer	Squamish
Alex	McDonald	Carman	Squamish
Scott	McDonald	Special Duty	Squamish
Alan	McDonald	Engineer	Squamish
Lorne	McNamee	Assistant Superintendent	North Vancouver
Norman	McPherson	Chief Dispatcher	Squamish
Charlie	Midnight	Engineer	Squamish
F.J.	Mulhern	Fireman	Squamish
Alex	Munroe	Engineer	Squamish
George	Nesbitt	Unknown	Squamish
Frank	Peveril	Conductor	Squamish
Mike	Powell	Engineer	Squamish
William	Rae	Superintendent of Motor Power & Equipment	Squamish
Pete	Rebegliati	Section Crew Head	Lillooet
Sonnie	Rennie	Crane Operator	Squamish
Harry	Seymour	Fireman	Squamish
Henry	Smith	Labourer	Squamish
Andy	Steele	Fireman	Squamish
Mr.	Stewart	Superintendent	North Vancouver
Mike	Stilwell	Wrecking Crew	Squamish
Clayton	Thorne	Wrecking Crew Crane Operator	Squamish
Gordon	Thornton	Loading Supervisor	Prince George
Robert	Wilson	General Manager	North Vancouver